Paul's Joy in Christ

Paul's Joy in Christ

Studies in Philippians

By
A. T. ROBERTSON

" To me to Live is Christ "

BAKER BOOK HOUSE
Grand Rapids, Michigan

ISBN: 0-8010-7602-1

Second printing, April 1980

PHOTOLITHOPRINTED BY CUSHING - MALLOY, INC.
ANN ARBOR, MICHIGAN, UNITED STATES OF AMERICA
1 9 8 0

Preface

THESE lectures were first prepared as expository talks from the Greek text for the Northfield Conference for Christian workers in August, 1913. They were delivered in Sage Chapel and their publication was requested by the hearers. The addresses have since been repeated at Winona Lake, Indiana, Columbus, Ohio, Virginia Beach, Moody Bible Institute, and to various other assemblies and churches. The Greek text is kept in foot-notes so that the average man can read the book with comfort without a knowledge of Greek. The volume is essentially popular in style and purpose, while the latest researches of modern scholarship are utilized for the illustration of this noble Epistle. Nowhere is the tender side of Paul's nature better shown than here, his delicacy, his courtesy, his elevation of feeling, his independence, his mysticism, his spiritual passion. My book is not so much a technical commentary, though it covers all the Epistle, as an interpretation adapted to modern needs on the part of all teachers, preachers and students of the New Testament. Nowhere does Paul have more " charm," to use Ramsay's phrase, than in Philippians. Nowhere is he more vital and more powerful. Paul was

7

not merely a man of supreme genius and high culture, but one who let himself go completely in spiritual abandonment to the love and life of Jesus. It is small wonder that the hypercritical spirit seeks to discount him as a paranoiac or a Pharisaic bungler who distorted the message of Jesus. Such modern critics fail to understand Paul because of failure to know Jesus as Paul knew Him by rich experience of heart and soul. I confess to a feeling of reverent hesitation as I venture to enter afresh this Holy of Holies of Paul's Life in Christ. Here we see in clear outline, not only Paul's Joy in Life, but his Joy in Death, a message sorely needed by many stricken hearts during these dreadful days of war. Paul was able to see the Face of Christ in Death since Death brought Christ in all His fullness.[1]

A. T. R.

Louisville, Ky.

---

[1] Once more, as I read the proof of this page, I am called upon to find Christ in Death, in the going of my young daughter, Charlotte, who loved Jesus utterly.

Contents

I.   THE BRIEF SALUTATION   .   .   .   11
           (*Philippians 1 : 1–2.*)

II.   JOY IN PRAYER   56
           (*1 : 3–11.*)

III.   GOOD OUT OF ILL   .   .   .   73
           (*1 : 12–20.*)

IV.   JOY IN DEATH AS WELL AS IN LIFE   .   92
           (*1 : 21–30.*)

V.   PAUL'S FULL CUP   .   .   .   110
           (*2 : 1–11.*)

VI.   REALIZING GOD'S PLAN IN LIFE   .   141
           (*2 : 12–18.*)

VII.   FELLOWSHIP   158
           (*2 : 19–30.*)

VIII.   THE HOLY QUEST   .   .   .   174
           (*3 : 1–14.*)

IX.   FOLLOWING THE ROAD   .   .   204
           (*3 : 15–21.*)

X.   THE GARRISON OF PEACE   .   .   225
           (*4 : 1–9.*)

XI.   THE SECRET OF HAPPINESS   .   .   245
           (*4 : 10–23.*)

I

THE BRIEF SALUTATION
(Philippians 1 : 1–2.)

THE formula for greeting in Paul's Epistles is now very familiar to all students of the Greek papyri. Here the technical word for greeting,[1] so common in the papyri and seen in James 1 : 1, is absent. But it is implied, of course, and is simply taken for granted by Paul. The full formula is to "say greeting,"[2] like our vernacular "say howdy," as we find it in 2 John 10, "give him no greeting,"[3] and 11, "that giveth him greeting."[4] This most familiar of all Paul's Epistles (or Letters, as Deissmann[5] insists on calling them all) is very simple and direct in the salutation. The outstanding facts of the situation come promptly before us.

1. Paul the Author.

No one of Paul's Epistles stands upon firmer ground than this one, in spite of Baur's vigorous attacks upon its genuineness. His arguments have been completely answered and McGiffert[6] sums the

---

[1] χαίρειν.   [2] λέγειν χαίρειν.   [3] χαίρειν αὐτῷ μὴ λέγετε.
[4] ὁ λέγων αὐτῷ χαίρειν.
[5] "Light From the Ancient East," p. 225.
[6] "The Apostolic Age," p. 393.

matter up by saying: "It is simply inconceivable
that any one else would or could have produced in
his name a letter in which no doctrinal or ecclesiastical motive can be discovered, and in which the
personal element so largely predominates and the
character of the man and of the apostle is revealed
with so great vividness and fidelity." Von Soden [1]
denies the genuineness of Ephesians and the Pastoral
Epistles, but he stoutly defends Philippians: "We
are treading upon very sacred ground as we read this
epistle. It is without doubt the last from St. Paul's
hand." The ground is holy beyond a doubt, but not
because this is the last of Paul's Epistles. Moffatt [2]
waves aside Baur's criticisms as to alleged imitation,
anachronisms, gnostic controversies, and doctrinal
discrepancies and argues also for the unity and in-
tegrity of the Epistle in spite of Polycarp's use of the
plural [3] in referring to Paul's Epistle which, like the
Latin *litteræ*, can be used of a single epistle. The
somewhat broken and disconnected style of Philippians is due rather to the incidental character of the
letter and its personal nature. It is in no sense a
formal treatise and has no announced theme as in
Romans I: 17. Critics who carp at the lack of order
in Philippians "forget that Paul was a man, and an
apostle, before he was a theologian; and are actually

[1] "Early Christian Literature," p. 107.
[2] "Introduction to the Literature of the New Testament,"
pp. 170–176.   [3] ἐπιστολαί.

surprised at his not giving to this familiar letter the methodical order of a treatise." [1] This "Epistle is like a window into the Apostle's own bosom." [2] Let us gratefully and reverently look in to see what Paul has revealed of Christ in himself. We do not know that he used an amanuensis for this Epistle, though that was his usual custom (as in Rom. 16:22). He may have written it all as he did the little letter to Philemon (verse 19, "I Paul write it with mine own hand"). Timothy and Epaphroditus were with Paul when he wrote to the Philippians and either of them (in lieu of another scribe) could have performed the function for Paul. And yet it is quite possible that he penned this love letter with his own hand. At any rate he put his heart into it and some of the noblest passages that were ever penned by mortal man are here. Paul was a versatile man and his style adapted itself to the subject matter and the mood of the moment, as is the case with all men of real eloquence and power of speech.

2. Paul in Rome.

He does not say so, nor does he necessarily imply it, though that is the most natural inference from the incidental allusions in the Epistle. There are some scholars who hold that Paul was in prison at Ephesus when he wrote the Epistle to the Philippians. The

[1] Sabatier, "The Apostle Paul," p. 252.
[2] Shaw, "The Pauline Epistles," p. 419.

Ephesian imprisonment is largely hypothetical and
the theory due to a possible interpretation of 1 Corinthians 15 : 32 (" I fought with beasts at Ephesus ") and 2 Corinthians 1 : 8–9 (" concerning our
affliction which befell us in Asia" and " the sentence[1] of death within ourselves "). The idea here
is, according to this theory, that Paul languished in
prison in Ephesus and came near to death. It is
possible to take " prætorian guard " (Phil. 1 : 13) for
a band of soldiers in Ephesus and by a stretch
" Cæsar's household " (Phil. 4 : 22) of messengers in
Ephesus, but the situation and outlook of the Epistle
do not belong to any known period in Ephesus.
Cæsarea can be made a much more plausible location
for Paul when he wrote the letter. The arguments
of Paulus (1799) and Boettger (1837) for Cæsarea
have been adopted and enlarged by O. Holtzmann.[2]
But at most only a possible case is made out. The
use of prætorium[3] for an imperial residence outside
of Rome is undoubted (Kennedy, Phil. in " Exp.
Greek Testament," Vol. III, p. 404) and it occurs for
Herod's palace also (Acts 23 : 35) in Cæsarea. We
know that the Augustan band (Acts 27 : 1)[4] was at
Cæsarea. But even if Cæsar's household[5] is equivalent to these soldiers or the prætorian guard, it is
still far more likely that the real household of Cæsar

---

[1] τὸ ἀπόκριμα τοῦ θανάτου, the answer of death.
[2] Theol. Lit., 1890, col. 177.   [3] πραιτώριον.
[4] σπείρης Σεβαστῆς.   [5] οἰκία Καίσαρος.

in Rome is meant. We know that later there were
Christians in the imperial circles and it is by no
means unlikely that Paul was able to reach some of
the slaves in the home of Nero by the help of the
soldier to whom he was chained. It is true that the
jealousy of the Judaizing Christians pictured in Philippians 1 : 15–17 does seem to suit Cæsarea better
than Rome, because of its proximity to Jerusalem,
but it is to be borne in mind that the Judaizers do
not appear against Paul in Cæsarea, and the onset
against Paul in Jerusalem in Acts 21 was due to Jews
from Ephesus and not to the Judaizers. It is not at
all unlikely that the Judaizers would reappear in Rome
after their defeat in Jerusalem, Antioch, Galatia, and
Corinth. It is very difficult, besides, to think of
Paul as expecting a speedy release in Cæsarea, either
at the hands of Felix or Festus, according to the narrative in Acts 24–26. There was delay also in Rome
since Luke in closing his story in Acts (28 : 30) states
that Paul had already spent two whole years [1] in his
own hired house. Nero, like Tiberius, was noted for
his dilatory habits and no accusers may have come
against Paul.

When Paul wrote to the Philippians time enough
had elapsed since his arrival in Rome for the Philippian church to hear of his arrival and condition and
to send Epaphroditus with messages and gifts, for
Epaphroditus to fall ill, for the Philippians to hear of

[1] διετίαν ὅλην.

it, and for Epaphroditus to be distressed over their
sorrow, and to recover his health (Phil. 2 : 25–30).
We do not know, of course, how long this was nor
precisely how long Paul was in prison in Rome before
his release, assuming, as I do, that he did not fall a
victim to the hate of Nero in connection with the
burning of Rome in A. D. 64. We may say then
that Paul had left Rome before the early summer of
A. D. 64. He may have reached Rome in the spring
of A. D. 59 or 60. Colossians, Ephesians, and Philemon were sent together by Onesimus and Tych-
icus (Philemon 10, 13 ; Col. 4 : 7–9 ; Eph. 6 : 21 f.).
They were also written from Rome, I hold, and not
from Cæsarea or Ephesus. It is not clear whether
Philippians was despatched before or after this group
to Asia. The common opinion is that Philippians
was sent afterwards and just before Paul's release,
because he expects to be set free when he wrote to
Philippi (1 : 25–26). But he is just as confident of
getting free when he writes to Philemon and asks for
a lodging to be made ready for him (22). The apparent absence of Luke and Aristarchus (Phil. 2 : 20)
is a puzzle, but we have no right to say that they
remained with Paul constantly in Rome. The presence of Timothy surely calls for no explanation.
The doctrinal aspect of the Epistle comes in well
between the Judaizing controversy in the great doctrinal Epistles (1 and 2 Corinthians, Galatians, Romans) and the Christological controversy raised by

incipient Gnosticism in the Lycus Valley and other parts of Asia (Colossians, Ephesians). Thus we have an echo of the Judaizing trouble in Philippians 1 : 15–17 and 3 : 1–2, while in Philippians 2 : 5–11 Paul has his greatest passage concerning the Person of Christ. There was probably no great space of time between Philippians and the other three (Philemon, Colossians, Ephesians) Epistles of the First Roman Imprisonment. Till we can get further light on this point I follow Lightfoot in placing Philippians before the others, though not long before. Lightfoot's essay on " St. Paul in Rome " (pp. 1–29 of his commentary on Philippians) is still the masterpiece on this topic. We can fill in some of the details in the picture of Paul's life in Rome, whither he had come at last. He had long planned to come to the Imperial City (Acts 19 : 21 ; Rom. 1 : 13 ; 15 : 22, 32). In spite of all the hindrances of Satan and the Jews Paul was to go to Rome (Acts 23 : 11) for he was to stand before Cæsar (27 : 24) to whom he had appealed. He had not expected to come to Rome as a prisoner, but he is not in despair because of that fact. Things might be worse. He has his own hired house (Acts 28 : 30), even if he is chained to a Roman soldier (28 : 20 " this chain "). He was allowed liberty to receive his friends by the Prætorian Prefect Burrhus, if so be Paul fell to his care. Ramsay indeed thinks that Paul was the rather under the care of the *Princeps Perigrinorum* (*stratopedarch,*

according to some manuscripts for Acts 27 : 16),
who was the head of the soldiers from abroad with
some of whom Paul had been sent to Rome. He
was a prisoner with dignity and some degree of
liberty. He paid for his own lodging (in his own
hired dwelling[1]) and so did not have to stay in the
soldiers' camp. He " received all that went in unto
him "[2] (imperfect tense and here shows his habit).
His friends had free access[3] (without hindrance) to
him and he preached to them the kingdom of God
and the things concerning the Lord Jesus Christ[4]
with all boldness.[5] His life was therefore a busy
one and he met Christians, Jews, and Gentiles, men
of all classes. To all of them he presented Jesus as
the Saviour from sin and the Lord of life. Lightfoot
emphasizes the sharp antithesis " between the Gospel
and the Empire " when Paul comes to Rome. He
had seen long ago that the Roman Empire was the
world-power of Antichrist (2 Thess. 2 : 6 f.), unless,
indeed, as Lightfoot suggests, Paul then looked on
the Empire as the power that was restraining Antichrist, a view I do not hold. But Paul with a states-
man's grasp of the situation saw that the kingdom of
Christ and the kingdom of Cæsar were at grips with
each other. He longed to win this world empire to
Christ and laid his plans to that end. His appeal to

---

[1] ἐν ἰδίῳ μισθώματι.   [2] ἀπεδέχετο.   [3] ἀκωλύτως.
[4] τὰ περὶ τοῦ κυρίου Ἰησοῦ χριστοῦ.
[5] μετὰ πάσης παρρησίας.

Cæsar sharpened the issue, though Nero as yet had taken no notice of Christianity. The official attitude of Rome was still probably the lofty indifference and tolerance of Gallio which looked upon Christianity as a variety of the Jewish superstition and hence a *religio licita*. At Rome the greatest preacher of Christianity necessarily gave fresh impetus to the cause of Christ, as we shall see, and made Christians " a mark for the wanton attack of the tyrant. The preaching of Paul was the necessary antecedent to the persecution of Nero" (Lightfoot, Phil., p. 2). The shadow of Nero falls across Paul's path because he had appealed directly to him. Even if Nero finally dismissed the case without a formal trial, Paul was still at the mercy of the Roman Emperor. Roman power and Roman citizenship loom large before Paul now and bring out more strongly the imperial aspects of the kingdom of God.

The character of the church at Rome was mixed, as seems probable from Philippians 1 : 12–20 and from Romans 1, 2, 15. They were partly Jews and partly Gentiles, though the Jewish element apparently

[1] Prof. D. Plooij, of Leiden (see *The Expositor*, December, 1914, February, 1917, and M. Jones' reply March, 1915), contends for the idea that Luke wrote the Acts as an apologetic for Paul to influence Jewish and Roman opinion about Paul favourably for his release from his first imprisonment. He does not mean that the book was ever formally presented to Nero, but that it was conceived as a defense of Paul's career. This interpretation explains the attention given to the arrest in Jerusalem and the imprisonment in Cæsarea.

predominated. Rome itself was the home of men of all races and all lands, a conglomerate like New York to-day. Paul had already many friends in Rome, if we still take, as I do, Romans 16 as a genuine part of the Epistle to the Romans. Rome drew people like a magnet from all parts of the world, and Christians came as well as others. Probably few people of social or political importance in Rome had as yet identified themselves with this "*superstitio externa*" (Tacitus), with which Pomponia Græcina, wife of Plautius, Britain's conqueror, was charged. A generation later, Lightfoot notes (pp. 21 f.), "Flavius Clemens and his wife Flavia Domitilla, both cousins of Domitian, were accused of 'atheism,' and condemned by the emperor." Legend has claimed as Christians " the poet Lucan, the philosopher Epictetus, the powerful freedmen Narcissus and Epaphroditus, the emperor's mistresses, Acte and Poppæa, a strange medley of good and bad," but without a particle of proof.

More interest attaches to the presence in Rome of the Stoic philosopher Seneca as Nero's friend and adviser. The subject has a fascination for Lightfoot (pp. 270–333) and there is small doubt that Paul had adequate knowledge of Stoicism. He had probably met it in Tarsus, the home of Athenodorus. In Athens Paul argued with the Stoics (Acts 17 : 18). Many of the ethical teachings of Paul's Epistles are parallel to those of the Stoics as seen in the writings of Seneca and Epictetus. Many of these were more or less current proverbs and sayings of the time. But there is no real evidence that Paul and Seneca met or that they had any literary connection. " The Letters of St. Paul and Seneca " are certainly spurious. Ramsay (" St. Paul the Traveller," p. 355) thinks that Seneca exerted a restraining influence of great value on Nero till his disgrace and retirement in A. D. 62, when Nero became much worse under the baleful influence of Tigellinus. The fact that Nero, Seneca, and Paul are in Rome at the same time appeals to one's imagination. Nero is the embodiment of will-ful power and wanton ambition. Seneca is the adroit and suave worldly-wise philosopher in the imperial court where he preaches lofty maxims for others to practice, a Stoic in creed and a hair-splitter in practice like the Jewish Pharisee. Both would scorn to no-tice Paul the provincial prisoner, a Jew and worse, a Christian, an intellectual outcast with no standing with gods or men. The very pride of Nero and Seneca lifted Paul to greater heights by contrast. This " prisoner of Christ " [1] (Eph. 3 : 1), this " slave of Christ Jesus " [2] (Phil. 1 : 1), this " ambassador in a chain " [3] (Eph. 6 : 20), is conscious of his spiritual, moral, and intellectual superiority to Nero, Seneca, and all the minions of the world-power of that age. He was the ambassador [4] from the Lord Jesus in heaven

---

[1] δέσμιος τοῦ χριστοῦ.
[2] δοῦλος, same root (δε-) as in δέ-σ-μιος bondsman.
[3] ὑπὲρ οὗ πρεσβεύω ἐν ἁλύσει.   [4] πρεσβεύς.

to the court of each soul in Rome and all the world.
The proud court of Nero was to Paul but an incident
and an item in his world program. The outcome has
vindicated Paul as all the world knows. The great
man is the man who does the really great task in
spite of appearances. The glitter of tinsel in Rome
did not confuse the eyes of Paul. He was able to
grasp the elements of real power in the world and to
work with God and to abide God's time. One is
tempted to linger with this hero of faith as he makes
Rome the new world capital of spiritual energy and
power. He vitalizes the Roman Church (Phil.
I : 12–20) and directs the enterprise of Christian
missions in the Lycus Valley, in Philippi, and
wherever there was call for cheer and guidance. He
is guiding the forces that will ultimately overthrow
the world-powers of evil and make Nero's power
puny and Seneca's sophistries puerile.

3. The City of Philippi.

The ancient name was Crenides (Strabo vii. 331)
or springs (" Little Fountains "). Philip II of
Macedon, father of Alexander the Great, gave his
name to each one of the springs and hence Philippi
(plural) for the town. The city occupied a strategic
position on a hill, between the rivers Strymon and
Nestus, which commanded a view of the plain of
Druma with the river Gangites or Angites (Herod.
vii. 113) and overlooked also the mountain pass be-

tween Pangæus and Hæmus. It is nine miles from
its seaport, Neapolis (the modern Kavala). Philip
seized it and exploited it for its gold and silver mines,
which were of great service for his wars and helped
him as much as his use of the Macedonian phalanx.
The gold went before and paved the way for the
phalanx. He gained a revenue from these mines of
a thousand talents a year (Diodorus xvi. 8).

With the battle of Pydna in B. C. 168 Macedonia
became Roman and in B. C. 146 one Roman province.
But Strabo (vii. 331) says that it was now " a small
settlement" (κατοικία μικρά) and the exhaustion of the
mines marked its decline as a commercial point. In
the autumn of B. C. 42 Cassius and Brutus successively
met defeat here (twenty days apart) at the hands of
Octavius and Antony; and the defeat and suicide
of Cassius and Brutus marked the end of the Roman
republic. Macedonia and Achaia were at first senatorial provinces, then at their own request imperial
under Tiberius (Tac. *Ann.* i. 76) and senatorial again
under Claudius (Snet. *Claud.* 25). Octavius was
much impressed by the position and importance of
Philippi and made it a military colony (*Colonia Iulia
Philippensis*) with the *jus Italicum*. Copper coins
of Philippi have the inscription *Colonia Iulia Augusta
Victrix Philippensium*. This title was given after the
battle of Actium B. C. 31, when the colony was largely
strengthened by Italian partisans of Antony displaced
at Rome by followers of Octavius. The city was

thus a colony [1] (Acts 16: 12) with many privileges, immunity from taxation being the chief one. The people also had the right to own and sell property like other Roman citizens and the right of civil action (*vindicatio*). The mother city was copied closely and the colony was in reality " a miniature Rome "(Vincent) even in the form and the appearance of the city. Roman inscriptions were on the coinage. The city had its own magistrates (*Duumviri*) who called themselves *Prætores* [2] (Acts 16: 20–38). The city was exempt from interference from the provincial government.[3] The famous Egnatian Way (*Via Egnatia*) ran by Philippi and added to its importance as an outpost of Rome. It is not clear what Luke means by " the first of the district " [4] (Acts 16: 12). Thessalonica was the capital of the province and Amphipolis, thirty-three miles away, was a larger city. But Philippi, because a colony and in such a strategic position, may still have been the most important in rank in this district of Macedonia.

The village of Filibedjik or Filibat, which preserved the name Philippi, has now vanished. Near by is the modern village of Ratchka, in a ravine to one side of the ancient city which was on the height. But " an enclosure of rough stones preserves traces of the Hellenic wall " (Vincent, Int. Crit. C., p. xvii.)

---

[1] κολωνία. [2] στρατηγοί.
[3] Mommsen, " Provinces of the Roman Empire," i., pp. 299–302. [4] πρώτη τῆς μερίδος.

upon the hill, while the plain below is covered with ruins and the theatre can still be seen on the face of the acropolis fronting Mount Pangæus. The rocks around are covered with inscriptions to the ancient gods, " a veritable museum of mythology " (Heuzy and Daumet, " Mission Archéologique de Macedoine," p. 86). Traces exist of a temple dedicated to the Roman god Silvanus, one of the popular deities of the imperial era. He was considered " the sacred guardian of the Emperor " (Kennedy, " Exp. Greek Testament," Vol. III, p. 400). Two statues of this god have been found, one of which may have stood in the temple here at Philippi. Tablets also have been found with the names of the members of the sacred college of the temple. Some of these names (like Crescens, Pudens, Secundus, Trophimus) are the same as those of some of Paul's friends. The god Mên was also worshipped here and Dionysus, the favourite god of Thrace, had his chief sanctuary in the mountains near by. There was plenty of religion, such as it was, in Philippi, when Paul and his party first appeared here.

4. Paul in Philippi.

Situated on one of the main trade routes east and west, Philippi offered a splendid opportunity for Paul's first work in Europe.[1] " Philip and Alex-

---

[1] Ramsay, " Church in the Roman Empire," pp. 56, 70.

ander, Æmilius, Mummius, and Octavianus had thus
prepared the way for Paul" (Vincent, p. xviii.).
The Macedonian Cry[1] (Acts 16:8-10) was not
specifically from Philippi. It was simply "a certain
Macedonian man"[2] who was standing in the vision
and urging Paul: "Cross over into Macedonia and
help us."[3] This incident is in one of the "we-sec-
tions" of Acts which fact shows that Luke, the author of the book, was present. Ramsay says that
Paul, since the Macedonians and Greeks dressed
alike, recognized the man in his dream by sight as
one already known to him. Hence he argues that
the man was Luke who had talked to Paul before he
had his vision about the need in Macedonia. Ramsay concludes further that Luke now lived in Philippi, as is shown also by the fact that Luke continued in Philippi for some five years after Paul's
first visit. We do not know whether Luke was a
Macedonian by birth if he now lived there. There
is some support for the idea that he was a native of
Antioch in Syria. It is not clear whether Luke first
met Paul in Alexandria Troas, or had already been
with him in Galatia during his illness there (Gal.
4:13)[5] But, at any rate, we know the names of
Paul's three companions (Silas or Silvanus, Timothy,

---

[1] In the second missionary journey, A. D. 50-51.
[2] ἀνὴρ Μακεδών τις.
[3] διαβὰς εἰς Μακεδονίαν βοήθησον ἡμῖν.
[4] "St. Paul the Traveller and the Roman Citizen," p. 201.
[5] Shaw ("Pauline Epistles," p. 400) thinks that Luke now

and Luke) who went with him from Alexandria
Troas to Philippi. They all " concluded "[1] (Acts
16 : 10) with Paul that God called them to evangelize
Macedonia. The cry was the cry of one man, but
he plead for his country, and it was the voice of God.

Paul is in Philippi three times. The first time is
recorded in Acts 16 : 11–40, and the narrative is full
and vivid and adds further point to the view that
Luke now made Philippi his home. Ramsay (" St.
Paul the Traveller and the Roman Citizen," p. 206)
thinks that Luke here shows " the true Greek pride
in his own city." One is struck at once by the absence of Jewish influence in Philippi and the prominence of the Roman element in the narrative (M. N.
Tod, " Philippi in Int. St. Bible Enc."). There was
no synagogue in the city, showing that the number
of Jews there were small. It was now a military
outpost rather than a great commercial emporium
like Thessalonica where Jews abounded. The praying place[2] (Acts 16 : 13) may have been in reality a
synagogue. There seems no doubt that *proseuche*
was used for synagogue.[3] The location of the praying place several miles out of town by the riverside
was due to the need of water for the Jewish ablu-
tions. The worshippers were mostly women, as Paul

lived at Troas and met Paul in a professional way as his physician and was thus converted.

[1] συνβιβάζοντες making go together.   [2] προσευχή.
[3] Schuerer, " Jewish People in the Time of Jesus Christ,"
Vol. II, Div. II, pp. 68–73.

and his friends found, and they did not seem to be
certain (we supposed)[1] of finding the place of worship
at all, having evidently failed to find a synagogue in
the city as had been so easy to do in Salamis (Acts
13 : 5), Antioch in Pisidia (13 : 14–43), Iconium
(14 : 1), etc.   Here by the Gangites Paul was on the
site of the battle of Philippi and near the old mines
(Shaw, " Pauline Epistles," p. 405).   Here, moreover,
the Jews seem to have been few, for Luke does not
say that Lydia was a proselyte, but a " God-fearer "[2]
(Acts 16 : 14), a Gentile who had come to worship
the God of the Jews, like Cornelius in Acts 10, but
not necessarily one who had gone over formally to
Judaism.   There is no mention of Jewish converts,
for the household[3] of Lydia, if her employees, were
probably simply " God-fearers " like herself.   Some
Jews may have been converted, or at any rate Paul
found it necessary in his letter to warn the church
against the activity of the Judaizers (Phil. 3 : 1–2).
It was a small enough beginning that Paul was able
to make.   " A man had summoned Paul to Macedonia in the vision.   Paul went to Macedonia and
found a _woman_ first of all " (Hayes, " Paul and His
Epistles," p. 411)[4]   But this Asiatic merchant-woman

[1] ἐνομίζομεν.   [2] σεβομένη τὸν θεόν.
[3] ὁ οἶκος αὐτῆς.
[4] Women seemed to occupy " a specially favourable position
in Macedonia " (Kennedy, Phil., p. 402).   Note mention of
the activity of women in Acts 16 : 13 ; 17 : 4, 12.   " The
extant Macedonian inscriptions seem to assign to the sex a

from Thyatira proved to be one of the greatest trophies in Paul's ministry. This church came to be the joy and crown of Paul (Phil. 4 : 1), and that fact was largely due to Lydia and Luke.

The Roman features of the story come out sharply in connection with the episode of the poor girl with the spirit of a python or divination.[1] Luke represents Paul as driving the spirit out of her (Acts 16 : 18) as of an unclean spirit or demon. A Pythoness was thought to have oracular power from the Pythian Apollo who had a shrine near here. She was able to earn many a penny for her masters [2] (16 : 19), whose slave she probably was, by her soothsaying or raving[3] (16 : 16). The ancients sometimes described such a gift as that of ventriloquism,[4] but, whatever the cause, the poor girl was exploited by a company of men for commercial purposes just as "white-slavers" exploit girls to-day for gold. We are making some progress in the United States when at last Congress has passed a child-labour law. It is an old trick, this use of helpless children and women to fill the pockets of greed. Paul touched this " syndicate in its tenderest spot " (Shaw, " Pauline Epistles," p. 406). He had no respect for the vested interests

higher social influence than is common among the civilized nations of antiquity " (Lightfoot, Phil., p. 56 ; cf. also Achelis, Zeitschr, f. N. T. Wiss. I, 2, pp. 97–98).

[1] πνεῦμα πύθωνα.   [2] οἱ κύριοι.   [3] μαντευομένη.
[4] ἐγγαστρίμυθος. Ramsay, " St. Paul the Traveller," p. 215, accepts the view that the girl was a ventriloquist.

of capital that traded in human life and human souls.
He set the girl free from the spell of Satan and from
the grip of her enslavers. Their fury knew no
bounds and was as violent as is the rage of men to-
day who are compelled to give up the liquor business,
gambling, or any other form of graft or greed that
fattens on the weaknesses of human nature. These
men (the girl's masters) were Romans, as is shown
by the appeal to race prejudice which they make in
the effort to stir up the Romans against the Jews
(Acts 16:20f.). The Romans were more than half
the population of the city, though there was still a
solid substratum of the old Macedonian stock. So
then the masters of the girl feel perfectly safe in the
spurious cry which they put forth to the archons [1]
(16:20, the common Greek term for chief magistrates) or the prætors [2] (16:21, the Latin term
claimed by the magistrates, though *duumviri* was the
technical title) in the market-place [3] like the Roman
forum. These officers are accompanied by lictors [4]
(16:35, 38) or sergeants who carry the *fasces* with
which they scourge Paul and Silas [5] (16:22). They
are charged with a breach of public order and the introduction of customs [6] unlawful for Romans to observe.
It was a skillful turn, for " the population prided
themselves on their Roman character and actually
called themselves Romans " (Ramsay, " St. Paul the

[1] τοὺς ἄρχοντας.   [2] τοῖς στρατηγοῖς.   [3] εἰς τὴν ἀγοράν.
[4] ῥαβδοῦχοι.   [5] ῥαβδίζειν.   [6] ἔθη.

Traveller," p. 218). No chance was offered for Paul and Silas to defend themselves, but they are at once condemned after an onset by the multitude who are completely deceived by the pious and patriotic claptrap of the accusers. The magistrates themselves give way to excited indignation and the farcical trial is over. Paul and Silas are placed in the inner prison for safety with their feet fast in the stocks.[1] The forms of Roman law are duly observed, but the spirit of justice is utterly violated. The sudden change of base by the magistrates next morning after the earthquake is not explained by Luke (Acts 16: 35)[2] when they sent the lictors and said to the jailor: " Let these men go." The magistrates may have heard what had taken place and may also have become ashamed of their conduct. But this request gave Paul his opportunity to state the fact of his own Roman citizenship and to recount how Roman law had been violated in his imprisonment. Everything done to him and Silas was illegal, they being Romans. They had been beaten publicly and uncondemned[3]

---

[1] εἰς τὴν ἐσωτέραν φυλαϰήν.

[2] The addition in Codex Bezae (" assembled together in the Agora, and remembering the earthquake that had taken place, they were afraid, and ") is hardly genuine. Cf. Ramsay, " St. Paul the Traveller," p. 223.

[3] Ramsay, " St. Paul the Traveller," p. 225, thinks that Luke has not accurately rendered Paul here, who probably spoke in Latin and said *re incognita*, " without investigating our case." But it did aggravate the matter for the imprisonment to happen without condemnation.

and cast into prison. It was a sudden turn of the
wheel of fortune and the magistrates are themselves
in grave peril. They come and in apologetic style
beg Paul and Silas to leave before further compli-
cations arise. They do go, but not before their own
innocence is established and Christianity is vindicated
in Philippi. We do not know how long Paul was in
Philippi, though Luke uses " many days" (Acts
16:18) of the case of the girl with the spirit of
divination. But a sturdy church of Gentile Christians is now established before Paul leaves. Paul
went to Lydia's house and "comforted the brethren," showing that men were won also to Christ
here, though the term for "brethren"[1] probably
included the "sisters" also. Lightfoot (Phil., p. 57)
notes how in Philippi the gospel exerted a powerful
effect on woman, on the slave, and on family life
(Lydia and the jailor). The church in the house
of Lydia, for they had no other meeting place at
first, grew to be the most loyal and helpful of all the
Pauline churches. When Paul and Silas left Philippi,
Luke and Timothy remained behind. Troubles came
to the Philippian church " in much proof of affliction" (2 Cor. 8:2) at a later time, we know, and
probably also soon after Paul left, for the Philippians
knew the "proof" of Timothy (Phil. 2:22). It is
meet, therefore, that Paul should associate Timothy
(now with Paul in Rome) with him in the salutation

[1] τοὺς ἀδελφούς.

of the Epistle (Phil. 1 : 1), though Timothy is in no sense co-author with Paul. Timothy joined Paul and Silas in Berœa (Acts 17 : 14) and probably before that in Thessalonica (Phil. 4 : 16), " for even in Thessalonica ye sent once and again to my need." Luke, however, apparently remained in Philippi.

Paul appears in Philippi again during the third mission tour (A. D. 55–57) when he hurried over from Troas to Macedonia ahead of time in his eagerness to see Titus on his way back from Corinth (2 Cor. 2 : 12; 7 : 5–14; Acts 20 : 1). We do not know that Paul stopped at Philippi and met Titus there, but there is every probability of it, though Paul tells us that " even in Macedonia " he had no relief till Titus came (2 Cor. 7 : 5 f.). We naturally think of him as waiting with Luke and Lydia in Philippi who could cheer his despondent spirit in the meanwhile. He was preceded by Timothy and Erastus (Acts 19 : 22). He had originally planned to go first to Corinth from Ephesus and then to Macedonia and back to Corinth and Jerusalem (2 Cor. 1 : 15 f.), but the acuteness of the crisis in Corinth made Paul decide to postpone his visit to Corinth till they had one more chance for repentance, and so he sent Titus to them with a rather sharp letter (2 Cor. 2 : 1–4), the effect of which he awaited with eager anxiety. The outcome was joyful on the whole (2 Cor. 7 : 5–15), though the minority remained stubborn (2 Cor. 2 : 5–11 ; 10–13). While in Philippi Paul apparently

wrote 2 Corinthians, if we take the Epistle as a unit,
as I still hold to be the most plausible theory. Paul
is still in Macedonia when he writes (2 Cor. 8 : 1–5 ;
9 : 2–4). But Luke, for some reason, tells us nothing
in Acts about this visit of Paul to Philippi and Macedonia.

After three months in Achaia (Acts 20 : 3) Paul
suddenly changed his plans again and, instead of sail-
ing direct to Syria, went on to Philippi, where he
met Luke again who remained with him till the close
of Acts. Luke gives the names of Paul's companions in travel (Acts 20 : 4), messengers of the churches
to accompany Paul in carrying the great gift to the
poor saints in Jerusalem, and he mentions the fact
that Paul remained in Philippi to keep the passover
there (Acts 20 : 6), probably a slight evidence of the
presence of some Jewish Christians by this time in
the church in Philippi.

We know, if we may follow the Pastoral Epistles
as letters of Paul as I do, that Paul was in Macedonia once more, though after he wrote the Epistle
to the Philippians. When he wrote to the church,
he expressed the hope that he would himself be able
to come "shortly"[1] (Phil. 2 : 24). He did come to
Macedonia again after his release from imprisonment
in Rome, and was there when he wrote the first
Epistle to Timothy (1 Tim. 1 : 3). It is certainly
highly probable that Paul went once more to Phi-

[1] ταχέως.

lippi where he could thank them face to face for
their many tokens of affection and support during
the years. There may, indeed, have been other
visits, but these four are reasonably certain.

5. The Philippian Church and Paul.

Paul himself tells us of the devotion and zeal of
the Philippian church. While Paul was in Thessalonica shortly after leaving Philippi (Acts 17 : 1–9),
the church in Philippi had sent twice at least gifts
for his needs (Phil. 4 : 16). They kept up this good
work when Paul went to Corinth and was in want,
for it was not Corinth, but Philippi alone that at first
supplied his wants above what he could make by his
own hands (2 Cor. 11 : 9; Phil. 4: 15). The example of Philippi was later followed by some other
churches, though never by all. "I robbed other
churches," Paul ironically says, "taking wages of
them that I might minister unto you" (2 Cor. 11 : 8).
"In the beginning of the Gospel, when I departed
from Macedonia, no church had fellowship with me
in the matter of giving and receiving but ye only"
(Phil. 4: 15). Probably Thessalonica and Berœa
soon fell into line with Philippi and helped Paul in
Corinth. Certainly Thessalonica became "an example to all that believe in Macedonia and Achaia"
(1 Thess. 1 : 7). From them "has echoed forth the
word of the Lord"[1] (1 : 8).

[1] ἐξήχηται.

But no one of the Pauline churches was so thoroughly missionary in spirit and deed as that in Philippi. The church in Antioch has as its glory that it rose above the narrow prejudices of the Judaizers in Jerusalem, the Pharisaic (anti-mission or "Hardshell" element there), and welcomed the propaganda among the Gentiles, though there is no evidence that the Antioch church contributed anything but goodwill to the enterprise. It was a Greek church and was open to this world-movement. But the Roman church in Philippi rallied heartily and steadily to the practical support of Paul's missionary campaign to win the Roman Empire for Christ. They set the pace for all time for the churches that wish to exemplify the love of Christ for men. It was all the more beautiful that it was voluntary and continuous. The Greek church at Antioch had responded to the appeal of Paul and Barnabas to send a contribution to the poor saints in Jerusalem in proof of the genuineness of their conversion (Acts 11 : 29 f.), but they did not at first catch the vision of practical coöperation with Paul in his great missionary enterprise. This glory belongs to the church in Philippi, who thus became Paul's "joy and crown" (Phil. 4 : 1). They had true "fellowship" with Paul in the work of the Gospel. At first they alone had this "partnership,"[1] for this is the true meaning of the word (Phil. 1 : 5 ; 4 : 14 f.). They alone at first were Paul's

[1] κοινωνία.

"co-sharers"[1] (Phil. 1 : 7) in this grace of giving the Gospel to the lost world. It may seem amazing that the early churches were so slow to respond to the missionary appeal. But it is not for modern Christians to say much on this subject till we do enough to entitle us to speak.

The church at Philippi probably did far more for Paul than he has told in his letters. The last instance of their "fellowship" after an interval when they "lacked opportunity" (Phil. 4 : 10) was while Paul was in Rome the first time when they sent Epaphroditus, "your messenger and minister, to my need" (Phil. 2 : 25). They seem to have fairly outdone themselves this time and their gift was "an odour of a sweet smell, a sacrifice, acceptable, well-pleasing to God" (Phil. 4 : 18). They may have sent a letter to Paul by Epaphroditus and he may have written other letters of thanks to them (Phil. 3 : 1).

Paul leaned on the church in Philippi heavily in raising the great collection for the poor saints in Jerusalem from the churches in Galatia, Asia, Macedonia, and Achaia. The churches in Achaia were quick to promise and slow to pay, like some modern churches. Under the spur of Titus's leadership they promised a whole year ahead (2 Cor. 8 : 10) and Paul used their prompt pledges to stir the Macedonian churches to activity (9 : 2). And now in turn he has to spur the Achaian churches on to actual payment

[1] συγκοινωνούς μου.

by the liberality and prompt paying of the Macedonian churches (8 : 1–15 ; 9 : 1–5). Paul does not
wish to be ashamed of the Achaian churches if he
comes with some of the Macedonian brethren to
whom he has boasted of the Achaian liberal promises.
It is all a very modern situation drawn from life.
But it is clearly the church at Philippi, poor and
generous, that has long had the habit of giving, that
set the pace for the other Macedonian churches and
for the Achaian churches as well.

The church in Philippi no longer exists. The
Turks have swept over Macedonia like the locusts of
Egypt. But its early fame is secure. Ignatius, Bishop
of Antioch, stops in Philippi early in the second century on his way to Rome where he is condemned as
a Christian and is thrown to the wild beasts. The
Philippian Christians treated Ignatius kindly and
wrote a letter of sympathy to his home church in
Antioch and to Polycarp, Bishop of Smyrna, asking
him to send them copies of any letters of Ignatius
which he might have, a side-light on the circulation
of Paul's Epistles. Polycarp complied with their
request and also wrote the church a letter of his own
full of comfort and cheer. Polycarp censures a
presbyter, Valens, and his wife for avarice, though
the church at Philippi seems to be doing well.
The church lived on apparently to modern times,
but no story of the destruction of city and church
is known. Le Quien (Or. Chr. II, p. 70) gives the

name of the Bishop of Philippi when he wrote in
1740.

6. Purpose of the Epistle.

In reality Paul's immediate purpose is to express
his appreciation of the love and kindness of the
Philippian church in their gracious generosity by the
hand of Epaphroditus (Phil. 1 : 3–11 ; 2 : 19–30 ;
4 : 10–20). Three times he takes up the subject.
He explains the occasion of the Epistle to be the return of Epaphroditus, the bearer of their gift and now
of his Epistle to Philippi after his dangerous illness.
It is all perfectly natural and obvious.   Paul tells also
something of his own situation in Rome and expounds
his comfort in Christ and urges the Philippians to
constant joy.   He strikes a jubilant note, though a
prisoner himself, as he and Silas sang praises at mid-
night in the Philippian jail (Acts 16 : 25).   Paul
sings the song of victory and not of despair.   It is
thus a letter of joy and a letter of love.   The sheer
simplicity and beauty of his rapture in Christ make
this Epistle a favourite with all who know the deep
things of God in Christ.   It is easy to take the
theology of Philippians and apply it to modern conditions.   The mass of modern men and women have
to live their lives in untoward circumstances.   They
must do their work and sing their song in spite of
prison or pain, of penury or pressure, of perversity or
pugnacity.   The very sanity and serenity of Paul's

piety bring his loftiest flights within the range of the humblest of us who gladly try to imitate Paul as he imitated Christ.   Lightfoot (p. 72) says : " The Epistle to the Philippians is not only the noblest reflexion of St. Paul's personal character and spiritual illumination, his large sympathies, his womanly tenderness, his delicate courtesy, his frank independence, his entire devotion to the Master's service ; but as a monument of the power of the Gospel it yields in importance to none of the Apostolic writings."

7. The Church and the Officers.

Paul does not here use the word church,[1] but he writes " to all the saints in Christ Jesus that are at Philippi, with the bishops and deacons."[2]   Evidently Paul has the church in mind because he mentions the two classes of officers, " bishops and deacons," and yet he addresses the Christians in Philippi as individuals (" all ") rather than as an organization.   The unit in the kingdom of God is not the local church and not the officers.   The church is made up of individual believers and the church chooses its own officers.   The believers are here addressed as " saints." The term was already in use for the covenant people of Israel as " the saints in Jerusalem " (1 Macc. 10 : 39), " the holy nation," " the holy people," " the saints "

---

[1] ἐκκλησία.

[2] σὺν πᾶσιν τοῖς ἁγίοις ἐν χριστῷ Ἰησοῦ τοῖς οὖσιν ἐν Φιλίπποις σὺν ἐπισκόποις καὶ διακόνοις.

(cf. Ex. 19 : 6; Deut. 7 : 6; 14 : 2; Dan. 7 : 18, 22).
It was natural to apply it to the true Israel, the believers in Christ, "a chosen generation, a royal priest-
hood, an holy nation" (1 Pet. 2 : 9). Lightfoot (*in
loco*) notes that even the irregularities and profligacies
of the Corinthian church did not prevent Paul's use
of the word for this church "called to be saints"
(1 Cor. 1 : 2).[1] It is really the technical term for
Christians on a par with "believers"[2] and carries
with it the atmosphere of consecration found in
the Old Testament usage (Septuagint) as in Leviticus
11 : 44–45. The term is used of the priests who
consecrated themselves to God, who were set apart
from the people for the service of God. So it is
used of the chosen people who were set apart from
the nations as God's instrument in the work of redemption. Now it is applied to those of all nations
who are set apart from both Jew and Gentile as the
elect of God. The idea of holiness[3] as a duty is
necessarily involved in the word, as appropriate and
obligatory, though not always actual. Its use in the
Gospels seems to be confined to Matthew 27 : 52.

---

[1] The adjective ἅγιος is common in the inscriptions as θεῷ
ἁγίῳ ὑψίστῳ OGIS 378[1] (A. D. 18–19). See Moulton and
Milligan, "Vocabulary of the Greek Testament."

[2] οἱ πιστοί.

[3] ἁγιωσύνη, ἁγιότης, ἁγιασμός. The verb ἁγιάζω is not
yet found outside of Biblical and ecclesiastical Greek. The
ancient Greeks used ἁγίζω, ἁγισμός in their religious language.
Cf. Moulton and Milligan, "Vocabulary of the Greek Testament."

Since the Jews would apply the term " the saints " to
themselves, Paul here adds " in Christ Jesus " (Chrysostom, *in loco*). This is Paul's common idiom for the
mystic union between the believer and Christ. Jesus
used the figure of the vine and the branches (John
15 : 1–8). The branch abides in the vine. Paul uses
" in Christ Jesus " forty-eight times, " in Christ "
thirty-four, " in the Lord " fifty (Vincent, Int. Crit.
Comm.).[1] " These words sum up Paul's Christianity "
(Kennedy, Exp. Gk. Test.). The idiom is apparently
original with Paul, but one must compare the words
of Jesus, "Abide in me, and I in you " (John 15 : 4).[2]
The most intimate and vital union with Christ is
Paul's idea, not a perfunctory ecclesiastical connection. Paul assumes that the nominal saints in Philippi
are real saints in the sense of actual life in Christ ;
not in the sense of absolute sinlessness, but of living
connection with Christ who vitalizes and sustains
each one. They are members of Christ's body of
which He is the Head (1 Cor. 12). It is not professional saints who pose as superior to other believers that Paul has in mind, but he makes his salutation to all those who live in Christ as the sphere
of the spiritual activity. This inclusive circle cuts
out other circles. But Paul does not ignore the

[1] Cf. also Deissmann, Die Neutestamentliche Formel " in
Christo Jesu " (1892).
[2] Cf. Robertson, " Grammar of the Greek New Testament
in the Light of Historical Research," pp. 588 f.

officers of the saints or church, though they occupy
a secondary [1] place in his mind.   The officers are important, but not primary.   The individual saint is
primary.   Church officers are made out of saints.
The fundamental reason that we do not have better
preachers (bishops) and deacons is that they come
from the body of the saints, a part of whom they still
are.   Paul does not draw a line of separation between
clergy and laity.   He rather emphasizes the bond
of union by the use of "together with." [2]   To be
sure, the progress and usefulness of a church are
largely gauged by the efficiency of the officers.
Like priest like people.   And yet the other side is
true also.   Like people like priest.   So long as the
saints are sound at heart Christianity will outlive the
vagaries and follies of sporadic preachers.   A corrupt
ministry will ruin any church if condoned.   Certainly
preachers and deacons are not free from the responsibility for sainthood by their official position.
Noblesse oblige.   Their very prominence imposes
higher burdens.   Fundamentally the average church
member has precisely the same obligations and limi-

[1] The use of σύν shows this.   It is not certain whether σύν
here has the idea of " plus " or " including " since the preposition bears either connotation.   The papyri show both ideas
(Moulton and Milligan, " Lexical Notes from the Papyri,"
Expositor, Sept., 1911).   The context favours the idea of
" including " here.   On the whole Paul uses μετά much more
frequently than σύν, particularly in the two last groups of his
Epistles.   He has μετά seven and σύν four times in Philippians.
[2] σύν.

tations that the preacher has, but practically the preacher and deacon cannot escape an extra responsibility because of their leadership (cf. Jas. 3: 1).

We are confronted here with the whole problem of the Christian ministry (its origin, character, and functions). Bishop Lightfoot[1] has proven that in the New Testament " bishop " and " elder " are used interchangeably for the same office as in Acts 20: 17, 28; 1 Timothy 3: 1–7 and 5: 17–19; Titus 1: 5–7; 1 Peter 5: 1–2. See also Clement's " Epistle to the Corinthians," § 42. Lightfoot translates the words[2] in Philippians 1: 1 " presbyters and deacons " to make it plain to his readers that Paul is not using " bishop " in the sense of Ignatius in the second century who gives a threefold[3] ministry, " the bishop, presbyters, deacons," and insists on the distinction. Ignatius makes the bishop supreme and the embodiment of ecclesiastical authority.[4] It is clear that in the New Testament usage the Christian ministry is in a more or less fluid state as to the functions of different members. General terms occur in 1 Thessalonians 5: 12, " them that labour among you, and

---

[1] Cf. note on " The synonymns bishop " ($ἐπίσκοπος$) and " presbyter " ($πρεσβύτερος$) (Phil., pp. 95–99) and dissertation on " The Christian Ministry " (Phil., pp. 181–269) and Lightfoot's " Apostolic Fathers " (Vols. I, II).

[2] $ἐπισκόποις\ καὶ\ διακόνοις$.

[3] $τῷ\ ἐπισκόπῳ,\ πρεσβυτέροις,\ διακόνοις$. Letter to Polycarp § 6.

[4] Cf. Ep. to Smyrn., Ch. VIII.

are over you in the Lord, and admonish you." [1]   In
Hebrews 13 : 7, 17, 21, we find " your leaders " com-
mended to their memory, obedience, welcome.[2]
The term " elders " (presbyters) first appears in Acts
11 : 30, but as an established body of officers who are
later active in the Jerusalem conference in Acts 15.
The term itself is very old in an official sense as is
shown by the Septuagint usage which merely reflects
the older Egyptian custom as has been amply shown
by Deissmann.[3]   The " elders of the village " were
town officers.   The term also occurs for pagan
priests.   The technical use appears in the inscriptions
of Asia Minor.   Even " bishop " (ἐπίσκοπος) appears
in " the technical religious diction of pre-Christian
times " in inscriptions in Rhodes, curiously enough
along with " scribes." [4]   Precisely " elder " means an
older man and " bishop " an overseer, but when both
became technical terms no such distinction is drawn.
Kennedy (in loco) suggests that " elder " applied
more to status and " bishop " to function.   Vincent
(Phil., pp. 36–49) argues for a distinction between
" bishop " and " elder," though he admits the vague-

---

[1] τοὺς κοπιῶντας ἐν ὑμῖν καὶ προιστάμενους ὑμῶν ἐν
κυρίῳ καὶ νουθετοῦντας ὑμᾶς.

[2] τῶν ἡγουμένων (-οις, -ους).

[3] " Bible Studies," pp. 154–157, 233–235.   We can no
longer follow Cremer in speaking of ἐπίσκοπος as " the Greek
coloured designation" and πρεσβύτερος as of " Jewish col-
ouring."

[4] Cf. Deissmann, " Bible Studies " γραμματεῖς, pp. 230 f.

ness of the early usage and renders (p. 4) " with the superintendents and ministers." Here at Philippi we meet a twofold ministry, though the definition of neither " bishop " nor " deacon " is given. One may note also that use of the plural " bishops " is like the plurality of " elders " found at Jerusalem (Acts 11 : 30) and Ephesus (20 : 17, 28). This fact shows clearly that " bishop " is not here used in the later ecclesiastical sense of Ignatius when one bishop is head of a large city or district with many elders and deacons under his rule.

The term deacon is of obscure etymology,[1] and is a general term for one who serves. It is common in the New Testament in the general sense of servants of God or Christ (1 Cor. 3 : 5 ; 2 Cor. 6 : 4). It is not always clear when the word has a technical use in the New Testament or precisely what the office is meant to be. The papyri and inscriptions show the word in the general sense and for religious officials.[2] It is probable, though not certain, that deacons in the technical sense are described in the group of seven chosen in Acts 6 : 2–6 to " serve tables."[3]

---

[1] Some derive διάκονος from διήκω or διώκω (eager pur- suit) and others even from διά, κόνις (dusty with running). Certainly some deacons can " raise a dust " if nothing more.

[2] Moulton and Milligan, " Vocabulary," quote *Magn.* 109 circa B. C. 100, where διάκονος is used for temple officials, and in CIG II, 1800, a " college " of διάκονοι is mentioned, while *ibid.*, 3037 we see two διάκονοι, and a female διάκονος as in Rom. 16 : 1. See further Dibelius, Phil., p. 45 in " Handbuch zum N. T."   [3] διακονεῖν τραπέζαις.

The qualifications given in 1 Timothy 3 : 8–13 are not wholly different from those for bishops (1 Tim. 3 : 1–7; Titus 1 : 5–9). Probably it cannot be shown beyond controversy that in the beginning the bishops had charge of the spiritual functions and the deacons the business side of the church life. There were at first apostles, prophets, evangelists, shepherds, and teachers "for the perfecting of the saints" (Eph. 4 : 11 f.), though strangely enough Paul does not mention bishops and deacons in this list. Both terms are likewise absent in 1 Corinthians 12 : 28 : "first apostles, secondly prophets, thirdly teachers, then miracles, then gifts of healings, helps, governments, divers kinds of tongues." Some have thought to see "bishops" in "governments"[1] and "deacons" in "helps."[2] In "The Teaching of the Twelve Apostles" the primacy still belongs to the apostles, prophets, and teachers (XI. 4–7; XIII. 3) as the spiritual guides of the churches, while bishops and deacons are local officers (XV. 1), though "elders" or "presbyters" are not mentioned. One may note the famous discussion on the Christian ministry in *The Expositor* for 1887, which was participated in by W. Sanday, G. Salmon, C. Gore, G. A. Simcox, A. Harnack, J. Rendel Harris, W. Milligan, J. Macpherson. The lower view of the origin of bishops and deacons as presidents and dispensers of the ordinance of the Lord's Supper in particular is advocated

[1] κυβερνήσεις. [2] ἀντιλήμψεις.

by Rev. H. F. Hamilton in " The People of God "
(1912, 2 vols.).[1] There seems little doubt that the
development varied in different regions. Perhaps
Ignatius represents one line of development while
" The Teaching of the Twelve Apostles " shows another. But in the course of time apostles, prophets,
and teachers disappeared and a consequent readjust-
ment of functions followed. The growth of the ad-
ministrative bishop was certainly later than the New
Testament period, as Lightfoot has proven. The
modern " pastor " (shepherd)[2] of the flock is expected
to be at once apostle (missionary,[3] or one sent of God),
bishop or overseer, shepherd to care for each lamb
in the flock, herald[4] or preacher to proclaim the
message, evangelist (gospelizer[5]) to win to Christ,
prophet[6] or for-speaker for God, teacher[7] to instruct
in the way of the Lord, deacon (in the general sense
of service) at the call of one and all in the com-
munity, elder or guide and counsellor. The demands upon the " bishops " have grown with the
years, while those upon the " deacons " have lessened
by comparison. The wise pastor seeks to throw
some of his burdens upon the deacons and upon the
church as a whole.

[1] See his theory ably reviewed by Rev. Maurice Jones in
The Expositor, August, 1916, pp. 118–135. See the other
side in Loenning, " Gemeindeverfassung des Urchristentums,"
Theol. Lit., 1889, coll. 418–429.

[2] ποιμήν.   [3] ἀπόστολος.   [4] κήρυξ.
[5] εὐαγγελιστής.   [6] προφήτης.   [7] διδάσκαλος.

8. The Fatherhood of God and the Lordship of Christ.

This is Paul's favourite greeting[1] as it appears also in 1 and 2 Corinthians, Galatians, Romans, and Ephesians, and in slightly modified form in one and 2 Thessalonians, Colossians, 1 Timothy, Titus, 2 Timothy. There seems little doubt that Paul means to place Jesus Christ on an equality with God the Father in spite of the absence here of the application of the term God to Jesus. Paul ascribes divine attributes to Christ in Colossians 1 : 15–19, and is credited by Luke in Acts 20 : 28 (true text, " Church of God ") with applying the term God directly to Christ. According to the probable punctuation in Romans 9 : 5 Paul calls Christ God, and that is the real idea in Titus 2 : 13.[2] Besides, in Philippians 2 : 5–11, Paul argues on the basis of Christ's being " in the form of God " and possessing " equality with God." In Colossians 2 : 9 he says that all the fullness of the Godhead dwells bodily in Jesus Christ. It is beside the mark, therefore, for Vincent (" Int. Crit. on Phil.," p. 5) to say : " The fact that God and Christ appear on an equality in the salutation cannot be adduced as a positive proof of the divine nature of Christ, though it falls in with Paul's words in chap-

---

[1] χάρις ὑμῖν καὶ εἰρήνη ἀπὸ θεοῦ πατρὸς ἡμῶν καὶ κυρίου Ἰησοῦ χριστοῦ.

[2] See margin of Am. St. Version " of our great God and Saviour Jesus Christ." Cf. Robertson, " Grammar of Greek New Testament in Light of Historical Research," p. 786.

ter 2, and may be allowed to point to that doctrine which he elsewhere asserts. We cannot be too careful to distinguish between ideas which unconsciously underlie particular expressions, and the same ideas used with a definite and conscious dogmatic purpose. This Epistle especially has suffered from the overlooking of this distinction." *Per contra*, the almost unconscious attribution of deity to Jesus Christ by Paul so often and in so many ways reveals better than anything else Paul's attitude of mind towards the Person of Christ. It is not positive proof of the deity of Christ for Paul to have this opinion, to be sure, unless one is willing to follow Paul's guidance in the matter, but the repeated implication is strong proof of Paul's conception of Christ's nature and relation to God. Certainly Paul is not meaning to give a mere Trinitarian formula, since he does not mention here the Holy Spirit, though Rainy (" Expositor's Bible," Phil., p. 16) suggests that the work of the Holy Spirit is really involved in the grace and peace from the Father and the Son. Sometimes at the conclusion of the letters Paul mentions only Jesus, as in 2 Thessalonians 3 : 18; Galatians 6 : 18; Philippians 4 : 23. No name at all may be used as in Colossians 4 : 18 (" Grace be with you "); Titus 3 : 15. But in 2 Corinthians 13 : 13 we have the full Trinity named: " The grace of the Lord Jesus Christ, and the love of God, and the communion of the Holy Spirit, be with you all."

The term " Lord " [1] is common in the Old Testament (Septuagint) for God, and there can be little doubt that Paul in his frequent use of this word means to affirm the essential deity of Jesus Christ. The word is common in the papyri and the inscriptions for the Roman emperors who claimed divine attributes and accepted worship. But Paul was not going to allow this pagan usage to rob him of the privilege of employing this noble word with its rich heritage. Indeed, it is quite possible that Paul made a point of applying " Lord " to Jesus so many times for the very reason that the emperors claimed it for themselves. The word in a way became the hallmark of Christianity in the Roman Empire. The Christians applied it to Jesus, the heathen to Cæsar. The Gentile Christians who once said " Lord Cæsar " now learned to say " Lord Jesus." Hence Paul says (1 Cor. 12 : 2 f.): " Ye know that when ye were Gentiles ye were led away unto those dumb idols, howsoever ye might be led. Wherefore I make known unto you, that no man speaking in the spirit of God saith, Jesus is anathema [2] ; and no man can say, Jesus is Lord, [3] but in the Holy Spirit." During the trial of Polycarp he was urged by Herod and Nicetes to say the words " Lord Cæsar " and live : " For what is the harm in saying ' Lord Cæsar ' and in offering sacrifices and doing the things

---

[1] κύριος.   [2] ᾿Ανάθεμα ᾿Ιησοῦς.

[3] Κύριος ᾿Ιησοῦς.

following these and being spared?"[1] A Phrygian Christian, Cointus, had just renounced "Jesus as Lord" and said "Lord Cæsar" and was spared. Polycarp stoutly refused to say "Lord Cæsar" when those words meant the renunciation of "Lord Jesus." He said in defense, "I am a Christian"[2] and was burned as he knew[3] he would be. It cost something then to say "Lord Jesus," and Paul was right in saying that no one could say these words (and mean them) except in the Holy Spirit. These three words (Lord, Jesus, Christ) present the various aspects of the work of Jesus. His human name "Jesus"[4] means "saviour of his people from sin" (Matt. 1 : 21) and the glory and dignity of the humanity is emphasized in Philippians 2 : 5–11 and in the Epistle to the Hebrews (in particular ch. 2). He is the new Joshua of the people of God. The name was common enough among the Jews as Josephus testifies and the papyri also show it. Christ was at first merely the description of His Messianic mission, the Hebrew Messiah,[5] the Anointed One. In the Gospels we usually have the article with it, the Anointed One[6] (the Messiah) as in Matthew 1 : 17;

---

[1] Martyrdom of Polycarp, VIII, 2. τί γὰρ κακόν ἐστιν εἰπεῖν Κύριος Καῖσαρ, καὶ ἐπιθῦσαι καὶ τὰ τούτοις ἀκόλουθα καὶ διασώζεσθαι.   [2] Ibid., X. χριστιανός εἰμι.

[3] Ibid., V. δεῖ με ζῶντα καυθῆναι.   [4] Ἰησοῦς.

[5] χριστός.

[6] Μεσσίας is transliteration as Christ is translation. χριστός is the verbal adjective of χρίω to anoint.

16 : 16. But its use as a title or mere proper name also occurs in the Gospels (as Matt. 1 : 1) as is the rule in the Epistles and Revelation. In Paul's later Epistles we usually have " Christ Jesus " instead of " Jesus Christ," a still further development in the usage (cf. 1 Tim. 1 : 1–2). Thus by " Lord Jesus Christ " Paul really presents the statement that Jesus is a real man, is the Jewish Messiah of promise, and is divine, Son of God and Son of man (cf. Luke 2 : 11 " the Saviour, who is Christ the Lord "). Paul does not explain in what sense he uses " Father " as applied to God, whether the general sense in which God is the Father of all men who are His offspring (Acts 17 : 26–29) or the more limited sense as Father of the redeemed (Rom. 8 : 14–16). The use of " God our Father " reminds us of the Lord's Prayer (Matt. 6 : 9).

9. Grace and Peace.

It has already been noted that Paul does not use the common word for greeting so abundant in the letters in the papyri. He may have felt that it was " too meagre for Christian intercourse " (Kennedy, *in loco*). Grace is from the same root[1] as the other word for greeting. Kennedy calls grace Paul's " own great watchword." It is the distinctive word for the new dispensation as John has it in his Gospel (1 : 17): " For the law was given through Moses; grace and truth came through Jesus Christ." It is Paul's word

[1] χαρ—root of both χαίρω (χαίρειν) and χάρις. Our word " grace " is the Latin *gratia*.

greeting = grace

in his famous antithesis between legalism and law,
" justified freely by his grace" (Rom. 3 : 24). " But
if it is by grace, it is no more of works : otherwise
grace is no more grace" (Rom. 11 : 6). The word is
constantly coming from Paul's pen and is akin to the
word for joy,[1] as has just been shown. It is used for
" gift" and " gratitude " and " charm " and " good-
will " and " lovingkindness." No one word in English can translate its wealth of meaning. This word,
" perhaps above all others, shows the powerful re-
moulding of terms by Christian thought and feeling "
(Kennedy, *in loco*). It lays emphasis on the *freeness*
of God's lovingkindness to men (Vincent, *in loco*). It
is the " free favour " of God, the state of grace (Rom.
5 : 2) and the power from that state (Eph. 4 : 7), the
overwhelming richness of the love of God in Christ
Jesus, which Paul wishes for the saints in Philippi.

The other word " peace "[2] is a picture of " the
harmony and health of that life which is reconciled to
God through Jesus Christ" (Kennedy, *in loco*), the
peace which follows from the grace. The two words
thus cover the whole of the Christian experience.
This word " peace " is used of nations and of individuals and implies a bond that is made, words that
are spoken, as the basis on which peace rests. The
Jews said " *shālōm*" (*salaam*, Arabic *salam*, peace)

---

[1] χαρά.

[2] Εἰρήνη may be either from εἴρω to join or εἴρω to say.
Our word " peace " is the Latin *pax* through the French *paix*.

as a greeting. The angels brought a message of
" peace " to men of good-will in their song of greeting
to the shepherds (Luke 2 : 14). It is the Messianic
greeting to those who welcome the preachers of Christ
(Luke 10 : 5). But peace in the Pauline conception
implies reconciliation with God in Christ (Vincent, *in
loco*). It is the tranquil soul at peace with God. God
is the God of peace (2 Cor. 13 : 11; Heb. 13 : 20).
Jesus gave His peace as a blessing to the disciples,
His parting blessing (John 14 : 27), a peace which the
world could not give. Paul has this same idea when
he speaks (Phil. 4 : 7) of the peace that passeth all
understanding. But let no one imagine that Paul
taught " peace at any price " either with man or devil.
No one exhibits the spirit of courage and conflict
more than Paul. He has no patience with cowardice
in preachers (2 Tim. 1 : 7). Christ bade His disciples
to be of good cheer in the midst of tribulation, for
He had overcome the world (John 16 : 33). Jesus
offers us repose in the midst of struggle. God's
peace makes us independent of man's petty wars.
Peace is not the greatest good. Righteousness out-
ranks peace. " First pure, then peaceable " (Jas.
3 : 17). Only those who " do peace " may expect
" the fruit of righteousness " which is sown in peace
(Jas. 3 : 18). It is not always possible to live at peace
with men, but the responsibility for breaking the peace
should rest upon others (Rom. 12 : 18). But peace at
the price of the triumph of evil is cowardly sin.

good ch.

II

JOY IN PRAYER
(Philippians 1 : 3–11.)

JOY is the key-note of Philippians. Here we see Paul's joy in prayer. It is a noble gift, this exultation and exaltation in prayer. The men of a former generation spoke of " liberty " in prayer. There is no higher spiritual exercise than this and it comes only from long practice. The Philippians knew of this trait of Paul, for in prison there he and Silas " were praying and singing hymns unto God [1] (Acts 16 : 25). Rainy (" Expositor's Bible ") calls this prayer " The Apostle's Mind about the Philippians." It is that, but it is his mind in prayer, a summary of his constant prayer for them, the deepest desires of his heart about them, the highest hopes he has for them. There are delightful words here that linger in the mind.

1. **Memory** (verse 3).

" Upon all my remembrance of you." The words could mean " upon all your remembrance of me," but the other is probably the idea. It cannot[2] be

[1] προσευχόμενοι ὕμνουν τὸν θεόν. Almost as if the prayer was a song.

[2] Because of πάσῃ τῇ μνείᾳ (the article). Cf. Robertson, " Grammar of the Greek New Testament in the Light of Historical Research," pp. 769 f.

56

" upon every remembrance." Paul is not thinking of isolated memories of Philippi, but of the total picture that is still vivid in his mind. There were unpleasant memories of Philippi if he cared to dwell upon them, the rage of the masters of the poor girl whom Paul set free and the conduct of the magistrates and the populace towards Paul. But these were not part of the flock in Philippi. Even there Paul knows of unpleasantness between two women (Phil. 4 : 2 f.) and of others who seek their own desires (3 : 17). But time and distance mellow one's memories in a gracious way, particularly in the case of an old pastor who no longer feels the petty irritations that once were so keen. Fortunately also the people forget their grudges against the pastor, now that he is gone. Paul will not allow specks to spoil the whole. So he meditates upon the names and faces of the saints at Philippi with his marvellous faculty for recalling them, happy trait for any preacher who can thus bind people to him. Time blurs names and faces for most of us, but Paul has zest in the life of people. He is fond of folks and joys in them through the haze of the past, in all of them. Indeed, it almost sounds as if Paul did nothing else but dream about the Philippians, " always in every supplication."[1] Memories of his work all over the world came to him often in moments of despair and of cheer

[1] He plays upon the word " all ": πάσῃ, πάντοτε, πάσῃ, πάντων.

(cf. 2 Cor. 11). These hallowed associations with
the elect of earth spur one on to fresh endeavour.
One feeds upon rich experiences of grace, like those
at Northfield, and can go in the strength of this
meat for many days.

2. Gratitude (verse 3).

Gratitude springs out of memory, bubbling up like
a fountain. His feeling of gratitude[1] rests upon[2]
the happy and holy memories of his days with the
Philippians and their kindness to him.   Paul always
has something to thank God for in the churches to
which he writes, save in the case of the Galatians,
whose sudden defection shocked him severely.   Even
in Corinth he finds much to praise.   Paul is a man
of prayer and gratitude to God is an essential element in real prayer.   " The great people of the earth
to-day are the people of prayer.   The greatest force
of the day is prayer " (Baskerville, " Sidelights on the
Epistle to the Philippians," p. 6).   But nowhere is
Paul in more grateful mood than in this Epistle of
joy and suffering.   He " dwells long and fondly on
the subject " (Lightfoot, *in loco*).   The Western

---

[1] εὐχαριστέω is condemned by the Atticists, but is good
Koine and occurs in the papyri (Deissmann, " Bible Studies,"
p. 122) and from Polybius on.   The vulgate *gratias ago* is a
good deal like εὐχάριστος (from εὖ and χαρίζομαι).

[2] ἐπί here in a semi-local (Ellicott) or ethico-local (Kennedy) sense.

text[1] makes Paul emphatic in the assertion of his gratitude, suggesting that the Philippians had written Paul a letter with the gifts which Epaphroditus brought. Perhaps also they may have imagined a slight lack of cordiality on Paul's part (Kennedy, *in loco*), because some time had elapsed with no word of appreciation from him. But the sickness of Epaphroditus explains his delay and he repeats his gratitude with emphasis. One of the common faults of men is failure to express gratitude for the simple courtesies and favours of life. It costs little to say " Thank you," and this word smooths out many wrinkles of care. Paul certainly had not meant to be derelict in this grace and amply atones for his apparent neglect by this beautiful Epistle which is a model of Christian courtesy. His gratitude is in no sense the Frenchman's definition, a lively sense of favours expected. This notion is repellent to Paul (Phil. 4: 17). It must be admitted that many a life is embittered by lack of gratitude and appreciation on the part of those who matter most.

> " How sharper than a serpent's tooth it is
> To have a thankless child."

3. **Supplication** (verse 4).

But Paul was not content with their spiritual state, many as were the grounds of thanksgiving. A holy discontent and high ambition for them led him to pe-

---

[1] DEFG defg have ἐγὼ μὲν.

titionary[1] prayer. One cannot well be in the presence of God without a sense of need. The words in this verse can be variously punctuated, but they probably go together as a single thought with its studied repetition of the word all (Lightfoot, *in loco*). One's mood in prayer varies according to the subject of the prayer. Here the Apostle prays " with joy,"[2] " with a sense of joy " (Moffatt). This note is the undertone of the whole[3] Epistle and sounds on through Paul's petition for them which partakes of the nature of a spiritual rhapsody. Christians often show emotion in prayer. Sometimes uncontrolled passion sweeps them away. At times feeling seems to be without thought and merely incoherent ecstasy or even worked-up artificiality as in some shouting, the " holy laugh," the " holy rollers " and similar performances. But dead formalism has little right to find fault with such excesses. With Paul joyful prayer is the normal atmosphere of his life with God. He had a " hallelujah chorus" in his heart. Christ to Paul was the spring of all joy. He could not be a pessimist. He was not a blind optimist. Joy is not mere excitement, not mere noise, but serenity of spirit that overcomes circumstance. His

---

[1] δέησις (twice in this verse) is, like εὐχαριστία, just one aspect of προσευχή (general prayer) addressed only to God, though δέησις, from δέομαι to need or to beg, is to God or man.

[2] μετὰ χαρᾶς.

[3] Summa epistolæ (Bengel).

" buoyant spirit can prevail
Where common cheerfulness would fail."

The happiest man in Rome is Paul the prisoner for Christ. Joy is the missing note in many
lives which are too easily upset by the little worries.
The little foxes eat away the vines. Christianity
will have more power when it recovers joyful prayer,
jubilant praying, mighty wrestling with God. Baskerville justly says that we need a revival in our
prayer-life: " Prayer may well be regarded as the
line of communication with the base of supplies."
We have let the stream get choked from this fountain of life. If we lay hold on God with great
energy, we shall have power with men.

4. **Partnership** (verse 5).

Partnership is one of the grounds[1] of Paul's
thanksgiving about the Philippians. It is their partnership[2] or fellowship with Paul in the furtherance
of the Gospel.[3] The specific reference is to the contributions made by this church " from the first day
until now,"[4] to Thessalonica and to Corinth at the
very start of the church's life (Phil. 4: 15 f.): At
first they stood alone in this cordial support of Paul's

---

[1] ἐπί.

[2] τῇ κοινωνίᾳ ὑμῶν (subjective genitive), from the adjective
κοινός (in common). The word κοινωνία is used in the
papyri of the marriage contract as well as of commercial partnership, a life-partnership βίου κοινωνία.

[3] εἰς τὸ εὐαγγέλιον. Note this use of εἰς.

[4] ἀπὸ τῆς πρώτης ἡμέρας ἄχρι τοῦ νῦν.

missionary labours, though others later followed this
noble example (2 Cor. 11 : 8). The Philippian
church was thus a missionary church from the start.
The word here for fellowship means coöperation in
the largest sense, though the particular application is
to their help to Paul in the work. James and John
were partners[1] with Simon in the fishing. Titus was
Paul's partner (2 Cor. 8 : 23). Paul uses this word
for partnership on the part of the Philippians in the
collection for the poor saints in Jerusalem (2 Cor.
8 : 4). The Philippians gave themselves to the mission cause heart and soul (Rainy, *in loco*). Here
was one church to which Paul could always turn,
upon whom he could always count for sympathy and
support. It is just the lack of this sense of fellowship
and of responsibility that makes so many Christians
ineffective and useless in aggressive work. After
Pentecost the Jerusalem Christians continued steadfastly in this fellowship or partnership (Acts 2 : 42).
This mutual bond of spiritual commerce should bind
together with hooks of steel people and pastor and
make the church glad to remunerate properly both
pastor and missionary (Gal. 6 : 6). It is the great
distinction of the Philippian church that they had
enlightenment enough to see their opportunity as co-
workers with Paul in the greatest enterprise of the
ages. They were only too glad of the chance of
taking stock in this chief business of the world.

[1] κοινωνοί (Luke 5 : 10). *aho 63*

Coöperation is still the great demand among modern Christians. Churches so often leave it all for the pastor to do. The forces of righteousness in our cities so easily disintegrate and fly apart. We have a common salvation, a common task, a common peril, and a common Captain of our salvation. When Christians, with frank recognition of their differences of standpoint and convictions, learn to pull together in all common interests against Satan, we shall see the beginning of the end of his dominion among men. But we have not even learned how to enlist all those in one denomination in any common cause.

5. **Confidence** (verses 6 and 7).

Paul's state of confidence [1] grew out of his experience with God and his knowledge of them. Paul places God first always. God began [2] a good work in them, took the initiative as He always does. God will also perfect [3] it, carry it on to perfection, will not take His hand from the task till the day of Jesus Christ, the day of consummation. God " will go on completing it " (Moffatt). Paul is cheered by the hope of the Parousia or Second Coming of Christ, though he sets no day for it. He nowhere says that it will be before his death, and in this very Epistle he faces his own death as a real problem (1 : 21 ff.). Paul does, however, maintain an expectant attitude

---

[1] πεποιθώς, second perfect participle.
[2] ὁ ἐναρξάμενος.   [3] ἐπιτελέσει linear future.

towards the return of Christ, and the hope has a
moulding influence on his life.   It is a pity that so
many modern Christians have lost any real joy in this
blessed hope and no longer look for the coming of
Jesus to claim His own.   Some, indeed, go to the
other extreme and have formal programs and details
and even dates for the Parousia.   One can admire
Paul's sanity and balance on this subject as on all
others that he discusses.   He counts it right[1] to
have the opinion about the Philippians that he cher-
ishes.   This church was good soil, no doubt, and
good seed was sown there, and good cultivation was
kept up also.   But the reason here given for Paul's
optimism is that he holds them in his heart.   Inter-
estingly enough the phrase in the Greek[2] can mean
" because you hold me in your heart."   Both things
are true, but Paul is speaking of his own love for his
children in the Gospel.   He was bound to believe
the best about them.   He has the shepherd heart
and grounds his confidence in his own love as well
as in God's purposes about them.   The Philippians
have shown the grace of continuance.   They are not
quitters.   They press on both in the defense[3] and in
the confirmation of the Gospel.   There are so many
unfinished books, pictures, sculpture, buildings.   It

[1] δίκαιον (*justum*, Vg.).   Right here, not righteous.
[2] Διὰ τὸ ἔχειν με ἐν τῇ καρδίᾳ ὑμᾶς.   Here καρδία includes the purposes of the will as well as the emotions.
[3] ἀπολογία is used of defense in a judicial action.

is a joy to see a church carry a thing through as they
are doing. This is like God whose work is thorough
(Baskerville). Hence Paul is proud to have the
Philippians co-partners [1] with him in grace, in all the
rich grace in Christ. They all share to the full with [2]
Paul. He claims no clerical grace above them.
They are fellows in Christ Jesus. It does Paul good
to brood over this noble band of brothers linked together in the mystic bond of love for God and man,
linked not merely in idea and theory, but in actual
practice. If all churches of Christ lived up to this
ideal, there would be no need and no room for any
other brotherhoods, much good as many of them do.
The church would fill all the life to the full.

6. Longing (verse 8).

Paul uses a very strong word [3] here, a word of intense feeling and yearning, sometimes transliterated
as *pothos*.[4] The solemn oath here adds to the emotion. Paul calls God to witness in no light or flip-
pant way (cf. Rom. 1 : 9–11). But Paul actually says
that he longs after them in the tender mercies [5] of

---

[1] συνκοινωνούς μου τῆς χάριτος.

[2] σύν.

[3] ἐπιποθῶ.

[4] We cannot press the force of the compound ἐπι- in the
κοινή.

[5] σπλάγχνα is used for the nobler viscera (heart, liver, lungs,
etc.), as opposed to the ἔντερα (lower intestines). It occurs
in the papyri in sense of pity ὑπὲρ σπλάγχνου " for pity's
sake " (BU 1139¹⁷, V. B. C.), Moulton and Milligan, " Lexical Notes from the Papyri," *Expositor*, June, 1911.

Jesus Christ, with all the heart-hunger of Jesus Himself. The ancient Greeks located the emotions of
love, pity, joy, etc., in the "stomach-brain," as it is
sometimes called. This word is used about Philemon, "my very heart"[1] (Phile. 12). Paul longs
for the Philippians, not only with the best of his own
heart but in mystic union with Christ with the very
heart-throb of Jesus Himself. He identifies his own
heart-life with that of Christ. Paul, though a man
of tremendous intellectual power, was even more a
man of heart. He was a spiritual dynamo for
Christ, a sort of electric battery, charged with the
love of Christ.

7. Discerning Love (verses 9–10[a]).

Petition (cf. 1 : 4) is now the form of Paul's prayer,
petition closely connected with the gratitude already
so richly expressed. Paul's prayers for the Christians are very suggestive. They are never perfunctory but always pertinent to the situation. "Prayer
makes the preacher a heart-preacher. Prayer puts
the preacher's heart into the preacher's sermon.
Prayer puts the preacher's sermon into the preacher's
heart" (Baskerville, *in loco*). This prayer has the
very breath of heaven. Paul prays for the overflow[2]

---

[1] τὰ ἐμὰ σπλάγχνα.
[2] περισσεύῃ (cf. περισσός from περί). In ancient Greek
this word meant to remain over. It is common in the Septuagint. Paul uses it commonly for "abound" (Vg. here
abundet). Cf. Thomas, "The Prayers of St. Paul."

of the love[1] of the Philippians for one another and
for himself. There is no danger of an excess. There
is still room, " yet more and more,"[2] Paul pleads
with his fondness for piling up adverbs. Some
coldly critical people dislike exuberance in Christian
affection, but Paul sets no limit[3] to the development
and expression of love except " in knowledge and
all discernment,"[4] " all manner of insight " (Moffatt),
a very important qualification. Love must not be a
raging flood like that in the Miami Valley that threat-
ened the very existence of Dayton and other cities.
It is a flood of love that Paul prays for and yet a
flood within the bounds of good sense and discretion.
He wishes that " the sensitiveness of touch may be
added to love" (Kennedy, *in loco*). There should be
sense in love and not blind impulse. Enthusiasm
needs common sense for poise and guidance. What
we call common sense is sense about common things,
and is itself an uncommon quality. The flood is
good if we know how to use it or to ride it. Love
grows best in the full light of knowledge.[5] Love has

---

[1] ἀγάπη is a " back-formation " from ἀγαπάω. There is
one doubtful example of ἀγάπη in a Herculaneum papyrus
(i. B. C.) δὶ ἀ[γ]άπης ἐ[ναρ]γοῦς. The verb ἀγαπάω in the
New Testament is a deeper and richer word than φιλέω which
is more human (Moulton and Milligan, " Vocabulary ").

[2] ἔτι μᾶλλον καὶ μᾶλλον.

[3] Paul here uses the tense for durative action (περισσεύῃ).

[4] ἐν ἐπιγνώσει καὶ πάσῃ αἰσθήσει. Vg. has *in scientia, et in
omni sensu*.

[5] Paul is fond of ἐπίγνωσις which is added (ἐπι-) knowledge.

nothing to fear from the light. Suspicion kills love.
" Perfect love casts out fear " (1 John 4 : 18). Intense love makes people hypersensitive to slights and
misunderstandings unless one is quick to apply full
knowledge to the situation. The word " discernment '① calls for the practical application of this
spiritual insight and sensitiveness. This word denotes the fineness of spiritual perception that comes
from alertness and practice. Hippocrates,[2] a med-
ical writer, employs the verb for perception with
sight, touch, hearing, the nose, the tongue, and
knowledge. The word suggests the nervous organ-
ism of the body, all the avenues of approach by the
senses of the mind, that wonderful sensitive plate,
more delicate than any seismograph for recording
earthquake shocks, or than any chemical apparatus
for detecting affinities between atoms, or than any
electrical machinery for noting the behaviour of
electrons. Wireless telegraphy requires apparatus
for sending and receiving the sound-waves. We
give various names to this ethical sensitiveness like
tact, spiritual sensibility, a trained conscience. One

See its intensive force in 1 Corinthians 13 : 12. Cf. Epictetus
II, 20, 21 ἐπίγνωσις τῆς ἀληθείας.

① αἴσθησις. Here only in the New Testament, but in
Proverbs 1 : 4, 7, 22, etc. Cf. εἰς αἴσθησιν τοῦ κακοῦ in
Epictetus II, 18, 8. In Hebrews 5 : 14 note αἰσθητήρια for
the organs of moral sense (Lightfoot).

[2] De Off. Med. 3 (quoted by Kennedy, *in loco*) ἃ καὶ τῇ ὄψι
καὶ καὶ τῇ ἀφῇ καὶ τῇ ἀκουῇ καὶ τῇ ῥινὶ καὶ τῇ γλώσσῃ καὶ
τῇ γνώμῃ ἔστιν αἰσθέθαι.

is reminded of the phrase in Hebrews 5 : 14 " who by reason of use have their senses exercised to discern good and evil," trained like athletes[1] " to discriminate between good and evil." [2] Sin blunts the moral sense and blurs the spiritual vision so that the eyes of the heart do not see correctly. Paul's wish about the saints at Philippi is that they may be in a position [3] where they can " approve the things that are excellent," [4] " have a sense of what is vital " (Moffatt). This is one of the translations of this expression and probably what Paul really means here. But the original idea is " to test the things that differ." The word for " excellent " [5] means to " bear apart " either in hostility or superiority. By comparison or examination [6] as in the testing of metals one learns wherein they differ and which is superior and at what points. Thus one is prepared intelligently to approve [7] the excellent. It is only when one has his ethical sense quickened and has also full knowledge of the facts that he is able to render a sound judgment on

---

[1] γεγυμνασμένα. Perfect tense, state of readiness.

[2] πρὸς διάκρισιν καλοῦ τε καὶ κακοῦ.

[3] εἰς τό with the infinitive. Probably purpose though contemplated result is possible.

[4] δοκιμάζειν τὰ διαφέροντα.

[5] διαφέροντα neuter plural participle from διαφέρω.

[6] Δοκιμάζειν. Very common in this sense in the papyri. It is used for assaying metals as in Proverbs 8 : 10 ; 17 : 3.

[7] The papyri have this sense also. Cf. ὁ]ποτέρως οὖν καὶ σὺ δοκιμάζεις, P. Pap. III. 41 (quoted by Moulton and Milligan, " Vocabulary ").

matters of right and wrong.   When the ethical sense
is dulled by misuse or blinded by misinformation or
prejudice, its decisions cannot be trusted.   So the
good is the enemy of the best.   One cannot be satisfied with what is " good enough " for others.   Few
things are more needed by modern Christians than
precisely this intelligent moral insight mingled with
a wealth of love.   It is needed to keep us from failure
to see sin.   We need it to help us to see spiritual
opportunity and privilege.   We need it to enable us
to see what things are relatively the most important
and to put the emphasis in the right place.   We need
it to keep us from becoming the dupes of slick-
tongued adventurers and religious mountebanks.
We need it to shield us from being ourselves the
victims of religious prejudice and narrowness.   It
is the only combination that insures loyalty to truth
with progress in grace and service.   God give us all
discerning love.

8.   Fruit (1 : 10ᵇ–11).

Paul has a series [1] of requests in this prayer, each a
link in the chain.   He prays for abounding and discerning love, that the Philippians may be drawn to
the highest and the best, that in [2] the day of Christ

---

[1] ἵνα, εἰς τό, ἵνα (verses 9–11), each dependent on the
other, the two last of an epexegetical nature.

[2] εἰς ἡμέραν Χριστοῦ.   Literally in or for the day of Christ,
the Parousia.   Cf. Phil. 2 : 16 ; Eph. 4 : 30 ; 2 Tim. 1 : 12.
Vg. has *in diem Christi.*

they may pass under the eye of the Judge with approval. The goal of Paul in his work is the Day of
Assizes when Jesus comes to judge. Then he wishes
the Philippians to be sincere.[1] The old etymology[2]
(T. H. Green quoted by Kennedy, *in loco*) defines the
word as " perfect openness towards God." Plato
uses the word for pure intellect, for the soul purged
from sense. Certainly the eye of Him with whom we
have to do sees us as we are (Heb. 4 : 12 f.). He is
the God of things as they are. But Paul prays
also that the Philippians may be " void of offence,"
a possible translation. The word is either intransitive as in Acts 24 : 16 and means " not stumbling " or transitive as in 1 Cor. 10 : 32 and means
" not causing others to stumble." Either will make
good sense here, for Jesus (cf. Matt. 25 : 31–46) mentions our treatment of others as one of the tests of
character on the Judgment Day. But Paul is not
satisfied with a negative statement of goodness. He
adds a prayer for " the fruit of righteousness," " that
harvest of righteousness " (Moffatt), for a full[3] crop
on a fruitful tree (cf. Ps. 1 ; Prov. 11 : 30). In the

---

[1] εἰλικρινεῖς. Unmixed, pure, unsullied. Vg. *sinceri*.

[2] From κρίνω and εἴλη (heat of sun) tested by sunbeams or
εἴλη separated into ranks is very doubtful. The word is common enough, though the etymology is unknown. Cf. 1 Cor.
5 : 8 ; 2 Cor. 1 : 12 for εἰλικρίνεια. Light would be in-
visible apart from obstructions against which it strikes.

[3] πεπληρωμένοι. Perfect passive, state of completion. Note
the accusative καρπὸν.

Sermon on the Mount Jesus gave fruit as the proof of one's sincerity in God's service. " By their fruits ye shall know them " (Matt. 7 : 16). The figure is common enough in all ages. Paul adds that this fruit of righteousness comes only through Jesus Christ.[1] The Pharisees did not possess it according to the indictment of Jesus in Matthew 6 and 23. Jesus is the vine on which this fruit grows (cf. John 15 : 1-8). Paul closes his prayer with the purpose of this glorious fruitage, " unto the glory and praise of God." The fruit is not for the glory of the Philippians nor for the honour of Paul. Redemption has its origin in God and its end in God. " For of him, and through him, and unto him are all things. To him be the glory for ever. Amen " (Rom. 11 : 36). The word for glory[2] originally meant opinion. But in the Septuagint it is used for the glory of the Lord, for the Shekinah. This is the conception here. The word had a popular sense also like our glory.[3] Paul means that men will be led to praise God because good fruit is found in our lives.

[1] τὸν διὰ Ἰησοῦ Χριστοῦ. Note the added article to the attributive clause.

[2] δόξα from δοκέω.

[3] Cf. δόξα πόλεως of the prytanis in P. Oxy. I. 41, 4 (iii, iv, A. D.) quoted by Moulton and Milligan's " Vocabulary."

III

GOOD OUT OF ILL
(1 : 12–20)

HE interpretation of Providence is not always easy if one looks at the whole problem. There are always glib interpreters, like Job's miserable comforters, who know how to fit the cap to others with complete satisfaction to themselves. Modern science has thrown the chill of doubt over many of those who find refuge in the love of a personal God, our Heavenly Father. It is grim comfort to find consolation only in the certain operation of inexorable law. Our problem is to be able to see the hand of God in a world of law and order when things go against us. Paul was able to get sweet out of bitter. It is easier to see the good after it has come out of the ill. But it would be a dreary world if one could not believe that God cares for His people and overrules the evils of life for the progress of man and of men.

1. **Progress of the Gospel** (verse 12).

It is possible that Epaphroditus brought a letter to Paul from the Philippian church which was full of concern for Paul's welfare. He had been a prisoner

for some years now, two at Cæsarea and one or two
in Rome. Kennedy raises the question whether
Paul may not have been by this time transferred from
his hired lodging (Acts 28 : 30) to the *castra perigrinorum* where provincial prisoners were kept in military
custody. If so, the Philippians would naturally expect Paul to have a harder time than he had so far
experienced in Rome. At any rate Paul is anxious [1]
for them to know the true state of the case about his
affairs.[2] Paul tells of his experiences in Rome because only thus can he relieve their anxiety. There
are two extremes in this matter. Some men talk
too much about themselves and some do it too little.
The use of " rather "[3] clearly implies that the Philippians had expected the worst for Paul. He hastens
to tell them that he has good news, not bad news,
about the progress of the Gospel in Rome. The
word for progress[4] seems to mean cutting a way
ahead, blazing a trail before an army to come afterwards. The pioneers, like Daniel Boone in Ken-

[1] The idiom γινώσκειν δὲ ὑμᾶς βούλομαι occurs only here
in the New Testament, but is like Paul's common θέλω with
the infinitive (1 Cor. 10:1; 11:3; Col. 2:1; Rom.
1:13). It is a common epistolary phrase (Kennedy).

[2] τὰ κατ᾽ ἐμὲ. This use of κατά is almost equivalent to
the genitive in the κοινή. Cf. Kælker, " Questiones de elocu-
tione Polybiana," p. 282. Cf. Eph. 6 : 21 ; Col. 4 : 7.

[3] μᾶλλον. Comparative without standard of comparison as
in Phil. 2 : 26 ; 1 Cor. 7 : 38 ; 2 Cor. 7 : 7 ; Rom. 15 : 15.
" Really tended to advance the Gospel " (Moffatt).

[4] προκοπή. Cf. 1 : 25 ; 1 Tim. 4 : 15. Common in the
later Greek. From προκόπτω, to cut forward.

tucky, blazed the path for civilization and Christianity. In the Stoic philosophy (Zeller, " Stoics," p.
294) the word is used for progress towards wisdom.
Paul uses it for the progress of a young minister in
culture and power (1 Tim. 4: 15). So then the opposition to Paul in Rome has kicked the Gospel up-
stairs. The Jews from Asia did not stop the onward
march of the Gospel when they raised their hue and
cry in the temple in Jerusalem. The hand of God
was with Paul when he was at the mercy of the mob
and before the Sanhedrin. Even Felix and Festus
did not stay God's arm. In spite of shipwreck and
delay on the part of Nero work has gone on. \Paul
had not courted imprisonment, but he does not fret
unduly because of his chain. This very chain has
been used of God to spread the Gospel.

2. Sermons in Bonds (verse 13).

The precise way in which good has come out of
ill Paul goes on to show in an explanatory clause of
result.[1] Paul's bonds[2] are literal bonds, for he was
constantly chained to a Roman soldier (cf. Acts
28: 20). He probably means to say that his bonds
have become manifest in Christ.[3] It has become

---

[1] ὥστε—γενέσθαι καὶ—τολμᾶν. Cf. Robertson, " Grammar
of the Greek New Testament in the Light of Historical Research," pp. 999 f.

[2] δεσμούς. Δεσμά (cf. Luke 8: 29) is more common, but
no real distinction is traceable.

[3] ἐν Χριστῷ γενέσθαι. Position is ambiguous, but Vg. has
manifesta fierent in Christo.

plain that he is a prisoner for no crime, but solely for
Christ's sake, so that Paul can properly call himself
" the prisoner of Christ "[1] (Eph. 3 : 1).   This fact at-
tracted attention to Christ and gave Paul a fresh opportunity to preach Christ to those interested.   Paul
is never ashamed of Christ.   He is not ashamed of
his bonds.   They become a badge of honour for they
come to preach Christ to all who see them and who
know why he wears them.   In particular Paul has a
fresh opportunity each day with the guard to whom
he is chained.   The soldiers relieved each other.   He
not only talks to this guard about his armour (cf.
Eph. 6 : 10–20) and his service, but he tells him of
Jesus.   By this means alone the knowledge of Jesus
would be conveyed to many.   But Paul insists that
the Gospel by means of his bonds has become known
" throughout the whole prætorian guard."[2]   The
expression is ambiguous in the Greek and can be
interpreted in four different ways.   It may mean the
ten thousand picked soldiers who formed this notable
guard.   It may be the barracks where the guard
were stationed in Rome.   It may refer to the imperial palace as it is used of the governor's palace in the
provinces (cf. Matt. 27 : 27; John 18 : 28, 33).   It
may refer to the judicial authorities of the imperial
court.   There seems to be no way of determining
the matter finally, for good arguments are adduced

---

[1] ὁ δέσμιος τοῦ Χριστοῦ.

[2] ἐν ὅλῳ τῷ πραιτωρίῳ.   Vg. has *in omni prætorio.*

for each meaning.[1] We know that there were converts in Cæsar's household (Phil. 4 : 22), though this
fact does not prove that Paul himself had access to
the emperor's palace. There were Jews connected
with the household of Nero (his wife Poppæa, for
instance). The Christians there probably were slaves
or other menials. It is possible that Paul was re-
moved to the prætorian camp (*castra prætoriana*)
and thus had ready access to the whole guard. But
if not, he was still able slowly to spread the knowledge of Jesus through this famous band of soldiers.
He would probably make visits to the camp with his
guard who went with him from his lodging. In a
way, therefore, Paul became the friend and chaplain
of these soldiers. Mithraism was already beginning
to get a powerful hold upon the Roman soldiers[2]
and Paul would not be slow to seize the opportunity
to counteract this influence and to tell the men about
Jesus. The Roman soldier probably took kindly to
Paul (cf. the centurion Julius in Acts 27 : 3 who
treated Paul " kindly "[3]). Certainly Paul had a manly
message to present. He is manifestly proud of the
fact that he has set all the prætorian guard, almost
the flower of the Roman army, to thinking and
to talking about Jesus. Preaching to soldiers has
always appealed to strong preachers.[4] The shadow

[1] See Kennedy, *in loco.*
[2] Cf. Kennedy, " St. Paul and the Mystery–Religions."
[3] φιλανθρώπως.
[4] Cf. Broadus in Lee's Army (Robertson, " Life and Letters

of death in the battle of to-morrow brings the message close home to strong men's hearts. One is
able to preach as a " dying man to dying men."
Whether Paul was able to address the soldiers in
large companies in formal sermons we do not know,
but he was able to make skillful use of conversaticn.
These rough and ready men of affairs saw the steady
joy of Paul the prisoner. They watched him day by
day and his buoyant optimism caught their fancy.
Jesus is the secret of Paul's life of joy. Thus the
contagion of Paul's love for Jesus spread to " all the
rest," whether to soldiers, or to people in Rome it is
not clear. He had spoken to the Jews we know
(Acts 28 : 17, 23). There was much in the soldier's
life that appealed to Paul's heroic nature and he
drew frequent illustrations from the life of the soldier.

3. Spurring Others to Action (verse 14).

This is the second result of Paul's imprisonment in
Rome. There are always timid souls who lose heart
in times of persecution. Some even go to the extent
of apostasy when the cause seems lost. The early
Christian centuries furnish examples of those who
renounced Christ for Cæsar under the pressure of the
Roman state (cf. 1 Cor. 12 : 1-3). Paul had long
foreseen the coming conflict between Christianity
and the Man of Sin or Lawlessness embodied in

of John A. Broadus," pp. 198–209 ; Jones, " Christ in the
Camp," pp. 312–326) ; and the opportunity during the Great
War.

the Roman Empire (2 Thess. 2 : 3–12). Here in
Rome itself that dark shadow loomed blacker than
ever in spite of the fact that Nero had not yet come
out openly against Christianity. The faint-hearted
in Rome knew the power of the state. Paul was a
prisoner and the outcome was uncertain. These
fearful saints would take no chances. There was a
minority of the brethren in Rome who exercised
extra caution because of Paul's activity for Christ.
They wished no responsibility for his conduct if
things went against him. There are always these
shirkers who practise absenteeism from church in
times of struggle, these cowards in a crisis who slink
away till danger is past. They come in for the
shouting after victory is won. In case of disaster
they are ready to say: " We told you so." But
" the most of the brethren " [1] constituted that inner
circle of the brotherhood that does and dares things
for Christ while the rest hang back. Paul was lucky
to have won a majority to this scale of activity. It
is usually the minority of Christians who put energy
into the work while the majority drift along or criticize what the minority do. The papyri [2] give plenty
of examples of " brothers " in the sense of " fellows "

---

[1] τοὺς πλείονας τῶν ἀδελφῶν. The comparative can thus
be translated. Cf. Robertson, " Grammar," p. 668.

[2] Thus a town clerk calls another ἀδελφός, P. Tebt. I.
12 (B. C. 118), members of a burial club are so termed in P.
Tor. I, 1. i. 20 (ii. B. C.). See Moulton and Milligan's " Vocabulary " for others.

in service or members of guilds or brotherhoods.
Paul's courage and contagious enthusiasm had
shamed many into action who had at first held back
through fear or indifference. These gain confidence
in the Lord, which is the probable [1] translation rather
than "brethren in the Lord." This confidence in the
Lord is caused by Paul's bonds.[2] Paul's chain re-
buked their lethargy and cowardice and stirred the
conscience so that they are now "bold to speak the
word of God without fear." [3] Manifestly they had
been afraid to open their mouths for a while till they
saw how brave Paul was in spite of his bondage and
impending trial. Some, never eloquent before, now
find tongues of angels as they catch the spirit of Paul.
The bolder spirits are rendered "more abundantly [4]
bold" than they were before. These cast caution to
the winds and are overwhelmingly daring in their
championship of Jesus. They speak "the message of God," Paul's phrase here for preaching and
telling the story of the gospel of grace. There
are always in a crisis some choice spirits ready to
die for Christ like the ten thousand native Chinese
Christians who at the time of the Boxer movement
died rather than renounce Jesus. Fortitude is con-

[1] ἐν κυρίῳ πεπεθοίτας. Cf. Phil. 2 : 24; Gal. 5 : 10;
2 Thess. 3 : 4. The order here is different, but that is not a
material point.

[2] τοῖς δεσμοῖς μου. Instrumental case.

[3] τολμᾶν τὸν λόγον τοῦ θεοῦ ἀφόβως.

[4] περισσοτέρως.

tagious. Paul's courage was like that of a brave general leading his troops. There is nothing that will quicken a dying church into life like courage on the part of the leaders. Prophets to-day have to call to the dry bones to live. Paul waked up the church in Rome by going ahead in spite of his limitations and doing his duty boldly as opportunity came to him. It is a great achievement to revive a dead church. There are plenty of them dead or dying or asleep. Much of the pastor's energy is required to keep his church awake or to wake it up. It is not enough to galvanize a corpse. Life must come back into the body. This is no artificial or mechanical process. Paul did his own part heroically. That is the way to wake up our churches. Let each one lay hold of his own task. That is better than conventions or conferences or resolutions. Life is more contagious than death. Life can put death to flight if it is given a fair chance. "And he hath put a new song in my mouth, even praise unto our God; many shall see it, and fear, and shall trust in the Lord" (Ps. 40 : 3).

4. **Preaching Christ from Envy of Paul** (verses 15,[a] 17).

But Paul had no bed of roses in Rome. The minority furnished plenty of thorns for his side. Some of these were provoked by Paul's activity, it

[1] τινὲς μὲν. He does not define them.

is true, to preach① Christ, but they did it " even of
envy and strife," [2] pitiful enough motives for Christian zeal.   Envy [3] is a powerful motive in human
life.   It played its part in the trial and death of Jesus
(Matt. 27: 18). There is a personal side to this
preaching which is as much against Paul as in favour
of Christ (cf. Eph. 2: 4).   Kennedy pleads for
" rivalry " [4] rather than " strife " in this passage and
the word often has this sense.   Envy and rivalry
often lead to open strife.   We do not, indeed, know
to what class of teachers Paul refers.   It may be
some of the old teachers of the church in Rome who
do not relish Paul's leadership since it displaces them,
a form of jealousy that one sees only too often.   In
that case their fresh activity would be with a view to
regaining their former prestige and influence and
partly by depreciating Paul.[5]   If it was not personal
pique that stirred these men, they may have been
Jewish Christians who disliked the note of universality
in Paul's message and feared that he did not suffi-
ciently guard the interests of Judaism.[6]   It may have
been the Judaizers, Paul's old enemies who did him
such harm in Jerusalem and Galatia and Corinth.
This is the usual view since Bengel, but it is open to

---

① κηρύσσουσιν to herald Christ.

[2] καὶ διὰ φθόνον καὶ ἔριν.

[3] Philemon, a comic poet of B. C. 330, says : πολλά με
διδάσκεις ἀφθόνως διὰ φθόνον.   [4] For ἔριν.

[5] Cf. Weiss, " Am. Journal of Theology," i. 2, pp. 388–389.

[6] Cf. McGiffert, " Apostolic Age," pp. 393–395.

the objection that Paul here apparently condones their preaching. That, however, is not quite true, as we shall see. We do not, indeed, know that the Judaizers had reached Rome, though there is no inherent difficulty in that supposition. As a matter of fact, it is quite likely that all of these elements enter into the situation, for Paul expressly says that these men proclaimed[1] Christ from mixed motives, " not sincerely." [2] In fact, they preach from a partisan[3] or selfish motive (cf. Gal. 5 : 20). It was primarily " labour for hire " (cf. Job 2 : 11) and the word was applied to those in official position who looked after their own selfish interests rather than the common good. Kennedy argues for " selfishness " as the meaning here. But, in any case, these selfish partisans cared as much for giving trouble to Paul as for preaching Christ. They thought[4] that they were stirring up tribulation[5] for Paul by making his chains gall him (Lightfoot). They found added zest in the thought that the growth of their peculiar type of Christian doctrine would irritate (" annoy," Moffatt) Paul. One must confess that some Christians seem to enjoy sticking pins in the preacher. It is possible

[1] Καταγγέλλουσιν.   A rather more formal word than κηρύσσω above.

[2] οὐχ ἁγνῶς.   Cf. 2 Cor. 11 : 13, 20 for the charge of insincerity.   So also in Gal. 6 : 22.

[3] The word ἐριθία is from ἔριθος, a hired servant.

[4] οἰόμενοι.   Planning and thinking it out.

[5] θλίψιν ἐγείρειν.   As if from the dead.

for one to be more of a denominationalist than a Christian, to care more for the progress of one's special views than for the kingdom of God. There are ministers with small jealousies who wreck churches like a tornado with their winds of doctrine. Paul's very success makes these men in Rome jealous and resentful and determined to nag him if they cannot stop his onward march. These men feel that they are entitled to success as much as men less able who get ahead of them. So the destructive spirit eats its way into their hearts and lives. It was a pity that this spirit should burst forth against Paul in Rome at the time of the crisis in his imprisonment. But at such a time small men feel like taking advantage of such a situation and they strike Paul when he is a prisoner. Wolves turn and rend one of their own pack who falls in the fight. It is a small thing to try to undermine another preacher's power. One may wonder that God should bless at all the message of men with such a spirit. But after all we should be glad that our own wrong motives do not wholly hinder the reception of whatever truth is preached to men. The power is from God and not from the preacher, in God's message and not in the preacher's heart.

5. **Preaching Christ from Love of Paul** (verses 15,[b] 16).

There is action and reaction in all things. The

factious opposition of the minority stimulated the
majority to increased efforts out of love for Paul.
They do it out of good-will [1] as well as love.   There is
this good that comes out of a church dissension.   Some
sluggish souls wake up and begin to take an interest
in the affairs of the kingdom who had not done so
before the disagreement arose.   There is this consolation to be found in the midst of the bitter strife of
the ages among various Christian sects which have
often caused sadness.   We can excuse much even
of rancour in theological debates and wranglings over
minor points because of the obvious sincerity and
conviction of the disputants.   We may rejoice in the
larger spirit of charity now in the world with the
hope for its increase provided the result is not a
spineless uniformity without point or pith.   Love
calls for no sacrifice of principle.   Love and good-
will moved the majority to stand valiantly by the
side of Paul in his exposition of spiritual Christianity.
One can be a conscientious denominationalist to-day
and full of love and the spirit of coöperation in all
wise and proper ways.   These men are active because of [2] good-will to Paul, and their zeal springs

----

[1] εὐδοκίαν.   This word (from εὐ and δοκέω) is used either
for desire (Rom. 10 : 1) or satisfaction (2 Thess 1 : 11) as in
the Father's good pleasure in Jesus (Matt. 3 : 17).   The best
manuscripts here in verse 16 give the order in the Revised
Version which is a chiasm or cross reference to verse 15.
Cf. Robertson, " Grammar of the Greek N. T.," p. 1200.
    [2] διά.

out of[1] love. Some even love Paul for the enemies that he has made, even among Christians, but most love him for his great achievements in Christ. When Paul is thus under attack in Rome, the faithful rally round him as the disciples did in a circle[2] at Lystra. The recognize[3] Paul as " set for the defence of the Gospel.[4] They rejoice in his courage in chains and take his view of his situation. His defence is an apology in the original force of the word (cf. 1 : 7). Paul is a living apologetic for Christ, a typical example of the word[5] in Jude 3. To desert Paul at this juncture is to desert Christ. The cause of Christ is here identified with the cause of Paul, its leading exponent. The cause is crystallized in the man. One cannot stand by Christ in theory and leave Paul in the lurch in practice. Alas, so often church members fail to rally to the support of the pastor or of the denominational servants. They are willing to give up the preacher to save the cause as Caiaphas proposed about Jesus in John 11 : 50, voluntary offering of some one else as a sacrifice. Sometimes, to be sure, the minister is at fault and has to go for the good of all concerned. Christianity is incarnated in men and women. This fact gives dignity to the Christian's task, but it makes it imperative that one

---

[1] ἐξ. [2] κυκλωσάντων τῶν μαθητῶν (Acts 14 : 20).
[3] εἰδότες.
[4] εἰς ἀπολογίαν τοῦ εὐαγγελίου κεῖμαι. The word κεῖμαι (positus sum, Vg.) means continued state like perfect of τίθημι.
[5] ἐπαγωνίζεσθαι. To contend steadfastly.

shall be really doing the work of Christ if people are to suffer with him for Christ's sake. Else the very love of the people for the man and minister may lead many into the pit. The words of Jesus here are final: " Inasmuch as ye did it unto one of the least of these my brethren, ye did it unto me—Inasmuch as ye did it not unto one of these least, ye did it not unto me " (Matt. 25 : 40, 45).

6. Paul's Conquering Joy (verse 18).

Nowhere does Paul appear to better advantage than in this verse. He faces frankly the limitations of ministers and men in the service of Christ, limitations in preacher and hearer. What is to be the attitude of the preacher towards other preachers who do not see things as he does in all points of Christian doctrine? This is a practical question and one that men must answer to-day. People are often diligent to stir up jealousy between preachers. The effort was made to make John the Baptist jealous of Jesus, but it failed miserably [1] (John 3 : 22–29). There is joy enough for all the workers in the kingdom, the one who sows and the one who reaps (John 4 : 36–38). People criticize the preachers in the most inconsistent ways and it is hopeless to try to please them all. They found fault with John and with Jesus for directly opposite things (Luke 7 : 31–34).[2] It has been ob-

[1] Cf. Robertson, " John the Loyal," pp. 165 ff.
[2] *Ibid.*, pp. 243 ff.

jected here that Paul seems to condone the errors
of the Judaizers which he had so severely criticized
in 2 Corinthians 10–13 and in Galatians. But this
estimate fails to understand Paul's spirit here. He
speaks out in Rome with the same courage and
clearness as heretofore. He abates no whit his own
convictions. But the issue before Paul is simply
whether or not he is to spend his time railing at
preachers who have the same right to preach as he
has and give ground for charges of pique and
jealousy besides filling the ears of the Roman soldiers with stories of the shortcomings of these en-
vious preachers. He could have done that and angels
would have wept and the ungodly would have sneered
at this exhibition of so-called Christian love. Jealousy had found a place even in the ranks of the
twelve apostles. Paul rises to the high plane of conquering joy in Christ. " What then ? " [1] The answer of Paul is " only that," [2] " in every way " [3]
or in any event " Christ is preached." [4] This is
what matters most. One must learn to see
things as they are and to find the consolation
in the big truths of life in spite of the minor
drawbacks. The alternative here between pretense [5]

---

[1] τί γάρ. A common classical idiom. Cf. Rom. 3 : 3.

[2] πλὴν ὅτι. Undoubtedly the correct text.

[3] παντὶ τρόπῳ.

[4] Χριστὸς καταγγέλλεται. Linear present.

[5] προφάσει. Our word " prophecy." It is the thing set
forth, the alleged or face value of a statement, whether true or

and truth[1] is a very common one. Some men
were using the name of Christ as a cover or mask
for personal and selfish ends (Vincent, *in loco*).
We are shocked at that statement, and yet we may
also thank God that He can use such poor preaching for His glory. God can even bless insincere
preaching. Even hypocritical preaching, alas, can
be blessed of God. Somehow God blesses the grain
of truth that is mixed in with error and bad motives.
He places no premium upon error or upon pretense.
But Paul's problem is one of personal adjustment. Is
he to embitter his own heart because all preachers
of Christ are not pure? Far from it. He the rather
seizes upon the salient point in the situation. Christ
is preached. This is what matters most. Other things
are important in varying degrees, but this is primal.
Paul knows how to put first things first and to keep
them there. So he takes his stand. " And therein I
rejoice, yea, and will rejoice." [2] He does not rejoice
in false preaching, but in the fact that even in such
preaching Christ is found by souls that hunger after
Him. Surely we can all rejoice that God does bless

false. Here the contrast with truth shows the meaning to be
pretext or pretense. Cf. 1 Thess. 2 : 5.
 [1] ἀληθείᾳ. The word means openness (ά privative and
λανθάνω to conceal, unconcealed), the very opposite of deceit.
   [2] καὶ ἐν τούτῳ χαίρω ἀλλὰ καὶ χαρήσομαι. Note the
affirmative use of ἀλλὰ here (Robertson, " Grammar of the
Greek N. T. in the Light of Hist. Research," p. 1185).
Note also the volitive linear future χαρήσομαι. Robertson,
ibid., p. 889.

indifferent preaching. Over and above all the clangour
of contending voices in modern Christendom rises the
fact of Christ. It is Jesus that saves men from their
sins. This is the universal note in the eternal Christ.
We look at Him from different angles and with imperfect eyes and we tell what we see in broken speech,
sometimes incoherent and contradictory. But, if by
means of it, men see Jesus, it is worth while.

7. Christ Magnified in Paul (verses 19 and 20).

Paul now turns to his own case and declares that
it matters little what happens to him in Rome. Already the imprisonment, as he has shown, has turned
out for the progress of the Gospel. He is grateful
for their prayers (" your supplication ") and " for the
supply [1] of the spirit of Jesus Christ " (both source
and gift). Paul's attitude is measured by [2] the earnest
expectation [3] and hope that Christ shall be magnified [4]
now as always in his body. Whether this is by life or
death is not material. If Christ is made great in the
hearts and eyes of men it is a small matter what hap-

---

[1] ἐπιχορηγίας. A word used for the chorus leader who
furnished entertainments for the chorus. Then for "supply"
in general. Cf. 2 Pet. 1 : 5, 11. The verb ἐπιχορηγέω
occurs in the papyri.

[2] κατά.

[3] ἀποκαραδοκίαν. A very strong and striking word (cf.
Rom. 8 : 19) used for intent watching with head bent or
stretched in that direction. It occurs in the papyri of the expectation of peasants about the visit (παρουσία) of a high official.

[4] μεγαλυνθήσεται. Made great.

pens to Paul. Then he shall not be put to shame[1]
in anything. Hence Paul knows[2] that his present
troubles will turn out[3] at last for his eternal salvation,[4] not merely rescue from imprisonment, for it
applies (verse 20) both to death and life. He will
get the spiritual development that God means for
him to receive from his imprisonment and from the
personal antagonisms in Rome. It is all one to Paul
what the future holds in store for him on earth. He
is sure of the prayers of the Philippians and of the
presence of the Spirit of Jesus and of the triumph
of Jesus in his work whether by life or death. So
he faces the future with calmness whatever doubt as
to the course of events may exist. As to that Paul
is not sure of his own mind as he now proceeds to
show.

[1] αἰσχυνθήσομαι.   [2] οἶδα. Intuitional conviction.
[3] ἀποβήσεται. Go off at last in this direction.
[4] σωτηρίαν.

IV

JOY IN DEATH AS WELL AS IN LIFE
(1 : 21–30)

PAUL'S indifference about his personal incon-
veniences and his confidence that Christ will
be magnified in his body whether by life or
by death (1 : 20) raise the whole question of what
life is and what death is. Every one has to face this
problem sooner or later. He must have his philosophy
of life. The Stoics preached apathy as the triumph
of the reason over the passions. But that cold and
colourless creed is not for Paul's warm heart. He
gives us in this paragraph his conception of real life,
the life worth while. Kabisch,[1] it is true, affirms that
with Paul life is simply existence and has no ethical
quality, an inadequate interpretation of Paul's view in
my opinion, though in verse 20 the contrast is between the present life and death.[2] He argues from
this basis.[3]

1. **The Gain of Death** (verse 21).

Life has different senses and different standards.

---

[1] " Eschatologie des Paulus," p. 134.
[2] Cf. Kennedy, *in loco.*   [3] γὰρ in verse 21.

Paul here announces the principle of life[1] so far as he is concerned. The personal pronoun has the emphatic place in the sentence.[2] It means more than in my opinion, but in my case, in my realization of life[3] (Ellicott, *in loco*). This is what life means to me, whatever it means to others. With many life means pleasure, sensual indulgence, money, power, having one's way, flattery. But with Paul the regulative principle of life is Christ. Jesus had said that He was the life[4] (John 11 : 25 ; 14 : 6) as well as the resurrection, the way, the truth. Jesus is the source of power in life in the cosmic sense of energy, in the moral sense of truth, in the practical sense of guide, and is the origin of spiritual vitality. So Baskerville (" Sidelights on Philippians," p. 25) says that " Christ Jesus must be the origin of life, the essence of life, the model of life, the aim of life, the solace of life, the reward of life." In Colossians 3 : 4, Paul speaks of " Christ our Life."[5] But what Paul here affirms is not " Christ is life," but " living is Christ, and dying is gain."[6] Paul does say in Galatians 2 : 20: " It is no longer I that live, but Christ liveth in me."[7] Christ has taken possession of Paul so

---

[1] τὸ ζῆν, not τὸ βιοῦν (manner of life). Elsewhere Paul has τὸ ζῆν for the process of life (verse 22 ; Rom. 8 : 12 ; 2 Cor. 1 : 8). Ἐμοὶ γὰρ τὸ ζῆν Χριστός.

[3] The ethical dative. [4] ἡ ζωή.

[5] Χριστὸς ἡ ζωὴ ἡμῶν.

[6] This is plain from the use of the article with the infinitive and its absence with Χριστός and κέρδος.

[7] ζῶ δὲ οὐκέτι ἐγώ, ζῇ δὲ ἐν ἐμοὶ Χριστός.

completely that Paul has lost his autonomy and will-
ful independence of Christ. He is the glad slave of
Christ. He "is crucified with Christ"[1] in spiritual
identity. This is mysticism, but reality, the deepest
reality of life for Paul, who has been initiated into
the mystery of Christ (Col. 2 : 2). So then Paul is
able to say that life with him has come to mean Christ,
no less and no more. " To go on living "[2] means
more of Christ, living the " Christ life" in the real
sense of that term. Bengel[3] has interpreted Paul
thus : " Whatever I live, I live Christ." I live only
to serve Christ and have no conception of life apart
from Christ (Lightfoot). Christ occupies the whole
of my life. I have no secrets apart from Him. I
have no locked doors to keep Him out of any part
of my life. Christ has full possession of myself.
Paul's life is not on the bulk-head principle (Hutton).
In a word, Paul leads a surrendered life and finds
the utmost peace and power in it. It is the victorious life in the truest sense. Mere existence is not
real life for Paul. He is not just marking time.
Christ covers the entire horizon for Paul, the whole
circumference of his interests. Christ fills all of
Paul's eye. Christ is his all and in all. But then
what about death ? Simply more of Christ. That
is all. " To die is gain." The word here for " gain "[4]

---

[1] $Χριστῷ$ $συνεσταύρωμαι$.
[2] $τὸ$ $ζῆν$ (present and durative).
[3] Quicquid vivo, Christum vivo.   [4] $κέρδος$.

is used for interest, gains, profits. All that death
can do for Paul is to give him more of Christ. It will
be like cashing in the principal and the interest. Then
he will gain all of Christ. It is this idea that he has
in mind in Philippians 3:8 when he speaks of " gaining Christ."[2] Paul feels like an eagle in a cage.
Death will be his liberation from the limitations
of the flesh. Death has no terrors for Paul (cf. Heb.
2:15). He looks upon death as a friend in disguise,
the door to complete and glorious union with Christ.
So then Paul is ready for death, but is not dissatisfied
with life here.

2. The Quandary About Life (verses 21-24).

Paul faces life or death with equanimity. He is
ready for either. He has shown that for him death
means fuller and richer life in gaining Christ. But
he is not discontented to live on in the flesh if that is
the will of God. He adds " in the flesh " here because he has used " life " about death. Lightfoot
quotes " the sublime guess " of Euripides:[3] " Who
knows if living is indeed dying, while dying is living." The comic poets ridiculed this saying of
Euripides, but Christians have found it to be the
truth in Christ. Verse 22 is capable of several translations. The most natural one is this: " But if life

---

[1] τὸ ἀποθανεῖν here is the act of dying (aorist), not the
process (present).   [2] ἵνα Χριστὸν κερδήσω.
[3] τίς οἶδεν εἰ τὸ ζῆν μέν ἐστιν κατθανεῖν τὸ κατθανεῖν δὲ ζῆν.

in the flesh (be my lot), this [1] (means) for me fruit
of work." In this translation, the copula has to be
supplied in both clauses; but this is no more difficult
than to repeat the " if " with a dash after " flesh " or
to make a question out of the first clause.[2] He is
sure that if he is to live on in the flesh, it means that
Christ has " fruit of work "[3] for him, a beautiful
phrase. Hence he does not complain in spite of the
attractiveness of death for him with the glory of
Jesus beckoning him on. So Paul goes on: " And
(in that case, fruit of work in life in the flesh) what I
shall choose I know not." [4] There would be not a
moment's hesitation with Paul if it were clear to him
that his work was done. Just to eke out a useless
existence has no charm for him. He does not wish
to be like a fruit tree that no longer bears and only
cumbers the ground. He has no desire to be laid on
the shelf, to be past the dead-line in the ministry.
Paul had no friends to take care of his old age. One
of the saddest of all spectacles is the sight of an old
minister whom no one wishes to hear preach and who
is no longer able to support himself.[5] So then Paul

[1] τοῦτο here then refers to τὸ ζῆν.

[2] See Kennedy, Lightfoot, Vincent.

[3] καρπὸς ἔργου. The very phrase occurs in Ps. 103
(104): 13.

[4] καὶ τί αἱρήσομαι οὐ γνωρίζω.

[5] It is gratifying to note the efforts in the United States to
raise adequate endowment funds to care for the aged servants
of Christ who need help. They should be pensioned like old
soldiers.

declines to commit himself in case there is still work for him to do. "I do not say."[1] But Paul has no hesitation in declaring his personal preference for death since that means the riches in Christ. But it seems clear to him that there is work for him yet and so he is "in a strait betwixt the two," [2] life and death. Once elsewhere (2 Cor. 5 : 14) Paul uses this verb of the love of Christ that "constrains" him, holds him together. He is in a vise between these two conceptions. He is caught on the two horns of this dilemma. He has "the desire," the real longing of his soul, "to depart and be with Christ," to loosen his ship from her moorings and put out to sea on "the Great Adventure" of death which fascinates Paul, not by its uncertainty, but by the certainty of being with Jesus. He is not abashed by the thought that no traveller has ever returned from the other shore. He does not wish to return, but to go and to stay with Jesus. That will be glory for Paul. One may note here that Paul speaks as if he expected to be with Jesus at death without an interval. The word "depart"[3] was variously used, for a ship's departure, for breaking up camp, and for death. Paul

---

[1] Οὐ γνωρίζω. The ancient meaning was I do not perceive, but in the New Testament it is as above (declare or say). In the papyri it is common in the sense of "recognize" or "identify." (Cf. Moulton and Milligan, "Vocabulary," etc.)

[2] συνέχομαι δὲ ἐκ τῶν δύο.

[3] ἀναλῦσαι (loosen up). The intransitive sense of depart is common in Polybius and the papyri (Moulton and Milligan, "Vocabulary," etc.).

himself uses a similar word [1] for death under the figure of breaking up camp or striking a tent (2 Cor. 5 : 1). And in 2 Tim. 4: 6 he speaks of his own death again with the same word [2] as here. Paul is willing to make an end of his tent life in the flesh, a stranger and a pilgrim on the earth like Abraham (Heb. 11 : 13). His Promised Land is beyond Jordan where Jesus is. He feels sure that for him this " is very far better," piling up comparatives,[3] a triple superiority, to express the intensity of his feeling on the subject. But Paul does not take a selfish view of his life. He is willing to " abide by the flesh " [4] since it is " more necessary for you." [5] After all this is one of the chief joys of life to know that your life is necessary or useful for that of some one else. There is the pang of parting from loved ones here, the sorrow of leaving others without one's help, the shock of an incompleted task. So then Paul faces his work with joy, only he would have more joy to go to be with Jesus. But the hero is no shirker. He has kept to his task even though a prisoner for these five years.

[1] καταλυθῇ.

[2] ἀναλύσεώς (cf. our analysis).

[3] πολλῷ γὰρ μᾶλλον κρεῖσσον. This doubling or trebling (πολλῷ) of comparison is common enough in the κοινή. Cf. Robertson, " Grammar of the Greek New Testament in the Light of Historical Research," pp. 663 f.

[4] τὸ ἐπιμένειν δὲ τῇ σαρκί. So it is to be rendered rather than " in the flesh."

[5] ἀναγκαιότερον δι' ὑμᾶς. Comparative again, a sort of momentum from the first clause.

3. The Reason for Longer Life (verses 25 f.).

Paul has no desire for longer life just to be alive, hanging on to the ragged edge of existence. To be sure, he does not advocate suicide. The matter is in God's hands and he would not have it otherwise. Old people can be very happy and very useful. If they become a problem, it is partly because they take a morose view of things. Even the sick bring a blessing, often just because they are sick and suffering. Robert Hall and Charles H. Spurgeon are instances of ministers who turned physical suffering to glorious gain. The same thing is true of Adèle Kamm, the wonderful invalid girl whose life blessed so many. Paul was already doing that very thing while a prisoner. Paul is not here claiming prophetic insight into the course of his career. He is confident[1] of this very hope of being useful to the Philippians. He uses the same word again in 2 : 24 about his plans. In Acts 20 : 25 Paul speaks of a presentiment[2] about not seeing the elders of Ephesus again, which apparently was not fulfilled (1 Tim. 1 : 3; 2 Tim. 1 : 15, 18; 4 : 20). But his personal conviction about seeing the Philippians again seems to have come true (1 Tim. 1 : 3). He plays on the Greek verb as he loves to do with words. It is all a mistake to think that such plays or puns are simply funny or idle conceits. " I know that I shall bide

[1] τοῦτο πεποιθὼς.   State of assurance.
[2] οἶδα.   His intellectual conviction.

and abide with you all."¹ The second word² has in the later Greek the notion of remaining alive. So Paul expects to remain alive and to be with the Philippians again by God's favour "for your progress and joy in the faith."³ He had spoken of "the progress of the Gospel" (1 : 12) in Rome in spite of his imprisonment, in fact largely because of it. Now he uses the same word about the progress of the Philippians. Joy will go along with progress in the faith. It is eminently worth while to see people make progress in the faith and to find joy in the faith. The preacher who sees people grow under his ministry has his reward here and now. So the people love to see the preacher grow in his insight and grasp of spiritual truth. There is joy, mutual joy, because of mutual progress, joy *pari passu* with the progress. Paul strikes again the triumphant victorious note in his message to the Philippians. There is no " hark-from-the-tomb religion " for him.

¹ μένω καὶ παραμενῶ πᾶσιν ὑμῖν. The first verb is absolute (for life), the second is relative and particular with the dative, by the side of you all. Cf. Plato's Phædrus 115 D οὐκέτι ὑμῖν παραμενῶ. The word is in common use for "serve" as an apprentice or slave-boy (Moulton and Milligan, "Lexical Notes in Papyri," *Expositor*, Sept. 1910). For other word-plays by Paul see 2 Thess. 3 : 11; Rom. 1 : 20; 5 : 19; 2 Cor. 4 : 8; 5 : 4. Cf. Robertson, "Grammar of the Greek New Testament," etc., pp. 1200 f.

² παραμενῶ. Cf. Schmid, "Atticismus," I, p. 132.

³ εἰς τὴν ὑμῶν προκοπὴν καὶ χαρὰν τῆς πίστεως. The one article goes with both substantives as in 2 Pet. 1 : 1 and 1 : 11. Cf. Robertson, "Grammar," etc., p. 785.

The Christian ought to be the happiest man alive,
full of spiritual ecstasy and rapture. Joy is more
than Epicurean sensualism. Baskerville quotes the
Yorkshireman who found so great joy in his religion
that he had "A happy Monday. A blessed Tues-
day. A joyful Wednesday. A delightful Thursday.
A good Friday. A glorious Saturday. A heavenly
Sunday." Indeed, Paul wishes that their "glorying "[1] may literally overflow [2] all bounds, provided it
is in Christ [3] (because of Christ primarily and under
the control of Christ, in the sphere of Christ). If
people have enough occasion to shout aloud their
joy, let them do it. Let the redeemed of the
Lord say so. Sing aloud the praises of our God.
The Philippians will have, so Paul hopes, a special
occasion of joy in his case [4] "through my presence [5] with you again." He lives to serve and to
give joy to others. That is his joy. Paul, like his
Master, came not to be ministered unto, but to minister. He is not a minister who has to be "molly-
coddled," but a virile spirit radiating life and joy to
all about him. The key-word to Paul's life is precisely the notion of service. There is no harm in a
spiritual flood if it does not get beyond the sphere
of Jesus Christ.

[1] καύχημα ground of boasting.
[2] περισσεύῃ. All around and over.
[3] ἐν Χριστῷ Ἰησοῦ.　　　　　　　　　　　[4] ἐν ἐμοί.
[5] διὰ τῆς ἐμῆς παρουσίας. Common in this sense of coming
in the papyri. Cf. the Parousia of Christ.

4. The Christian as a Citizen (verses 27 f.).

Paul's coming to them cannot do it all. They must do their part if his coming is to be of any value to them. So he conditions[1] his hope of helping by a striking clause : " Only be citizens of the Christian commonwealth in a manner worthy of the Gospel of Christ." The Authorized Version preserves a curious mark of the inevitable change in words during the centuries for it has : " Only let your conversation, etc." In modern English " conversation " is confined to talk, whereas in old English it signified manner of life according to its etymology[2]. Christian conversation now means Christian talk. But the Revised Version has " manner of life " which is the old idea in " conversation." The Greek, however, has a more precise idea than that and gives the picture of a city-state or commonwealth, from which we get our words politic, political, polite.[3] Paul uses the word once also of his life in good conscience before God.[4] The Stoics had familiarized the public

---

[1] See a similar use of μόνον in 1 Cor. 7 : 39; Gal. 2 : 10; 2 Thess. 2 : 7.

[2] *Conversatio* from *converso* to turn round, then *conversor* to turn oneself, to live.

[3] πολιτεύεσθε. Act your part as citizens. From πολίτης citizen, and that from πόλις city. Cf. Fowler, " The City-State of the Greeks and Romans " (1895) ; Coulanges, " The Ancient City " (1916). Cf. πολίτευμα in Phil. 3 : 20. Josephus (" Life," § 2) says ἠρξάμην πολιτεύεσθαι τῇ φαρισαίων αἱρέσει κατακολουθῶν. The Pharisees were both a political and a religious party.

[4] πεπολίτευμαι (Acts 23 : 1).

with the idea of a world-wide state (Lightfoot on
Phil., pp. 270 ff.). " Stoic philosophy had leavened
the moral vocabulary of the civilized world" (Vincent, *in loco*). The life of Paul in Rome had made
him think afresh of the great Roman Empire and he
himself was a Roman citizen (Acts 22 : 28) by birth
and was proud of it. From the great center of the
Roman world he would naturally think of Christianity in Roman terms as Jesus so often spoke of the
kingdom [1] of God, a Jewish conception. But the
Philippians themselves lived in a city that was a
Roman colony and so were perfectly familiar with
the rights and dignity of Roman citizenship. Clement of Rome also (*ad Cor.* iii, xxi, liv) shows how
Christians owe obligations to a spiritual polity as
citizens do to the state. Christians are to live
worthily [2] of the Gospel of Christ. This is the
standard. They are " no more strangers and so-
journers," but " fellow-citizens [3] with the saints "
(Eph. 2 : 19). One of the great lessons for to-day is
just this matter of Christian citizenship. The age-
long conflict between church and state has caused
such a reaction that too many Christians fail to bring

---

[1] $\beta \alpha \sigma \iota \lambda \epsilon \iota \alpha$ from $\beta \alpha \sigma \iota \lambda \epsilon \upsilon \varsigma$.

[2] $\dot{\alpha} \xi \iota \omega \varsigma$. Cf. Inscr. of Pergamum in 2 cent. A. D. Bd. ii,
p. 496, for $\dot{\alpha} \xi \iota \omega \varsigma \tau \eta \varsigma \pi \dot{\sigma} \lambda \epsilon \omega \varsigma$. Deissmann (" Bible Studies,"
pp. 248 f.) gives five examples of inscriptions from Pergamum
with this use of $\dot{\alpha} \xi \iota \omega \varsigma$ with the genitive. So a priest of Dionysus
is praised as $\sigma \upsilon[\nu] \tau \epsilon \tau \epsilon \lambda \epsilon \kappa \dot{\sigma} \tau \sigma \varsigma \tau \dot{\alpha} \ \iota \epsilon \rho \dot{\alpha}$ ———— $\dot{\alpha} \xi \iota \omega \varsigma \tau \sigma \upsilon \ \theta \epsilon \sigma \upsilon$.

[3] $\sigma \upsilon \nu \pi \sigma \lambda \hat{\iota} \tau \alpha \iota \ \tau \hat{\omega} \nu \ \dot{\alpha} \gamma \iota \omega \nu$.

their consciences and their votes to bear upon the
problem of civil government. The divorce between
church and state has been entirely too complete.
Churches have no right as organizations to infringe
upon the prerogatives of the state. But after all the
Christian citizen is still a citizen and must not forget
that when he takes a hand, as he must, in civic affairs.
A new conscience has come to our citizens who are
no longer willing for the laws to be made and to be
executed by men who make a specialty of placing
their own interests above the public welfare and who
ruthlessly sacrifice ethical ideals to carry their point.
This new conscience in American business and political life is doing away with many old abuses that
flourished because Christians were not worthy citizens.   Child labour, white slavery, the liquor traffic,
the sweat shop, bribery in elections, the city boss are
just a few of the evils that must disappear before the
concerted effort of Christian citizens.   The party em-
blem must not be more sacred than the Gospel of
Christ.   The Christian has at least as much right in
city politics as the ward politician or the dive-keeper.
The time has come for Christians to clean up the
cities of the country and to keep them clean.   The
day will come when the modern city will be a safe
place for women and children to live in.   As it is,
the city streets are the last place on earth for our
boys and girls as Miss Jane Addams has so well
shown.   It is not good citizenship when money is

ground out of the pinched faces of the children and out of the souls and bodies of helpless girls. A citizenship worthy of the Gospel of Christ cannot be indifferent to the social ills in the body politic.

Paul is not sure when he can come, but he is anxious for unity and coöperation on their part in their life together in the Christian Commonwealth in Philippi. But his purpose[1] is that, whether he comes and sees them or only hears in his absence[2] about them, it may be true that they stand together in one spirit.[3] It is a great deal to be able to stand when under attack and sometimes it is very hard to do so, especially when others run away. They must stand fast like the famous Macedonian phalanx. Paul made fine use of the military figure of standing one's ground against the hosts of evil in Ephesians 6 : 13 ff. Team work in the games is absolutely essential. It is so to-day in baseball or football. It was so in the ancient games. Paul knew the spirit of the athletic games and makes frequent use of metaphors from them. He had probably seen the games in the Greek stadium (cf. Phil. 3 : 14). In 1 Cor. 4 : 9 he speaks of himself as a " spectacle "[4] to the world. In 2 Tim. 2 : 5 Paul speaks of contending[5] in the

[1] ἵνα.

[2] This sentence is not evenly balanced in the Greek. One would expect ἀκούω to be ἀκούων like ἰδών.

[3] πνεύματι (spirit) in contrast to ψυχή (soul) just below. But the words are sometimes interchanged.

[4] θέατρον.

[5] ἀθλῇ νομίμως.

games according to the rules. Here he uses the
compound verb[1] as in Phil. 4 : 3. It is the *esprit du
corps* or *camaraderie* of college boys in the games or
of soldiers in battle. There should be church spirit
in every local church that binds all together in Christ
" for the faith of the Gospel" (cf. Jude 3 " contend
earnestly[2] for the faith once delivered to the saints ").

In particular, those who thus strive in concert for
the advance of the faith of the Gospel, the new rule
of life, must not be frightened by the adversaries.
The word here for frightened[3] means to be startled
like a scared horse or fluttered like a surprised bird.
War horses will stand the booming of cannon and
the bursting of shells at their feet. Some Christians
are like scared rabbits. They jump and run at the
first adversary[4] who says " Boo !" They have no
more courage than grasshoppers and shy at every
shadow. They have to be nursed and coddled if
they do their ordinary duty as Christians and church
members. Panic is the worst sort of defeat. It is
rout. This[5] refusal to be fluttered is proof[6] to the
adversaries of their eternal destruction[7] and of your
eternal salvation.[8]   And this proof comes from God.

---

[1] συναθλοῦντες. Acting as athletes in concert. ἀγών,
[2] ἐπαγωνίζεσθαι. Another athletic word from ἀγών contest.
[3] πτυρόμενοι. Cf. Diod. Sic. XVII, 34, 6.
[4] ἀντικείμενος. Lined up against, face to face opposition.
[5] ἥτις. Explanatory relative.
[6] ἔνδειξις. Attic law term.
[7] ἀπωλείας.

[8] σωτηρίας.

The signal of life or death comes from God, not from the fickle crowd at a gladiatorial show.

5. The Gift of Suffering (verses 29 f.).

The "proof" of God's love, of which Paul spoke in verse 28, is seen[1] precisely in the fact that the Philippians have been honoured by God with the gift of suffering. This sentence is quite broken and Westcott and Hort have tried to mend it by a parenthesis, but the punctuation of the Revised Version is clear enough.[2] The Philippians not only have the gift[3] of faith in Christ, but also of suffering in His behalf. This is one of the great paradoxes of God's love. In Isaiah 48 : 10 note : " I have chosen thee in the furnace of affliction." The Servant of Jehovah was to be "a man of sorrows and acquainted with grief" (Isaiah 53 : 3). The Captain of our salvation was made perfect through sufferings (Heb. 2 : 10). Jesus suffered as we do and is able to sympathize with us and to help us because of His experiences in the flesh (Heb. 2 : 17 f. ; 4 : 15 f.). The fellowship with

[1] ὅτι. Because.
[2] There are here two instances of the broken structure. One is the suspension of the clause after τὸ ὑπὲρ Χριστοῦ which is left without an infinitive, and the addition of οὐ μόνον τὸ πιστεύειν which necessitates ἀλλὰ καὶ and the repetition of τὸ before πάσχειν. Paul was no stylist when his passion surged over all grammatical bounds (cf. Rom. 4 : 16), but his meaning is clear. The other instance is the nominative ἔχοντες after ὑμῖν. This is again a common idiom with Paul. See Robertson, " Grammar," etc., pp. 129 f., 439 f.
[3] ἐχαρίσθη. Aorist tense, but they still have the gift.

the sufferings of Christ is a favourite idea with Paul
(cf. 2 Thess. 1 : 5 ; Rom. 8 : 17 ; 2 Tim. 2 : 12). In
Colossians 1 : 24 he even speaks of "filling up in
his turn"[1] the sufferings left over by Christ. Paul
already had the stake[2] in the flesh which was given[3]
to him to keep him humble (2 Cor. 12 : 7 f.). The
Philippians had seen[4] Paul suffer as a prisoner while
with them (Acts 16 : 23 "many stripes." Cf. 1 Thess.
2 : 2). Now they hear[5] of his sufferings in Rome as
a prisoner. At last it has come their turn to undergo
like[6] sufferings themselves. It is their time to strive
in the arena as Christian gladiators in the same conflict.[7] He uses the common word (cf. Col. 2 : 1 ;
1 Tim. 6 : 12 ; Heb. 12 : 1) for athletic contests (our
"agony," "agonize"). The lesson of suffering as a
chastisement is one that is learned by experience.
Happy is he who learns the Father's hand in the
stroke of love (cf. Heb. 12 : 4–13). Some Christians
do not learn it and grow bitter instead of sweet.
They are not worthy of the high privilege of suffering
for Jesus' sake. The ministry of suffering is one of
the blessings of life. It equips us for service in a way
that nothing else does or can. Preachers are enriched
who themselves drink this cup. Their sympathy is

---

[1] ἀνταναπληρῶ. Note both prepositions ἀνά (up to the
brim) and ἀντί, in Paul's term.

[2] σκόλοψ.   [3] ἐδόθη.   [4] εἴδετε.

[5] ἀκούετε ἐν ἐμοί.   [6] τὸν αὐτὸν—οἷον.

[7] ἀγῶνα. Cf. 1 Thess. 2 : 2. Paul thus uses the same
word about his experiences.

no longer perfunctory. They know by experience what it is to suffer. So the Philippians are now qualified by this new bond of sympathy to understand Paul as they have never done before. "Blessed are they who are persecuted for righteousness' sake."

V

PAUL'S FULL CUP
(2 : 1–11)

"MAKE full my joy" Paul pleads. His
cup is not full to the brim. It is not
running over with bubbling joy. The
Philippians had begun well and were doing well on
the whole, but Paul was not satisfied with their attainment. He had a holy dissatisfaction about them
as shown in his prayer in 1 : 9 ff. He longed for
them all to see the possibilities of growth in Christ
and to be shaken out of a pious complacency. And
then there were already signs of strife in the church
at Philippi. Rumours of this contention had come
to Paul's ears probably through Epaphroditus. Paul
reveals concern in this whole paragraph, in his plea
with Euodia and Syntyche (4 : 2), in his words about
moderation (4 : 5) and the peace of God (4 : 7). He
had just made a fervent exhortation for unity of effort and courage in the face of adversaries (1 : 27 f.).
Paul refers now to this appeal by the use of " therefore,"[1] skipping the digression in 1 : 29 f. He takes

οὖν. Argumentative here, not transitional. Cf. Robertson, " Grammar," pp. 1191 f.

up again and presses the exhortation to unity in
order to fill up his cup of joy.

1. The Grounds of the Appeal (2 : 1).

There are four grounds given here by Paul for his
plea for unity. He puts his grounds in the form of
conditional clauses, but he assumes in each instance
that the condition is true.[1] This " if " is simply a
rhetorical device to get a grip on their attention.
He places in the form of hypothesis their fundamental experiences of grace in Christ. " The rapid
succession and variety of the appeals and the repetition of ' if any ' are peculiarly impressive " (Vincent,
in loco). The first ground of Paul's appeal is the
" stimulus in Christ " (Moffatt). " If there is any
power of exhortation in your connection with and
experiences in Christ." The Latin vulgate has
consolatio, but exhortation (cf. Rom. 12 : 8; Titus
2 : 15),[3] not comfort (2 Cor. 1 : 3; 7 : 4), is the real
idea. There is comfort in Christ beyond a doubt, all
the real comfort of life, for God is the God of all
comfort (2 Cor. 1 : 3) in Christ Jesus (1 : 5). " There
is a Friend that sticketh closer than a brother "

---

[1] The condition here is that of the first class, εἰ with the indicative, though the predicate is not expressed. See Robertson, " Grammar," pp. 1007–1012. Cf. Virgil, Aen. i. 603
for similar rhetorical form (*si qua, si quid*).

[2] εἴ τις παράκλησις ἐν Χριστῷ.

παράκλησις (from παρα—καλέω, to call to one's side)
means " exhortation " first, then " comfort." Cf. double
meaning of παράκλητος (Paraclete).

(Prov. 18 : 24). "The Lord will even light my candle" (Ps. 18 : 28). But that is not the idea of Paul here. Jesus is both Advocate and Comforter, but here He is presented by Paul as the Advocate who pleads the cause of God to the Philippians. The whole case of Christ, His Person and His Work and in particular the experience of the Philippians is here offered for consideration. "If your life in Christ, your knowledge of Christ, speaks to your hearts with a persuasive eloquence" (Lightfoot). Paul's mystic phrase "in Christ" which he uses so often here has all the rich content that he can pour into it. Let Christ speak to you in the hush of your own hearts. I have seen a physician try to find a response to all sorts of stimuli in a victim of apoplexy. He used needles, he touched the ball of the foot, he used every known physiological device to find signs of life. If Christ makes no appeal to the professed Christian, he is not "in Christ." He is out of contact with Christ. He is spiritually dead. If one's own life in Christ does not stimulate the soul to the noblest effort, it is useless to go on with the appeal. Response to stimuli is the sign of life. The absence of it is the proof of death.

The second ground of Paul's appeal is the "incentive of love." Here again the word means encouragement, not consolation, though the Vulgate has *solatium caritatis*. Paul uses the two words side by side also in I Thessalonians 2 : 11. The idea is the *moral influence*

tender persuasiveness of love. If love has any power by its tenderness to stir your hearts, then listen to me. It is the incentive that springs from love. He does not define whose " love " he has in mind and probably leaves it vague on purpose. He may be thinking of his own love for the Philippians, but he may also be presenting to their contemplation Christ's love for them. " Love makes the world go round." Love spurs to one last endeavour. Dr. John A. Broadus used to close his last lecture to the class in Homiletics in the Southern Baptist Theological Seminary with a plea for the young ministers to do their very best for Jesus' sake. And then, with tears in his eyes and in the eyes of his pupils, he begged that they would do just a bit better for their old teacher's sake. A man who is deaf to love is deaf indeed, deaf to the love of mother, of father, of wife, of child, of Jesus, of God the Father. Love of man may let us go, but not the love of God. We can all understand George Matheson's " Oh, love that will not let me go," the deathless love of Jesus.

The third ground of appeal is the participation in the Holy Spirit. " If fellowship in the Spirit is a reality," Paul means. It is a phrase that meant a great deal for Paul (cf. 2 Cor. 13 : 13 ; Rom. 15 : 30). People use it glibly and without meaning. The Holy Spirit is very vague to many Christians who refer to the Third Person in the Godhead by " it." The Greek used grammatical gender which has no

bearing in English.[1] The word here for "fellowship"[2] we have had already (1 : 5) and means participation or partnership. If we have any partnership in the life and blessings of the Holy Spirit,
then we are ready to listen to Paul's plea for unity.
The Holy Spirit is the unifying principle in the local
church (cf. 1 Cor. 12:4–11). He alone can bring
order out of chaos and preserve harmony in the body
of Christ. Unless the Holy Spirit rules, there is
mere excitement and confusion (1 Cor. 14). Instance to-day the "Holy Rollers" and other fanatics.
Without the Holy Spirit there is no life and no
power.

The fourth ground of appeal is compassion in the
heart. Paul uses two words here. One is the seat
or organ of the compassion ("tender mercies"[3]), the
other is the pity itself ("compassion"[4]). My physician, the late Dr. J. B. Marvin, a brilliant scientist
and earnest Christian, used often to speak of the

[1] $\pi\nu\epsilon\hat{\upsilon}\mu\alpha$ is grammatically neuter. But in John 14 : 26 $\epsilon\kappa\epsilon\hat{\iota}\nuο\varsigma$
skips over $\pi\nu\epsilon\hat{\upsilon}\mu\alpha$ δ to $\pi\alpha\rho\acute{\alpha}\kappa\lambda\eta\tauο\varsigma$. The Holy Spirit is a
person and we should say "He."

[2] $\kappaοι\nu\omega\nu\acuteί\alpha$.

[3] $\sigma\pi\lambda\acute{\alpha}\gamma\chi\nu\alpha$. The organ of the higher viscera (the heart, the
stomach, etc.).

[4] $οι\kappa\tau\iota\rho\muοί$. In Col. 3 : 12 Paul combines them $\sigma\pi\lambda\acute{\alpha}\gamma\chi\nu\alpha$
$οι\kappa\tau\iota\rho\muο\hat{\upsilon}$ as the Vulgate does here *viscera miserationis*.
There is a difficulty in the Greek text ($\epsilon\acute{\iota}$ $\tau\iota\varsigma$ $\sigma\pi\lambda\acute{\alpha}\gamma\chi\nu\alpha$) that
has various explanations. Paul may have written $\epsilon\acute{\iota}$ $\tau\iota$ in all
four clauses, the $\tau\iota$ being in the predicate in each instance.
$\tau\iota\varsigma$ here may be a scribal error due to the σ in the next word.
There is an early error undoubtedly.

Y " stomach-brain " in justification of this ancient
idiom, a sort of sensitive plate in the stomach that
corresponded to the brain. If you have a heart and
if your heart has any compassion, listen to me, says
Paul. If you love me at all, hear me. Could they
resist that plea ?

2. **The Nature of the Plea** (2 : 2).

Paul's cup of joy will indeed be full if the Philippians respond to his fourfold appeal. There is, forsooth, real joy in having our own way, but that is not
Paul's feeling. His word here for " make full " is the
original meaning of the word [1] so often translated
" fulfill." John the Baptist uses the word about his
joy in the joy of Jesus the Bridegroom : " This my
joy therefore is made full " (John 3 : 29).[2] The substance or purport [3] of Paul's plea is that the Philippians exhibit the unity of the spirit of which he
spoke in 1 : 27 f. Paul cannot rest content while the
spirit of faction exists in this generous, glorious
church at Philippi. He uses " the tautology of
earnestness " (Vaughan), but it is not quite " hypercritical" to see some distinction in the expressions
employed to emphasize unity.

There is first the unity of thought (" think the

---

[1] πληρώσατε.

[2] αὕτη οὖν ἡ χαρὰ ἡ ἐμὴ πεπλήρωται.

[3] ἵνα here is not final, but sub-final. Cf. Robertson,
" Grammar," pp. 991–994.

same thing 'ζ̔η even identity of thought (" of one mind," " thinking the one thing " [2]). Surely this is not an easy thing to do, especially where people have active minds and independent spirits. It is only true where minds are in tune that two minds think as one. Then one will say : " I was just thinking," and both say the same thing at once. There is something in telepathy when mind answers to mind like wireless telegraphy with transmitter and receiver. To be sure, one can be acquiescent without thinking and parrot-like repeat what he hears. This is a mechanical echo and not real harmony of thought from conviction and sympathy. There should be also unison of affection, " having the same love." [3] We have the phrase " two hearts that beat as one." If this were true, preachers would remain longer in their pastorates, churches would be more fruitful in good works, there would be fewer losses in the membership.

There should be also harmony of feeling, " of one accord." [4] A common disposition will ensue where there is unity of thought and of affection. Our word

τὸ αὐτὸ φρονῆτε. Deissmann (" Bible Studies," p. 256) quotes an inscription of Rhodes of 2 cent. B. c. which has ταὐτὰ λέγοντες ταὐτὰ φρονοῦντες ἤλθομεν used of a married couple.

[2] τὸ ἓν φρονοῦντες. Sometimes both constructions occur together. Cf. Aristides de Conc. Rhod., p. 569 ἓν καὶ ταὐτὸν φρονοῦντες, Polybius V. 104, λέγοντες ἓν καὶ ταὐτό.

[3] τὴν αὐτὴν ἀγάπην ἔχοντες.

[4] σύνψυχοι. Soul with soul.

accord (heart to heart, ad+cor) suggests two hearts
in perfect key, a symphony of the spirit. Certainly
there would be fewer divorces if husband and wife
never got out of tune. There is a music of the
spheres. The same note will respond when in key
with another instrument. If one note is struck, the
one in key answers to it. Everything has its note.
The whole church is a choir and must be kept in
tune. Musical natures are sensitive and high strung
and readily get out of tune. But, if each one of us
keeps his life in tune with God, " in tune with the
Infinite," it will not be impossible to get in tune with
each other.[1] The discord will all be lost in the
glorious orchestra that blends in common praise to
God. Such a church will have variety in plenty, but
it will be the variety of concord, not jarring notes out
of tune with the rest.

3. The Preëminent Social Grace (2 : 3 f.).

What is it ? Elegance of manners ? The gift of
saying agreeable things ? Courtesy ? These are all
worth while and courtesy comes very close to Paul's
idea of humility, if it is courtesy of the heart and not
of the mere occasion or fashion. " Paul's ethic is
at least as much a social as an individual ethic."[2]
Church life is a social fact and humility is a prime
factor in it. Egotism and party spirit destroy the

---

[1] συν ——
[2] Holtzmann, " N. T. Theol.," ii., p. 162.

unity essential to healthy church life. The antidote
to these evils is humility. It is absolutely essential
to social harmony. The egotist is a bore in any
circle. The partisan is tiresome to all save his circle.
Egotism and partisan pride seem to be the chief perils
to the Philippian church.[1] The Jewish element had
the pride of privilege, the Gentile element the pride
of culture. The Pharisee was an egotist and a partisan by inheritance of seclusive virtue and grace. The
cultured Greek or the oriental Gnostic had a profound
sense of his own superiority over the outside bar-
barians. So Paul attacks earnestly the sins that lie
in the way of spiritual unity in Philippi. Humility
is essential to concord in the church.

· There is no participle in the first clause in verse 3,
but we need only repeat the last one in verse 2,
" thinking[2] nothing by way of faction or vainglory."
The word for " faction "[4] Paul has used already (1 : 17)
of a party in Rome that loved to trouble him. He is
reluctant to see that spirit break out in Philippi. Perhaps already the church members are beginning to
take sides in the dispute between Euodia and Syntyche. There is danger of a conflagration if the fire is
not stamped out at once. Vainglory[5] is emptiness

---

[1] Vincent, *in loco*.   [2] φρονοῦντες.
[3] κατὰ. The standard of measure. Cf. Robertson,
" Grammar," pp. 608 f.   [4] ἐριθία.
[5] κενοδοξία. See Gal. 5 : 26 for κενόδοξοι where envy is
also mentioned. Ignatius (*Magn.* XI.) has ἄγκιστρα τῆς
κενοδοξίας. The Vulgate has *inanem gloriam*.

of ideas. The man who is puffed up with conceit is regarded as empty headed. Censoriousness and conceit are the marks of the zealous braggart whose loud protestations do not conceal his poverty of ideas. Vanity (from *vanus*) means emptiness. Moody has a good word here: "Strife is knocking another down —vainglory is setting oneself up."

The antidote is humility. "But in lowliness of mind,"[1] Paul says. This word is very common in the New Testament, but does not appear earlier, though it may turn up in the papyri of an earlier date any time. Plutarch has an adjective[2] kin to it. Epictetus[3] uses the very word, but in the ancient sense of meanness of spirit: "Where is there still room for flattery, for meanness?" The ancients meant abjectness of spirit or a grovelling condition or rank self-abasement by the adjective. Plato and the Platonists do sometimes use it for submission to the divine order or modesty of attitude, a preparation for the use of the word by Christ. Jesus raised humility to the rank of a grace and spoke of Himself as "lowly" (Matt. 11 : 29) and often praised the humble and condemned the proud and self-seeking.

---

[1] $\tau\tilde{\eta}$ $\tau\alpha\pi\epsilon\iota\nu o\phi\rho o\sigma\acute{\nu}\nu\eta$. For the case cf. Robertson, "Grammar," p. 530.

[2] $\tau\alpha\pi\epsilon\iota\nu\acute{o}\phi\rho\omega\nu$. Cf. Deissmann, "Light From the Ancient East," p. 72, n. 3.

[3] Bk. III, ch. xxiv, § 56 $\pi o\tilde{\nu}$ $\check{\epsilon}\tau\iota$ $\kappa o\lambda\alpha\kappa\epsilon\acute{\iota}\alpha\varsigma$ $\tau\acute{o}\pi o\varsigma$, $\pi o\tilde{\nu}$ $\tau\alpha\pi\epsilon\iota\nu o\phi\rho o\sigma\acute{\nu}\nu\eta\varsigma$; see frequent use of $\tau\alpha\pi\epsilon\iota\nu\acute{o}\varsigma$ by Epictetus quoted by Sharp, "Epictetus and the New Testament," pp. 130 f.

He made " low " mean " lowly " and gave dignity to
this despised word.   Once Paul (Col. 2 : 18) uses the
word for " mock humility," an echo of the ancient
usage.   The word has played a large part in Christian ethics.[1]   Absolute humility we learn at the feet
of Jesus before God.   Relative humility we practice
towards each other.   It is the crowning social grace
and is Christian in origin and spirit.

    " Each counting other better than himself."[2]   This
is a very astonishing clause, to be sure, from the
standpoint of the natural man.   Paul has the same
idea in Romans 12 : 10 " in honour preferring one
another."[3]   It is the deliberate estimate and preference of others, not a momentary impulse of polite-
ness.   I have heard Paul's principle here pointedly
challenged by a Christian minister as making too
great a demand on one's self-esteem.   But there is
no doubt at all as to the meaning of Paul and that he
is in harmony with the teaching of Jesus on the subject.   It is difficult to practise this Christian chivalry
to women, to aged men, to ministers for Christ's
sake, to all men for humanity's sake.   Deference is a
beautiful word and the absence of it in the family is
" pig manners," every one for himself.   A girl at
school surprised her friends by a motto on the wall
of her room which read: " I am willing to be third."

---

[1] Cf. Neander, " Planting of Christianity," I, p. 483.
[2] ἀλλήλους ἡγούμενοι ὑπερέχοντας ἑαυτῶν.
[3] τῇ τιμῇ ἀλλήλους προηγούμενοι.

God was first with her, others second, self third.
That is the spirit of Christ. This is the secret of the
life of William Booth. Once, when he was unable to
come to a meeting in New York, he sent the cable-
gram " Others." That is the key to the life of David
Livingstone dying in the heart of Africa.

Proper self-respect does not demand selfishness.
" Not looking each of you to his own things, but
each of you also to the things of others."[1] Paul
does not mean that a man should not attend to his
own business. If one does not do his own work,
no one else will do it for him. Paul is not advocat-
ing our being busy-bodies in other people's affairs.
His use of " also "[2] shows that he has no such idea.
But he means that one must not fix his eye[3] (like
the runner on the goal) upon his own interests to the
exclusion of those of others. The Christian has no
right to conduct his life by the law of the jungle.
He cannot look out simply for " number one." The
Golden Rule must be applied to business and to
politics as well as to private life. There is no love
in the rule of might, in ruthless overriding of the

[1] The plural ἔκαστοι is unusual in the New Testament,
though common elsewhere. The participle σκοποῦντες is the
correct text, not σκοπεῖτε, but it is tantamount to an imperative. Cf. Robertson, " Grammar," pp. 1132–1135. The
word here for " others " is ἑτέρων, not ἄλλων, even people of
another class. The caste spirit is all over the world. " People like that," we hear in a sniff of contempt.

[2] ἀλλὰ καί.

[3] σκοποῦντες. From σκοπός goal, aim.

rights of others. Might does not make right in the
state or in the individual. That is the rule of the
bully and the braggart. The Juggernaut method is
the spirit of the devil, and rides rough shod over all
in the way whether men, women, or children. There
is no surer way to wreck a church than this spirit of
selfishness, the rule or ruin policy. Social justice is
impossible without courtesy, love, sympathy. This
is what Paul pleads for and to enforce it he gives the
supreme example of the ages.

4. The Example of Jesus (2 : 5–11).

(a) *For Our Imitation* (verse 5). Look at Jesus:
" Have this mind in you which was also in Christ
Jesus." Kennedy (*in loco*) makes a striking suggestion as to what this sentence means. It is very
awkward in the Greek.[1] He takes it to mean:
" Think this very same thing in yourselves that you
think in Christ Jesus." That is, apply the same rule
to yourselves that you see and approve in Jesus our
Lord and Saviour. It is not always true that Christians put religion into their business relations or feel
the same call for consecration that they love to note
in Christ. " The keenest zeal may be displayed in
religious work, accompanied by singular laxity of
principle in the common concerns of daily business
and social intercourse " (Kennedy). This is certainly

[1] Kennedy would supply φρονεῖτε after ὅ instead of ἐφρονεῖτο
or ἦν. The use of ὑμῖν as a reflexive is common enough.
Cf. Robertson, " Grammar," pp. 680 f., 687 f.

a possible meaning.   Some people are piously humble on Sunday, but a terror on Monday.   Sheldon's
" In His Steps" did not quite state the case.   We
are to do what Jesus wishes us to do, not always just
what He did.   Paul cites the example of Jesus (cf.
verse 8, " humbled himself") with the command that
the Philippians imitate it.

(b) The Preincarnate Glory (verse 6).   Every
word in this verse has been the subject of fierce
controversy.   Kennedy makes two very sensible ob-
servations.   One is that Paul is not here giving a
technical theological discussion.   The other is that
he is not using the language of philosophical meta-
physics.   He is probably familiar with the chief terms
of Greek philosophy and of rabbinical theology.   The
Gnostics in a way combined both sets of terms.
But here Paul is making a practical use of the Incarnation of Christ to enforce the great lesson of
humility as essential to unity.   Christ was humble.
Therefore we should be.   It is a piece of popular
theology that Paul gives us in this great passage
(2 : 6–11), but the words are balanced with rhetorical
rhythm (two strophes of four lines each).   He is not
formally discussing Christology, but he does lift the
veil and shows us Jesus Christ in His Preincarnate
Glory as John's Gospel does in 1 : 1–10.   As there,
so here Paul shows identity of personality in the two
states of Christ.[1]   There is no " Jesus or Christ"

---

[1] By the use of ὅς for both spheres of existence.

controversy for Paul.[1] Christ, according to Paul
here, is divine in nature and glory before the Incarnation. Bacon,[2] forsooth, thinks that John's Gospel
merely copies Paul's Christology here. The preëx-
istence of Christ does not carry with it the preëxist-
ence of others. (See Wordsworth's "Ode on Immortality.") It is poetical to say "trailing clouds of
glory do we come," but not necessarily true.

The definite statement is here made by Paul that
Christ "existed"[3] before His Incarnation (cf. also
2 Cor. 8:9[4]). This Preincarnate state of Christ was
"in the form of God,"[5] a difficult phrase to translate.
God, of course, has no "form" in the usual sense
of that term. It is used of Christ's human form in
Mark 16:12 and of Christ's Incarnation in "the form
of a servant" here in verse 9. Lightfoot argues that
the word means here "the essential attributes of
God" as below in verse 9 "the essential attributes
of servant." Paul has no notion of a body or form

[1] Cf. *Hibbert Journal Supplement* (January, 1909).
[2] "The Fourth Gospel in Research and Debate," 1910, p. 7.
[3] ὑπάρχων. This word denotes prior existence. Cf. ἐν
ἀρχῇ in John 1:1 and πρωτότοκος in Col. 1:15, 17. But
ὑπάρχων comes in the κοινή to be a mere copula = being.
Cf. Robertson, "Grammar," p. 394.
[4] Here we have ὤν.
[5] ἐν μορφῇ θεοῦ. Vulgate *in forma Dei*. The word does
differ from οὐσία, φύσις, εἶδος, εἰκών, and σχῆμα, but one
must not go into psychological or philosophical refinements in
these words. Sharp ("Epictetus and the New Testament,"
pp. 32 f.) shows that Epictetus used ἐκ ψιλῆς μορφῆς = ἡ
ἐκτὸς περιγραφή (Bk. IV, ch. v, §§ 19, 20).

for God, but simply the character of God in His real essence. In Colossians 1 : 15 Paul describes Jesus as the Image[1] of God, as the author of Hebrews (1 : 3) calls Him "the Radiation[2] of His Glory and the Character[3] or Stamp of His Substance[4] or Nature." We cannot comprehend the nature of God's Person. John applied Logos[5] to Christ as the Expression of God. Paul means to affirm that Christ had not the accidents of the divine glory and environment, but the essential attributes of God's nature, actual deity, not mere divinity such as is dimly seen in all men who were made in God's image.

This "equality with God"[6] refers only to relation, which "in the form of God" refers only to nature. Jesus could not give up His essential character of Sonship. He was the Son of God in the Preincarnate state. He was the Son of God during the Incarnation after He became also the Son of man. So John says that the Logos became flesh (John 1 : 14). Jesus did not consider[7] this state of "equality with God," His glory at the right hand of the Father, a thing to be held on to[8] at any cost when, by giv-

---

[1] εἰκών.   [2] ἀπαύγασμα.   [3] Χαρακτήρ.
[4] ὑπόστασις. These are all philosophical terms.
[5] ὁ λόγος τοῦ θεοῦ (John 1 : 1).
[6] τὸ εἶναι ἴσα θεῷ. It is doubtful if much can be made of the distinction between ἴσα and ἴσον (cf. John 5 : 18 ἴσον τῷ θεῷ). Lightfoot makes ἴσον refer to the person, ἴσα to the attributes.   [7] οὐχ ἡγήσατο.
[8] ἁρπαγμός. Words in μος express the action of the verb as a rule, but they often come to mean the result of the action

ing up the glory and holding on to the nature of
God, He could enter upon His redemptive work for
mankind. This is my view of this *crux interpretum.*
The notion of " robbery" is not the idea of Paul in
spite of the Vulgate " *rapina* " which itself is ambigu-
ous and may mean only a highly-prized possession.
Kennedy argues cleverly for the interpretation that
Jesus was not willing to compel men by a display of
His Godhood to recognize His deity, but preferred
that men acknowledge Him by gradual conviction.
This is a possible interpretation, but nothing like so
probable as the one just given.

(*c*)　*The Humiliation* [1] (verses 7 f.). These two
verses give a wonderful portrayal of what was in-

like those in μα. Cf. in the New Testament ἱλασμός=
propitiation, not the act of propitiating; ἁγιασμός, not the act
of consecration, but sanctification. Other words so used are
θερισμός, ἱματισμός, ψαλμός, ὑπογραμμός.

[1] One thinks at once of Bruce's great book on " The Humiliation of Our Lord " (1902). Many other books are
worth consulting like Bruce, " St. Paul's Conception of Christianity " (1898); Denney's " Jesus and His Gospel " (1908);
Dorner, " History of the Development of the Person of
Christ " (5 vols., 1878); Fairbairn, " The Place of Christ in
Modern Theology " (1893); Forsyth, " The Person and
Place of Jesus Christ " (1909); Gifford, " The Incarnation "
(1897); Gore, " The Incarnation of the Son of God "
(1891); Liddon, " Our Lord's Divinity " (1889); Mackin-
tosh, " The Doctrine of the Person of Jesus Christ " (1912);
Sanday, " Christologies Ancient and Modern " (1910);
Schweitzer, " The Quest of the Historical Jesus " (1910);
Somerville, " St. Paul's Conception of Christ " (1897);
Stalker, " The Christology of Jesus " (1901); Warfield,
" The Lord of Glory " (1907).

volved in Christ's Incarnation. Bacon[1] says that the
key-note of the synoptic story of Jesus " is not incarnation, but apotheosis," while in Paul's Epistles and
John's Gospel it is incarnation. There is undoubtedly in the Synoptic Gospels the account of the slow
recognition of Jesus as the Son of God, but that
appears in the Fourth Gospel also. Besides, the
Synoptic Gospels present Jesus at first as the Son of
God (Luke 1 : 32–35; Matt. 1 : 18, 23; Luke 2 : 11;
Mark 1 : 11; Matt. 3 : 17; Luke 3 : 22). The Bap-
tism of Jesus by John and the recognition of Jesus as
the Son of God by the Father occurs in each of the
Synoptics, and belongs therefore to Q or the Logia
of criticism, the oldest form of the tradition. From
the first Jesus is presented as both the Son of God
and the Son of man. He was the Son of God before
He was the Son of man. He continued to be the
Son of God after He became the Son of man.

He did give up much in order to become the Son
of man. That was inevitable and foreseen by Christ.
Paul has said in verse 6 that Christ did not cling to
" the equality with God " when He faced the redemptive work for man, but " he emptied himself "[2] of the
visible glories and the manifest prerogatives of deity.
We may pass by the various *Kenosis* theories which
seek to explain of what Christ emptied Himself and
confine ourselves to the details of the humiliation

---

[1] " The Fourth Gospel in Research and Debate," p. 11.
[2] ἑαυτὸν ἐκένωσεν. Vulgate *semetipsum exinanivit.*

mentioned in these two verses. We can feel certain
that He did not empty Himself of His divine nature
("the form of God" of verse 6), which He could
not do in the nature of the case (no son can change
the fact of his sonship), but only "of the insignia of
His majesty" (Lightfoot), the outward manifestation
of His deity. Jesus did not appear to men in the
likeness of God, but of man. He suffered in so
doing in ways that are beyond our comprehension.
"We may do well to cherish the impression that this
self-emptying on the part of the eternal Son of God,
for our salvation, involves realities which we cannot
conceive or put into words. There was more in this
emptying of Himself than we can think or say" (Rainy,
Philippians, p. 119). We catch glimpses of the
yearning of Christ for the glory which He had with
the Father before the Incarnation and even before
the world was by the Father's side[1] (John 17: 5).
There is a fullness of knowledge[2] between the Son
and the Father not true of others and Jesus often
goes alone[3] to pray with the Father. How the Son
missed the glories of heaven we can only imagine.
How the sin and desolation of earth jarred upon His
sensitive soul we do have some comprehension, but
only a little after all, for we have become used to the
dullness and the hardness of our world. Perhaps, it
was in mercy to Jesus that there was some humilia-

---

[1] $\pi\alpha\rho\grave{\alpha}\ \sigma o\acute{\iota}$.   [2] $\grave{\epsilon}\pi\iota\gamma\iota\nu\acute{\omega}\sigma\kappa\epsilon\iota$ (Matt. 11: 27).
[3] $\alpha\grave{\upsilon}\tau\grave{o}\varsigma\ \mu\acute{o}\nu o\varsigma$ (John 6: 15).

tion in His Incarnation, else He could not have endured His earthly estate. We are expressly told here
that the emptying was voluntary on Christ's part.
The emphasis is on the act (the verb). It applied to
the state of glory, to some extent to His knowledge,
and to His power. Into that subject I do not here
enter. I do not believe that Jesus subjected Himself to error of any kind. He mentions His lack of
knowledge about the time of His second coming
(Matt. 24 : 36). He shows surprise and weariness.
He was a real man, free from sin and from errors of
ignorance, I believe. No effort to explain the combination of deity and humanity has succeeded. We
do not understand the nature of God. We do not
understand our own human nature (spirit and matter
in combination). It is not surprising that we fail in
the union of the divine and the human. Certainly
Dr. William Sanday's excursion [1] with the "sublimi-
nal consciousness" does not explain it. But let us
turn from merely speculative theology to Paul's
interpretation of the details involved in the Incarnation.

"Taking the form of a servant," [2] Paul says, by
way of explanation of "emptied himself." Here Paul
employs the same term for "form" that he did
in verse 6. As Christ possessed the real attrib-

[1] "Christologies Ancient and Modern," 1910.
[2] μορφὴν δούλου λαβών. Cf. μορφῇ θεοῦ in verse 6. The
aorist participle is here simultaneous with the verb ἐκένωσεν
and explanatory (Robertson, "Grammar," pp. 860 f., 1127).

utes of deity, so He took upon Himself the real attributes of servantship.   Here there is a change in the
condition of Christ.   He was [1] in the form of God, but
He took [2] upon Himself the form of a servant.   However, we must not understand that Christ lost " the
form of God " in so doing.   He lost only the appearance as God, not His essential nature as God.   It is
the reality of Christ's humanity that is here affirmed
by the side of the reality of His deity.   He did not
become an actual " slave " [3] of any single man, but
was an actual " servant " (or slave) of mankind.
Paul thus " describes the humility to which He con-
descended " (Kennedy, *in loco*).   The Master [4] of all
became the slave of all (Matt. 20 : 27 f.; Mark 10 :
44 f.).   Jesus entered upon the condition of service
as He had before the condition of equality with God
(Vincent, *in loco*).

" Becoming in the likeness of men," [5] a further explanation of the self-emptying of Christ.   Here again
Paul states that Jesus entered [6] upon the state of His
humanity as we have it in John 1 : 14.   But the word
here is " likeness," [7] not " form " as in verse 6.   It is
a real likeness, but not identity that is meant.   All
of Jesus is not human.   Hence Paul could not use the

---

[1] ὑπάρχων.   [2] λαβών.   [3] δοῦλος.
[4] Κύριος.   Cf. John 15 : 20 οὐκ ἔστιν δοῦλος μείζων τοῦ
κυρίου αὐτοῦ.
[5] ἐν ὁμοιώματι ἀνθρώπων γενόμενος.
[6] γενόμενος, not ὑπάρχων.   So θεὸς ἦν and σὰρξ ἐγένετο in
John 1 : 1, 14.   [7] ὁμοιώματι.

word for "form."[1] Christ "was no mere phantom, no mere incomplete copy of humanity" (Kennedy, *in loco*). "To affirm likeness is at once to assert similarity and to deny sameness" (Dickson, Baird Lectures, 1883). The humanity of Jesus, though thoroughly real and not merely apparent as the Docetic Gnostics held, yet did not express the whole of Christ's self. He was still "in the form of God" in His essential nature in spite of His Incarnation. He still has the essential nature of God while in the similitude[2] of man. The plural[3] here shows Christ's relation to the race. Christ no longer wore His "Godlike majesty and visible glories" (Ellicott), but appeared as a man and to most only as a man.

"And being found in fashion as a man."[4] Here the word for "fashion"[5] refers more to the outward appearance of Christ. It is like the word "habit"[6] as applied to dress. The "form of a bondservant" expressed the essential nature of the servantship of Christ and the "likeness of men" showed the reality of His humanity (Vincent, *in loco*). This word

---

[1] μορφή.

[2] *In similitudinem hominum factus* (Vulgate).

[3] ἀνθρώπων.

[4] καὶ σχήματι εὑρεθεὶς ὡς ἄνθρωπος.   [5] σχήματι.

[6] Vulgate has *in habitus inventus ut homo*. *Habitus* is from *habeo* as σχῆμα from ἔχω. The word σχῆμα is used of God in Test. XII Patr. Zab. 9 ὄψεσθε θεὸν ἐν σχήματι ἀνθρώπου. In Benj. 10 note ἐπὶ γῆς φανέντα ἐν μορφῇ ἀνθρώπου.

"fashion" expresses the appeal that Christ made to the senses, to human observation. "His outward guise was altogether human" (Kennedy, *in loco*). The words for "form" and "fashion" are contrasted by Paul in Romans 12 : 2 : "And be not fashioned [1] according to this world," the outward expression in conduct and manners, "but be ye transformed [2] by the renewing of your mind," the inward spiritual change. Jesus was discovered [3] or recognized as [4] a man, though He was more than man, and in His very humanity revealed God to men if they had eyes to see (cf. John 14 : 7–9 ; Matt. 11 : 27).

"He humbled himself." [5] This is not a mere repetition of "emptied himself" in verse 7. This verb expresses plainly and simply the fact of the Humiliation [6] of Christ. "The depth of the self-renunciation" (Kennedy) is brought out by the following phrases. The great act was voluntary on Christ's part and hence has moral value. This idea is set forth clearly in Hebrews 9 : 12 "having found by himself eternal redemption" [7] (the middle voice)

---

[1] συνσχηματίζεσθε.

[2] μεταμορφοῦσθε. Cf. also Phil. 3 : 10 συμμορφιζόμενος and 1 Pet. 1 : 14 συνσχηματιζόμενοι. In Phil. 3 : 21 we have μετασχηματίσει and σύμμορφον.

[3] εὑρεθεὶς.

[4] ὡς. Implying that he was more than man.

[5] ἐταπείνωσεν ἑαυτὸν. The emphasis is here on the verb as in verse 7 on ἑαυτὸν.

[6] The Vulgate has *humiliavit semetipsum.*

[7] αἰωνίαν λύτρωσιν εὑράμενος.

and in 9:14 " he offered himself," [1] a construction like the one in Philippians 2 : 8.

" Becoming obedient unto death." [2]   Jesus followed the Father's will obediently in the path that led straight to death.   The hate and guilt of His enemies do not at all remove the dignity and the glory of Christ's death for sinners.   Paul speaks of the obedience [3] of Christ also in Romans 5 : 19.   It was an obedience that Jesus had to learn from suffering as is true of all sons (Heb. 5 : 8) and won Jesus the right and the power to offer eternal life to all those who obey Him (Heb. 5 : 9).   There were moments when Jesus was tempted to turn back from the road that led to death, moments of anguish that rent His very soul with a cry to the Father (John 12 : 27 f. ; Matt. 26 : 39; Mark 14 : 35 f.; Luke 22 : 42), times that brought sweat like blood from His forehead (Luke 22 : 44) and tears to His eyes (Heb. 5 : 7). Jesus saw the end from the beginning, saw His " hour " coming, saw the gathering cloud about to break upon His head, but resolutely set His face to go on to Jerusalem to meet it.   The very reality of His humanity made Him flinch as He saw that He was to be regarded as sin by the Father while He bore the sin of the world in His death, and made

---

[1] ἑαυτὸν προσήνεγκεν with the emphasis on ἑαυτὸν.

[2] γενόμενος ὑπήκοος μέχρι θανάτου. The Vulgate has *factus obediens usque ad mortem*.

[3] ὑπακοῆς.   Note force of ὑπό (*sub*) under.

Him cry aloud when the Father's presence left Him
in the dread darkness and loneliness (Matt. 27:46).
But Jesus held on His way "unto death"[1] and was
able to look on His death as a "glorification"
(John 13:31 f.; 17:2). He went as far as death in
His humiliation. "Yea, the death of the cross,"[2]
Paul adds, as the lowest rung in this Jacob's Ladder
of Christ's humanity of which Jesus had spoken to
Nathanael (John 1:51). Christ left His place in
glory and majesty by the Father's side with all the
Father's wealth of grandeur and became a poor man
on earth (2 Cor. 8:9). He took the estate of a servant and bore the likeness of men and no longer
seemed to be God to the multitudes. He Himself
was like a bondservant and served others on earth.
He humbled Himself to the end and met death as a
condemned criminal with all the shame of the Cross.
Down, down Christ went to the bottom of darkness,
the very depth of humiliation and shame. The body
of one that hung on a tree was accursed according
to the Mosaic law (Deut. 21:23) and Paul knew this
well (Gal. 3:13). Cicero spoke of crucifixion as the
most cruel of punishments (Verr. V. 64). The Roman boasted of his right to die a freeman, free from

---

[1] μέχρι θανάτου. Cf. μέχρις αἵματος (Heb. 12:4) of
those who had not yet resisted unto blood and μέχρι δεσμῶν
(2 Tim. 2:9) "unto bonds."

[2] θανάτου δὲ σταυροῦ. Note this use of δέ as addition.
Cf. Rom. 3:22; 9:30. Robertson, "Grammar," pp.
1183–1185.

the very name of cross.[1]   Paul, as a Roman citizen,
was free from this shame.   He was beheaded, though
the tradition is that Peter was crucified head down-
ward.   The Jews stumbled [2] at the cross of Christ and
the Greeks thought it foolishness,[3] but Paul came to
see in it the wisdom and the power of God (1 Cor.
1 : 23 f.).   Jesus saw the shame of the Cross and felt
it keenly, but He endured it for the sake of the joy
that would be His when He reached the goal and
finished His atoning death (Heb. 12 : 2).   Therefore
Jesus despised the shame.[4]   The Cross of Christ has
come to be His Crown of Glory.

   (d) The Exaltation (verses 9–11).   Paul has
taken us down to the bottom of the Valley of Death
into which Jesus went, the valley of darkness and
shame.   He has not forgotten his purpose in appeal-
ing to the example of Christ.   It is to enforce the
lesson of humility, " lowliness of mind " (2 : 3), the
mind of Christ Jesus (2 : 5).   Jesus Himself is the
supreme illustration of His own saying : " He that
humbleth himself shall be exalted " [5] (Luke 14 : 11 ;
18 : 14).   Paul seems to know this Logion of Jesus
for he says : " Wherefore also God highly exalted

   [1] Cf. Cicero pro Rabir., V. 10 Nomen ipsum crucis absit non
modo a corpore civium Romanorum sed etiam a cogitatione,
oculis, auribus.
   [2] σκάνδαλον.
   [3] μωρία.
   [4] ὑπέμεινεν σταυρὸν αἰσχύνης καταφρονήσας.
   [5] ὁ ταπεινῶν ἑαυτὸν ὑψωθήσεται.

him." [1] The " wherefore " is not reason, but conse-
quence (cf. Heb. 2 : 9 ; 12 : 2). The exaltation is the
result of the humiliation. " The idea of Christ's receiving His exaltation as a reward was repugnant to
the Reformed theologians " (Vincent, *in loco*), but
there is no objection certainly to regarding it as the
natural result of His service. " Christ's saying in
Matthew 23 : 12 was gloriously fulfilled in His own
case " (Meyer, *in loco*). It is not clear whether Paul
means to say that Jesus had a higher state of glory
than before His Incarnation or not. That is the
natural way to take the verb [2] here. He had not lost
" the form of God," but He had " emptied himself "
of the majesty and dignity in His Pre-incarnate state.
This He received again and sat in transcendent glory
at the right hand of God on high (cf. Rom. 1 : 3 f. ;
8 : 34 ; Col. 3 : 1 ; 1 Cor. 14 : 25). Paul does not
here say in what the " superior " dignity consists
which Christ did not have before His Incarnation. I
agree with Ellicott that it is His Humanity which
was permanently added to His Divinity. He is the
Son of man now as well as the Son of God which
He was before. The argument in Hebrews 2 : 5–18
illustrates the point which comes out also in Paul's
own argument here.

" And gave unto him the name which is above

---

[1] διὸ καὶ ὁ θεὸς αὐτὸν ὑπερύψωσεν. Vulgate *exaltavit*.

[2] ὑπερύψωσεν. Cf. Psalm 97 (96) : 9 σφόδρα ὑπερυψώθης
ὑπὲρ πάντας θεούς.

every name." [1] The obvious implication of this language is that the gracious bestowal of this name upon Christ as the prerogative of the Father was because of the Incarnation. The Son had voluntarily given up His position of " equality with the Father " and taken a subordinate one on earth (cf. John 14 : 28, " for the Father is greater than I "). " Christ obtained as a gift what He renounced as a prize " (Vincent, *in loco*). But what is " the name which is above every name " ? There is great diversity of opinion. Lightfoot and Haupt make it simply " title " or " dignity " as " name " [2] often represents " power," " authority." Vincent takes it to be " Jesus Christ," " combining the human name, which points to the conquest won in the flesh, and the Messianic name, ' The Anointed of God.' The two factors of the name are successively taken up in verses 10, 11." Ellicott makes it Jesus, " the name of His humiliation, and henceforth that of His exaltation and glory." Kennedy (*in loco*) considers it " amazing " how one can hold this view, but the very next verse (" in the name of Jesus ") certainly lends colour to this interpretation. Besides, it strengthens greatly the point of Paul's use of the example of Jesus if the added glory after Christ's Ascension is precisely the human nature of Jesus which was His state of humiliation. This point appeals to me, I confess, in

---

[1] καὶ ἐχαρίσατο αὐτῷ τὸ ὄνομα τὸ ὑπὲρ πᾶν ὄνομα.

[2] ὄνομα. So in the papyri as in the Septuagint.

spite of the fact that the name " Jesus " was already (Matt. 1 : 21) given to Christ before His Ascension. Still, there is force in the argument for " Lord "[1] as the word meant by Paul in lieu of the Tetragrammaton (the unpronounceable name of Jehovah). The Jews often used " the Name " when referring to this word.[2] Jeremy Taylor so interpreted it : " He hath changed the ineffable name into a name utterable by man, and desirable by all the world ; the majesty is arrayed in robes of mercy, the tetragrammaton or adorable mystery of the patriarchs is made fit for pronunciation and expression when it becometh the name of the Lord's Christ." The confession of Jesus as " Lord " in verse 11 gives colour to this view. But even so, we must not forget that it is Jesus who still preserves His human nature who is termed Lord. He is our Elder Brother at the right hand of God.

" That in the name of Jesus every knee should bow."[3] It is not " at " the name of Jesus, not mere genuflection. There is no essential merit in that attitude every time the name of Jesus is pronounced or heard. It is reverent worship that is here presented. Jesus is the object of worship. Surely it is worth while to note that Paul makes a point to use the name for Christ's human life, the name Jesus. Many had this

---

[1] $K\acute{\nu}\rho\iota\sigma\varsigma$. Used in the Septuagint for Jehovah (Jahwe).
[2] Cf. C. Taylor, " Sayings of the Jewish Fathers," iv., 7.
[3] $\emph{\i}\nu a\ \emph{\`e}\nu\ \tau\tilde{\wp}\ \emph{\'o}\nu\acute{o}\mu a\tau\iota\ \emph{`}I\eta\sigma o\tilde{\upsilon}\ \pi\tilde{a}\nu\ \gamma\acute{o}\nu\upsilon\ \kappa\acute{a}\mu\psi\eta.$

name, the Greek form of Joshua,[1] but they were not saviours from sin (Matt. 1 : 21). Jesus was worshiped while in the flesh and He is still the Son of man. The Epistle to the Hebrews uses constantly the name Jesus and defends gloriously the dignity of Christ's humanity. Jesus purchased the right to this universal adoration with the price of His blood. It is interesting to compare Revelation 5, where Jesus is pictured as receiving worship in heaven from all created things, with this verse. This idea of the mystic sympathy of the whole universe with the Cosmic Christ occurs also in Romans 8 : 21 f. ; 1 Cor. 15 : 24; Ephesians 5 : 20–22; Hebrews 2 : 8. Paul's language in Philippians 2 : 10 f. seems to reflect the Gnostic terminology so freely condemned in Colossians and Ephesians. " And that every tongue should confess that Jesus Christ is Lord."[2] The Lordship of Jesus came to be the test of loyalty. The password in the dark days of persecution came to be " Jesus as Lord." This was the Shibboleth of the faithful. It is so yet. Vain is the praise of those who refuse to bow the knee to Jesus and to confess Him as Lord. One is reminded of Charles Lamb saying that, if Shakespeare appeared in the company of literati, they would all rise, but, if Jesus came, they would all kneel. This word for " Lord " does

---

[1] Ἰησοῦς.

[2] καὶ πᾶσα γλῶσσα ἐξομολογήσηται ὅτι Κύριος Ἰησοῦς Χριστός.

not in itself imply divinity. It was used for Master as opposed to slave (Eph. 6:9), and even for "sir" in address (Matt. 13:27). But in the Septuagint it was a common translation for the Hebrew words for God. It was used also for Cæsar. "Lord Cæsar" was a common term in the papyri and inscriptions. The Emperor cult was the chief religion of the Roman world in the time of Paul. Life was offered to Polycarp if he would only say "Lord Cæsar."[1] "No one is able to say 'Lord Jesus' except by the Holy Spirit" (1 Cor. 12:3). To confess Jesus as Lord was the mark of a true believer, a Christian in reality (Rom. 10:9). "God made this Jesus both Lord and Christ" (Acts 2:36). "Christ the Lord" the angels said (Luke 2:11) the Saviour would be. It is not apotheosis or deification of Jesus that we here see, but the taking up of the humanity of Jesus into His deity with new glory, the glory of the humiliation, the glory of the accomplished redemption, the glory of the battle-scarred hero whose scars are his crown. It is all "to the glory of God the Father." The confession is for the glory of God. It is all of the Father's will and for His glory and gives Him joy. The glory of Jesus gives glory to the Father.

[1] τί γὰρ κακόν ἐστιν. Κύριος Καῖσαρ; Martyrium Polycarpi, viii. 2.

VI

REALIZING GOD'S PLAN IN LIFE
(2 : 12–18)

PAUL is eminently practical as well as really profound. He is equally at home in the discussion of the great problems of theology and in the details of the Christian life. He is a practical mystic who does not leave his mysticism in the clouds, but applies it to the problem in hand. There is in Paul no divorce between learning and life. Speculative theology as philosophy he knows and uses as a servant to convey his highest ideas, but he never forgets the ethics of the man in the street or at the desk. He has just written a marvellous passage on the Humiliation and Exaltation of Christ Jesus, scaling the heights of Christ's equality with God and sounding the depths of the human experience of Jesus, from the throne of God to the death on the Cross and back again. But Paul has no idea of leaving this great doctrinal passage thus. " So then,[1] my beloved,"[2] he goes on with an exhortation based on the experience of Christ. He returns to the

---

[1] ὥστε. On the use of ὥστε at the beginning of principal clauses (paratactic use) see Robertson, " Grammar," p. 999.

[2] ἀγαπητοί μου. Vulgate has *carissimi mei*.

practical note of 2:5. God has a plan in each of
our lives as in that of Jesus. It is worth a great
deal for us to recognize this blessed fact. Lightfoot
puts it that as you have the example of Christ's humiliation to guide you and His exaltation to encour-
age you, so continue.

1. Two Kinds of Obedience (verses 12ª).

Paul picks out the obedience of Christ in verse 8
(" obedient unto death " [1]) as the point of contact for
his exhortation. This sort of obedience is the result
of listening or hearkening and not absolute obedience
to authority.[2] The obedience that Paul commends
in the Philippians is obedience to God, though he
uses the word here absolutely. Certainly it is a remarkable compliment that Paul pays the church at
Philippi. Technically here the structure[3] of the
sentence shows that the clause about presence and
absence belongs to " work out." Still, the idea
covers obedience also. The energy which Paul
commands is a form of the obedience. So then we
may apply the picture to that. Vincent objects
that in such case Paul would say that the Philippians
did better in his absence than in his presence. By
implication he does say that. He directly affirms

---

[1] ὑπήκοος. Here ὑπηκούσατε. The use of ὑπό (sub) suggests reverent hearkening.

[2] πειθαρχεῖν.

[3] μή goes with the imperative κατεργάζεσθε.

that they "always"[1] obeyed God. He exhorts
energetic action " not as in my presence only,"[2] not
mere " eye-service," when the master (or mistress) is
present. They are not like children who obey till
the mother's back is turned. Spurgeon tells of a
servant girl who gave as the proof of her conversion
that now she swept under the mats and behind the
door. It is poor obedience that only does what will
be noticed, as little as possible. Paul is not regarded
as a mere moral policeman. The pastor is not a man
simply to watch over the church and keep it in line.
There are people who go to church only when the
pastor is present and will notice their absence. The
preacher is surely more than a spiritual watch-dog to
bark at the sheep and keep them together. Obedience like that is very shallow and superficial.

" But now much more is my absence."[3] This is
real obedience of the heart. It is the spirit of the
workman who does his best work on the high ceiling
where no one will see it save God. Paul urges this
highest form of spiritual energy at the time when he
is away. There are men who do their best work
when left to their own initiative. This is true only
of the choice spirits who listen to the voice of conscience. These are the salt of the earth who savour

---

[1] πάντοτε.

[2] μὴ ὡς ἐν τῇ παρουσίᾳ μόνον. Note παρουσία the word
used of the Second Coming.

[3] ἀλλὰ νῦν πολλῷ μᾶλλον ἐν τῇ ἀπουσίᾳ. Note the pun
παρουσία, ἀπουσία.

the whole lump. There are men and women in our churches who remain true when pastors come and go and when others fall away.

2. Working In and Working Out (verses 12[b] f.).

In Paul's absence he desires that the Philippians shall press right on with the work of their own salvation in so far as the development is committed to their hands. The eye should rest upon the final goal and so Paul uses a verb [1] that puts the emphasis on the final result. Salvation [2] is used either of the entrance into the service of God, the whole process, or the consummation at the end. The Philippians are to carry into effect and carry on to the end the work of grace already begun. Peter (2 Pet. 1 : 10) likewise exhorted his readers to make their calling and election sure. They must not look to Paul to do their part in the work of their salvation. His absence cuts no figure in the matter of their personal responsibility. It is "your own [3] salvation." It is the aim of all to win this goal at last. If so, each must look to his own task and do his own work. The social aspect of religion is true beyond a doubt. We are our brother's keeper and we do owe a debt of love and service to one another that we can never

---

[1] $κατ$-$εργάζεσθε$. The perfective use of $κατά$.

[2] $σωτηρίαν$. Used also of safety. Cf. 1 : 18.

[3] $ἑαυτῶν$. Not = $ἀλλήλων$, though grammatically possible. It is reflexive here, not reciprocal. Cf. Robertson, " Grammar," pp. 689 f.

fully discharge (Rom. 13 : 8).   But it is also true that
each of us is his own keeper and stands or falls to
God.   Kipling has it thus : " For the race is run by
one and one and never by two and two."

Work it out " with fear and trembling,"[1] Paul
urges ; " with a nervous and trembling anxiety to
do right " (Lightfoot).   People to-day do not tremble
much in the presence of God and most have little sense
of fear.   Jonathan Edwards' great sermon on " Sinners
in the Hands of an Angry God " finds little echo
to-day.   We live in a light-hearted and complacent
age.   The Puritans went too far to one extreme, but
we are going too much to the other.   We all need
afresh a sense of solemn responsibility to Almighty
God.   Paul did not feel blindly complacent about
himself (1 Cor. 9: 27).   Religion is both life and
creed.   The creed without the life amounts to little.
We touch a hard problem here, to be sure, but Paul
feels no incompatibility between the most genuine
trust and the most energetic work.   The two supplement or rather complement each other, though we
cannot divide them.   Divine sovereignty is the fundamental fact in religion with Paul.   He starts with
that.   But human free agency is the inevitable corol-
lary, as Paul sees it.   The two are not inconsistent
in his theology.   Hence Paul is not a fatalist like
the Essenes and the modern Hyper-Calvinists nor is

[1] μετὰ φόβου καὶ τρόμου.   The τρόμος strengthens the
φόβος.

he a mere Socinian like the Sadducees. The Pharisees held to both divine sovereignty and human free
agency as most modern Christians do in varying
degrees, to be sure. Paul seems to see no contra-
diction between them as Jesus did not (cf. Matt.
11 : 27 f.). All our modern efforts to explain the
harmony between these two necessary doctrines fail,
but we must hold them both true nevertheless. God
must be supreme to be God at all. Man must be
free to be man at all. The difficulty probably lies in
our imperfect processes of reasoning for two such
far-reaching truths. But Paul gives the divine sovereignty as the reason[1] or ground for the human
free agency. He exhorts the Philippians to work
out their own salvation with fear and trembling precisely because God works in them both the willing
and the doing[2] and for His good pleasure. We can
at least feel that the working of God's will has provided the whole plan of salvation in which we are
included and at which we are at work. We toil in
the sphere of God's will. But far more is true than
that, though we are conscious also that our own
wills have free play in this sphere. God presses His
will upon ours. We feel the impact of the divine

---

[1] γὰρ. Not so close and formal as ὅτι. Paratactic, not
hypotactic.
[2] καὶ τὸ θέλειν καὶ τὸ ἐνεργεῖν. The articular infinitive
singles out more sharply both activities. We need not press
the difference between θέλω and βούλομαι.

energy upon our wills which are quickened into activity thereby. A child can grasp this, and rest upon
it. A boy of four said joyfully to his mother, " When
we do anything, it's really God doing it." So then
in one sense God does it all. God is the one who
energizes[1] in you both the impulse and the energy
to carry out the impulse. No one knows what
energy is. It is the scientific name for God. It is
ceaseless as the sea, restless as the rapids of Niagara.
One of the theories of matter is that all matter is in
a vortex of inconceivable velocity, whirling round
and round these bombarding electrons. What makes
them whirl so? The particles of radium can be seen
darting violently into space. We were dead in tres-
passes and sins till God's Spirit touched us and we
leaped to life in Christ. This is the mystery of grace.
They that are in the flesh cannot please God (Rom.
8 : 7 f.). God plants in our souls the germ of spiritual life and He does not let it die. His Spirit broods
over us and energizes us to grow and work out what
God has worked in us. This is the ground of hope
and joy that makes Romans 8 so different from
Romans 7. We are in league with God. God's
grace is not an excuse for doing nothing. It is
rather the reason for doing all. In religion as in
nature we are co-workers with God. We plant the

---

[1] ὁ ἐνεργῶν. Works in or inworks. Note James' mention
of energetic prayer (Jas. 5 : 16). Cf. Ἐνεργεῖσθαι in the
New Testament by John Ross (*Expositor*, Jan., 1909).

seed and plan the plant and hoe it and harvest it.
But God gave us the seed and the soil and sends the
rain and the sunshine and supplies that wondrous
thing that we call life and makes it grow to perfection. " God has more life than anybody," said a
child. It is idle to split hairs over our part and
God's part. We must respond to the touch of God's
Spirit else we remain dead in sin. Jesus is the
author and the finisher of faith (Heb. 12 : 2), of our
faith, but we must believe all the same and keep on
looking to Him, the goal of faith and endeavour.
There is no higher standard of rectitude than God's
good pleasure[1] by which He regulates our lives.
Happy is the man who finds God's plan for his life
and falls in with it.

3. Cheerfulness Under Orders (verse 14).

Having committed our lives to the control of God's
will we are under orders. It is unmilitary and peev-
ish to fret at God's commands. " Do all things[2]
without murmurings."[3] The allusion may be to the
conduct of Israel in the wilderness (cf. Ex. 16 : 7 ff.;

[1] εὐδοκία. Picture of serenity and power, common to the
will of God.

[2] πάντα ποιεῖτε. Linear action. Habit.

[3] Χωρὶς γογγυσμῶν. Onomatopoetic word like murmur.
Ionic word as is the verb γογγύζω. The Athenians used
τονθυρισμός. Cf. Thumb, " Hellenismus," p. 215. The
verb occurs fairly often in the vernacular κοινή. Moulton and
Milligan, " Vocabulary," p. 130.

Num. 16: 5, 10). The Israelites murmured bitterly against Moses and against God repeatedly and with dire results. " Neither murmur ye, as some of them murmured,[1] and perished by the destroyer " (1 Cor. 10: 10). These inward murmurings against God's will would easily turn to grumblings towards each other. People do not usually stop with resentment against God, but wish to blame somebody. Disunion had already manifested itself in the church at Philippi. If God is supreme and does all things why did He allow *this* thing to happen? It is easier to ask than to answer that question. The next step is to become sour towards one another.

" Without disputings."[2] This word is used for questionings, then doubtings, then disputings. This is the usual course of our intellectual revolt against God. Probably the moral revolt (murmurings) comes first. The sceptical spirit follows resentment against some crossing of our will by God's will. The final result is " intellectual rebellion " (Lightfoot). Thoughts of hesitation[3] or doubt turn to distrust. Distrust ripens into open disputes when a public stand is taken with others against God (cf. Hatch, " Essays in Biblical Greek," p. 8). Doubt leads to dispute even over trifles (Kennedy). So then, as good

---

[1] μηδὲ γογγύζετε, καθάπερ τινὲς αὐτῶν ἐγόγγυσαν.

[2] διαλογισμῶν.

[3] The Vulgate has *hæsitationibus.*

soldiers, Christians are to carry out the orders of the
Captain of their salvation. Explanations, if they
come at all, come after obedience, not before. Into
the Valley of Death rode the Six Hundred.

> " Theirs not to make reply,
> Theirs not to reason why,
> Theirs but to do and die."

Soldiers go to the charge with a smile on their faces.

4. Perfection in the Midst of Imperfection (verses 15–16[a]).

Paul here expresses his purpose [1] about the Philippians. It is a double purpose, their own highest
development and the greatest service to others. The
first is a prerequisite to the other, though they cannot be wholly separated. They are to " become " [2]
" blameless and harmless." [3] They are not so in the
state of nature and do not easily become so in a state
of grace. Certainly none are absolutely free from
blame in the eye of God and men can usually find
some fault with most of us. But, at any rate, we can
give men as little ground as possible to pick flaws in
our character. Whimsical critics cannot be satisfied,
but we do have to regard the sober judgment of God's
people in ethical matters. Lightfoot takes " harmless " to refer to the intrinsic character as in Matthew

---

[1] ἵνα.   [2] γένησθε, not ἦτε.
[3] ἄμεμπτοι καὶ ἀκέραιοι.   Vulgate *sine querula et simplices.*

10 : 16 " harmless as doves." The word means literally " unmixed," [1] " unadulterated " like pure milk or
pure wine or unalloyed metal. In Romans 16 : 19
Paul says: " I would have you wise unto that which
is good, and simple [2] unto that which is evil," a noble
motto for young and old. It is a great mistake to
feel that one must know evil by experience in order
to appreciate good. An unsullied character a man
wants in his wife and the wife equally so in her husband. It is this sheer simplicity of character that is
so delightful in children and, *par excellence*, in the
" children of God [3] in the full spiritual import of this
term. The children of Israel, when they murmured,
were not acting like children of God. Paul here
quotes [4] Deuteronomy 32 : 5 and applies it to the
Philippians. The children of Israel were full of
blemish, while the Philippians are to be " without
blemish " [5] like the freewill offering (Lev. 22 : 21).
The Israelites had themselves become " a crooked
and perverse generation." But the Philippians must
not fall to that low level, as they will if they give
way to inward discontent. They must exhibit marks

[1] ἀ privative and κεράννυμι. The word occurs in the
papyri.
[2] ἀκεραίους δὲ εἰς τὸ κακόν.
[3] τέκνα θεοῦ. Both τέκνον and υἱός " signify a relation
based on parentage " (Vincent). Both are used also in the
ethical sense of the spiritual relation to God. Cf. Vincent, *in
loco*.
[4] οὐκ αὐτῷ τέκνα μωμητὰ, γενεὰ σκολιὰ καὶ διεστραμμένη.
[5] ἄμωμα. Cf. Eph. 1 : 4 ; 5 : 27 ; Col. 1 : 22.

of perfection " in the midst¹ of a crooked and perverse generation." It is an indocile or froward and
so " crooked "² (cf. Acts 2: 40; 1 Pet. 2: 18) generation. The word was used of crooked paths (Luke
3: 5) and so of crooked steps and crooked ways.
The word " perverse "³ means twisted or distorted
and is a bolder word like the Scotch " thrawn," with
a twist in the inner nature (Kennedy). Surely our
own generation is not without its moral twist and
means many straight men when so many are crooked
(" crooks "), twisted out of shape.

Paul changes his figure, but goes on with the same
idea, " among whom ye are seen as lights in the
world." ⁴ These are the very people, the twisted and
blinded by the darkness of sin, who need the light.
Jesus is the real light of the world (John 8: 12), but
the followers of Christ also pass on the torch and so
bear light to others (Matt. 5: 14). Here the Philippians are pictured as " luminaries "⁵ rather than as
lights⁶ in the world of darkness. As the moon and

---

¹ μέσον. Used as a preposition like so many other adverbs
in the κοινή. Cf. Robertson, " Grammar," p. 644. See
Epictetus, Bk. II, ch. xxii, § 10 for similar use of μέσον.

² σκολιᾶς. The opposite of ὀρθός.

³ διεστραμμένης. Perfect passive participle from διαστρέφω.
Cf. Epictetus III, 6, 8 οἱ μὴ παντάπασι διεστραμμένοι τῶν
ἀνθρώπων.

⁴ ἐν οἷς φαίνεσθε ὡς φωστῆρες ἐν κόσμῳ.

⁵ φωστῆρες. Cf. Gen. 1: 14, 16; Dan. 12: 3; Rev.
21: 11.

⁶ φῶτα. Cf. φῶς in Matt. 5: 14.

the stars "appear"[1] in the night, so the Christians
come out to give light in the darkness.   In the dark
night of sin the church of Philippi is a lighthouse in
the breakers, " holding forth the word of life."[2]   The
gospel has the principle of life in it.   John's Gospel
unites light and life as descriptive of the Logos
(1:4) and Christ offers to men " the light of life "
(John 8:12).   Paul naturally blends the two figures
here.   Vincent rightly calls it "hypercritical" to
change the figure in "holding forth."[3]   " It is common
to personify a luminary as a lightbearer."   The figure
can be either holding on to the word of life or presenting the word of life.   In this latter sense one
naturally thinks of the Statue of Liberty in New York
Harbour, holding forth the torch of freedom.   Every
church is a lighthouse in a dark place.   The darker
the place the more the light is needed.   It is sad to
see so many churches deserting the down-town dis-
tricts where they are so much needed.   Rescue work
must be carried on where sin has done its worst.
It is like fighting the plague.   Thank God for the
men and women who do take the light into the dark
corners of our cities.   What would our modern cities
be like without our churches ?   The answer is the
cities of Japan, of China, of India to-day.   The word

[1] φαίνεσθε, not φαίνετε (shine).
[2] λόγον ζωῆς ἐπέχοντες.
[3] ἐπέχοντες.   Literally to hold upon or apply to and so
fasten attention (Luke 14:7; Acts 3:5; 19:22).

of life quickens to life and brings light to the dark-
ened soul.

5. Paul's Pride (verse 16ᵇ).

" For a ground of glorying in the day of Christ." [1]
This clause is related to all of verse 15 and the preceding part of 16. It is epexegetical or further
purpose. The day of accounts comes to figure more
largely in Paul's mind as he grows older (Kennedy).
The writer of Hebrews speaks of the sleepless watch
of the shepherds of souls " as they that shall give account ; that they may do this with joy, and not with
grief ; for this were unprofitable for you " (Heb. 13 : 17).
Paul longs [2] to have " whereof to glory [3] in the day
of Christ." The success of the Philippians will give
Paul something tangible to present to Christ. They
will be stars in his crown. He means by " day of
Christ " the judgment day, commonly termed the day
of the Lord outside of this Epistle. Paul does not
wish to be saved " so as by fire " with all his works
gone (1 Cor. 3 : 15). When that day comes and
Paul looks back upon his work in Philippi, he does
wish to feel " that I did not run in vain neither labour
in vain." He has the metaphor [4] of the stadium before him as in Galatians 2 : 2 when he expresses the

---

[1] εἰς καύχημα ἐμοὶ εἰς ἡμέραν χριστοῦ. Note both uses of
εἰς. No reason for saying " until " the day.

[2] ἐμοὶ is the ethical dative. Cf. Robertson, " Grammar,"
pp. 536, 539.

[3] καύχημα is result.   [4] ἔδραμον. The race.

same dread about the Galatians.   He does not wish
it all to come to nothingness.   The word for labour[1]
here means the weariness of labour.   Toil and sweat
and weariness were all for naught.   It is a pitiful case
when the preacher has to see the people go back to
the flesh-pots of Egypt and leave his work null and
void.   The Philippians will be Paul's jewels in the
presence of Christ as the mother of the Gracchi
boasted of her boys.

6.   Paul's Sacrifice (verse 17[a]).

" Yea, though[2] I am offered upon the sacrifice and
service of your faith, " Paul adds.   He will not shrink
from death in order to be of service to them and to
help them in their efforts to press on in the Christian
life.   He hopes to live, but he stands in the constant
presence of death, and he is not afraid.   He had
faced death at Philippi and often since.   It will come
some day.   He is ready now.   It is not his apostolic
office, but his very life that he offers.   The picture
here is of their faith[3] in the sense of their Christian
life as a sacrifice[4] and priestly service.[5]   The Philip-

---

[1] ἐκοπίασα.   From κόπος exhausting toil (1 Cor. 15 : 10;
Gal. 4 : 11).   In Rev. 14 : 13 see distinction drawn between
ἔργα (works) and κόπων (toils).

[2] εἰ καί.   " Even if " would be καὶ εἰ as some manuscripts
have it.

[3] πίστεως.   [4] θυσία.

[5] λειτουργία.   From λαός and ἔργον, work for the people.
Cf. our " liturgy."

pians as priests lay down upon the altar their Christian lives (faith and fidelity). Upon[1] this Paul is ready to pour out[2] his own life as an additional sacrifice in their service. It is not necessary to press the point whether Paul has in mind the Jewish custom of pouring the drink offering around the altar or the heathen of pouring the libation upon the altar. The latter would be more familiar to the Philippians, but the point holds good in either case. Paul is willing to spend and be spent in the service of the Philippians (cf. 2 Cor. 12 : 15[3]). One thinks of the student volunteers who offer their lives for mission service and challenge the churches to furnish the money for their support. One thinks of David Livingstone who gave his life gladly for the healing of the open sore of the world in Africa.

7. **Mutual Joy** (verses 17[b]–18).

" I joy and rejoice[4] with you all," says Paul. He is glad by himself to make the offering of his life, if this supreme sacrifice is demanded. He will not shrink back, but will meet it gladly, and all the more readily since he can share his joy with them. Fel-

---

[1] ἐπί.

[2] σπένδομαι. The verb is used in the *libelli* (certificates of pagan worship). Those who poured out libations to the gods obtained immunity. Cf. Milligan, " Selections from the Greek Papyri," pp. 114–116.

[3] δαπανήσω καὶ ἐκ δαπανηθήσομαι.

[4] Χαίρω καὶ συγχαίρω. The point in the repetition is συγ ——

lowship is a blessed reality. Paul is glad on his own
account that he has been the instrument in their salvation (Kennedy). He is still more joyful at the experiences of grace which they have in Christ. Joy
is not selfish, but wishes company. The woman in
Luke 15: 9 who found her lost piece of money
called in her women friends and said: " Rejoice with
me, for I have found the piece which I had lost."
So the shepherd who found the one lost sheep said
to his friends: " Rejoice with me, for I have found
my sheep which was lost" (Luke 15 : 6). So the
father says : " Make merry, for this my son was
dead, and is alive again; he was lost, and is found"
(Luke 15 : 24). The child all aglow with his Christmas toys wishes other children to come and share
his joys. " And in the same manner¹ do ye also joy,
and rejoice with me." Play up to your part of the
joy. Plutarch² tells of the messenger from Marathon
who expired on the first threshold in Athens with
these words on his lips: " Rejoice and we rejoice."³
Nowhere in the Epistle is Paul so insistent about joy
as here. The Christian is rich in his joy in Christ.
What joy it will be in heaven to tell the story of the
triumph of Christ over sin in your life and in mine.

---

¹ τὸ δὲ αὐτὸ. Adverbial accusative (of general reference).
Cf. Robertson, " Grammar," p. 487.

² Mor., p. 347 C.

³ Χαίρετε καὶ χαίρομεν.

VII

FELLOWSHIP
(2 : 19–30)

MUCH as Paul loved doctrine, he also greatly loved people. He had a passion for folks and had hosts of friends wherever he laboured and even where he had not been as Romans 16 shows. Dan Crawford, the remarkable missionary of Central Africa and author of " Thinking Black," speaks quaintly of fishing in the eyes of his friends. Paul knew how to do that and dearly loved the fellowship of the saints. We have many glimpses of his personal relationships in the Acts and in his Epistles. Paul had the most delightful ties with his fellow-workers. He had foes in plenty, but he also made friends fast and true. In the midst of this Epistle Paul talks in a charming way about his plans for communicating with the Philippians, a human touch that breaks the strain of theological argument. This Epistle seems to have no formal or logical order.[1] It flows along in the most easy and

---

[1] Clemen (" Einheitlichkeit der paulin. Briefe," p. 138) thinks that verses 19–21 do not belong here, but that is hypercriticism in a letter like this.

natural way and treats the weightiest topics and the most incidental with equal ease and grace.

1. Paul's Plans for Timothy (verses 19–23).

He writes as the Master about the disciple. Timothy has evidently placed himself wholly at Paul's service in the matter of going or not going to Philippi. Perhaps the Philippians had wondered why Paul had not sent them more frequent messages. So then he writes in an apologetic vein about his conduct in the matter.

(a) *Timothy's Interest in the Philippians* (verses 19–21). The possibility of Paul's martyrdom (Phil. 2 : 17) was only a remote one and did not interfere with his plans for sending word to Philippi. Paul has a very definite hope to send Timothy "shortly"[1] to them, though how soon he cannot tell. His hope is centered "in the Lord Jesus."[2] This favourite Pauline idiom is not a mere pious phrase, but represents the very core of Paul's philosophy of life. Jesus is the circumference of all his thoughts and activities. Christ is both the center and the circumference of the circle of life for Paul. Christ is the key to the universe and to Paul's own life. He has no life outside of Christ (cf. 1 : 8, 14; 2 : 24; 3 : 1; Rom.

---

[1] ταχέως. The use of the aorist infinitive πέμψαι after ἐλπίζω rather than the future is in accord with κοινή usage. Cf. Robertson, "Grammar," pp. 1081 f.

[2] ἐν Κυρίῳ Ἰησοῦ.

9:1; 14:14, etc.). Evidently Paul had tried to send messengers to Philippi, but had been unable to do so. Epaphroditus had been here in Rome a good while and Paul had grown anxious about the Philippians, " that I also may be of good cheer, when I know your state."[1] He himself will be of good spirit, good heart, good courage. He needed the good cheer that would come from good news about them.

His reason for wishing to send Timothy in particular is plainly given: " For I have no man like-minded, who will care truly for your state." He means, of course, one like-minded[2] with Timothy. This is high tribute to the fidelity and disinterestedness of Timothy who richly deserved it. He was such a friend that[3] he would be genuinely[4] anxious[5] about the Philippians. He was Paul's companion and helper in the establishment of the Philippian church. Besides, like Paul, he had the shepherd heart and knew what anxiety for all the churches was (2 Cor. 11:28), a daily pressure[6] upon Paul's

---

[1] ἵνα κἀγὼ εὐψυχῶ γνοὺς τὰ περὶ ὑμῶν. This verb is rare (but cf. Josephus, Ant. XI, 6, 8), save that εὐψύχει is common in epitaphs. But εὔψυχος is in 1 Macc. 9:14; 2 Macc. 7:20; 14:18. Γνοὺς here is ingressive aorist, come to know.

[2] ἰσόψυχον. It is a rare word. Cf. Æschylus, Agam. 1470 and Psalm 54 (55):14 (13). Vulgate has unanimem.

[3] ὅστις almost consecutive (certainly sub-final) here. Cf. Robertson, " Grammar," p. 996.

[4] γνησίως. By birth relation, naturally, sincerely.

[5] μεριμνήσει. Common word for anxiety (cf. Matt. 6:25).

[6] ἐπίστασις. A load standing or staying upon Paul's soul.

heart. No other preacher is really worth while. The minister who is out for money will not win souls and feed them. The man who puts his own selfish interests before the Kingdom of God will not have the sacrificial spirit. Paul has a hard word to add: " For they all seek their own, not the things of Christ."[1] This is a very severe indictment of the rest of Paul's friends in Rome. We do not know all the circumstances. Perhaps Paul is only speaking of those who were in a position to make the long (for that time) trip from Rome to Philippi and back. It is possible that Luke and Aristarchus were absent from the city at this time. Paul is a man of quick impulses and we may have here a pessimistic note in this optimistic letter. The very exceptional conse- cration of Timothy set in relief the hesitation of the rest. But there is small wonder (Kennedy) that Paul should feel hurt at the lack of inclination on the part of any of his friends save Timothy to make the sac- rifice of time and energy necessary for the journey. " The whole number," says Paul, put their own inter- ests before the interests of Christ. Augustine says that Paul's companions here in Rome were merce- nary. Paul certainly loved Luke, the beloved physi- cian (Col. 4 : 14), and it is hard to think of him as mercenary and selfish. He was, as already suggested, probably out of town. It may be urged by some that Paul allowed himself to go too far in interpreting

[1] οἱ πάντες γὰρ τὰ ἑαυτῶν ζητοῦσιν, οὐ τὰ χριστοῦ Ἰησοῦ.

his own eagerness to hear from Philippi as the clear will of God. Certainly the interpretation of Providence is not always easy. More than one angle of vision is often possible. But, after all, it is amazing what good excuses men can find for doing their own way, the easy way, in a crisis rather than the hard way which may be God's way. If the duty seems unpleasant, we often seek reasons for thinking that it is not duty at all. At any rate, one is not wide of the mark if he says that nothing so hinders the effectiveness of our churches as just this tendency to put our own interests before those of the Kingdom of God. Many a pastor is dreary and despondent as he faces progressive enterprises in the church work because so many ask to be excused. They say that they really do not have time. These stern words of Paul come to one's mind, if not his lips, at a time like that. But Paul is not a man to be blocked by the refusal of men to do the work that is called for. If one way fails, there is always another way open.

(b) *Timothy's Devotion to Paul* (verse 22). Paul has no need to tell the Philippians about Timothy, whose character is in such contrast[1] to "the all" who put their own interests first. "Ye know (by experience[2] as seen in Acts 16 and 17) the proof

[1] δέ. Adversative here, not continuative. Cf. Robertson, "Grammar," p. 1186.

[2] γινώσκετε, not οἴδατε.

(approved character [1]) of him." When put to the test in Philippi, Timothy proved true. His love and loyalty they well know and they need only a reminder to bring it all back to them. Paul starts to say that, as a child served a father,[2] so Timothy served [3] me, but his refined feeling and instinctive humility (Kennedy) and delicacy lead Paul to change the structure of the sentence. He is checked also by the thought (Vincent) that both he and Timothy are servants of Christ (Phil. 1 : 1). So he says : " served with me " [4] as father and son in the common cause, side by side, " in the gospel " or " for the gospel " [5] however we take it. Either is possible and either sphere or purpose makes sense. The feeling of *camaraderie* and companionship is uppermost in Paul's mind. Timothy and Paul have served together in the trenches as comrades in the army of Christ. Paul elsewhere bears hearty testimony to the service of Timothy as " my beloved child and faithful in the Lord " (1 Cor. 4 : 17), " for he does the work of the Lord as I also " (1 Cor. 16 : 10). Cf. also 1 Tim. 1 : 2; 2 Tim. 1 : 2. This devotion was all the more appreciated by Paul if we admit that Timothy was not vigorous in health

---

[1] δοκιμὴν. Used for process of trial (2 Cor. 8 : 2) and result of trial (2 Cor. 2 : 9) and here (Vincent). Vulgate has *experimentum*.

[2] ὡς πατρὶ τέκνον.

[3] ἐδούλευσεν. Figure of slave (δοῦλος) and master.

[4] σὺν ἐμοί.

[5] εἰς τὸ εὐαγγέλιον. Robertson, " Grammar," pp. 591 f.

and had a natural timidity of disposition.   His loyalty
was unimpeachable.   He stood ready to serve Christ
anywhere.

(c)   *Paul's Need of Timothy* (verse 23).   As things
are with Paul now in Rome, he cannot spare Timothy till the cloud has vanished and Paul is free again.
Then he will dispatch Timothy *instanter*, for he
knows that the Philippians will wish to know how it
goes with Paul.[1]   Paul here resumes the standpoint
of verse 19.   Meanwhile Paul needs Timothy by his
side and can only cherish the hope of sending him
soon.   Then he can tell about the outcome of the
trial.

2.   Paul's Trust About Himself (verse 24).

He has a hope[2] of sending Timothy, a trust[3]
in the Lord (cf. 1 : 14; 2 : 19) of coming himself
soon.[4]   There is a curious parallel in Paul's language about his proposed visit to Corinth after he
had sent Timothy thither: " But I shall come to you
shortly, if the Lord will " (1 Cor. 4 : 19).   If Paul

[1] τὰ περὶ ἐμέ, the things concerning me.   The use of ὡς ἂν
as a temporal conjunction occurs also in Rom. 15 : 24 ; 1 Cor.
11 : 34.   It occurs in the papyri.   Cf. Robertson, " Grammar," p. 974.   The aspirated form ἀφίδω is here correct and
is amply supported in the papyri.   Cf. Robertson, " Grammar," p. 224, and Lightfoot, *in loco*.   Ἐξαυτῆς occurs chiefly
in Acts.   The Vulgate has *mox*.

[2] ἐλπίζω.

[3] πέποιθα.   Second perfect, state of confidence.

[4] ταχέως.   Shortly or swiftly.

wrote Philippians before Colossians, Ephesians and Philemon, he was not able to come right away, but only after a year or so. We do not know precisely what Paul's expectations were about this "shortly." The whim of a Nero was an elusive thing to count upon. But he no longer thinks of going on to Spain first as he had once planned (Rom. 15 : 28). His heart now turns to the east (Phile. 22). His long imprisonment in Cæsarea and Rome has made it necessary for Paul to set things in order in the east. The Gnostic disturbers had already appeared on the horizon before Paul left Asia (Acts 20 : 29 f.). These "grievous wolves" had taken full advantage of Paul's absence to play havoc with the flock in various parts of Asia. Philippi also tugs at Paul's heart which now definitely turns eastward. When he was released, it seems probable that he did go east at once. We catch traces of Paul's tracks at Miletus (2 Tim. 4 : 20), Ephesus (1 Tim. 1 : 3), Macedonia and so probably Philippi (1 Tim. 1 : 3), Troas (2 Tim. 4 : 13), Nicopolis (Titus 3 : 12). We may believe therefore that in time the Philippians did see Paul again as well as Timothy who was certainly in the east (1 Tim. 1 : 3).

3. **The Immediate Return of Epaphroditus** (verses 25–30).

The way is clear for this at any rate and now at last. For long this boon seemed remote if not impossible. But God has been good to Epaphroditus, to

Paul, and to the Philippians in sparing the life of this
good man. So Epaphroditus is to go at once as the
bearer of this Epistle and of Paul's love and blessing.

(a) *His Return Necessary* (verses 25 f.). His
" hopes " aside, Paul faces[1] the immediate necessity[2]
of sending Epaphroditus at once. It is important for
Paul to keep in vital touch with the work lest it lan-
guish and die, but the special reason for the urgency
is the anxiety of Epaphroditus and theirs about him
as Paul explains. There is no reason for confusing
this Epaphroditus of Philippi with Epaphras of
Colossæ (Col. 1:7; 4:12; Phile. 23), even if the
latter is a shortened form of the other name,[3] for the
name in both forms is common enough all over the
empire. There is nothing in the tradition that this
Epaphroditus was Nero's secretary, due to allusions in
Suetonius (Nero, 49; Domitian, 14). Paul describes
him as his brother[4] in the Christian brotherhood, as
his fellow-worker[5] in the cause of Christ, as his fellow-
soldier[6] in the conflict with Christ's enemies. He is

[1]ἡγησάμην is epistolary aorist like ἔπεμψα in verse 28.
Proof also that Epaphroditus bore the Epistle.

[2] ἀναγκαῖον. Cf. 2 Cor. 9:5 for same idiom.

[3] Cf. Robertson, " Grammar," p. 172; Lightfoot, *in loco.*

[4]ἀδελφόν.   [5] συνεργόν.

[6]συνστρατιώτην. Cf. Philemon 2. Very common metaphor with Paul. Moulton and Milligan (" Lexical Notes,"
Expositor, Sept., 1911) quote from BU 814²⁷ (iii. A. D.)
κέκρημαι χαλκὸν π[α]ρὰ συστρατιώτου when a soldier in a
letter to his mother says: " I have borrowed money from a
fellow soldier."

Paul's comrade in love, in work, and in peril, " common
sympathy, common work, common danger " (Lightfoot). But the Philippians regard him as their
" apostle (ᵃ¹) or " messenger " to Paul as he was in
truth and also their " minister," [2] " sacrificial minister " it almost turned out to be, to Paul's need. He
rendered a priestly service at any rate. Epaphroditus
brought their gifts (Phil. 4 : 18) which Paul there calls
a " sacrifice " [3] as in 2 : 30 a " service," [4] an oblation
to God.[5] The qualifications of Epaphroditus for
service to both Paul and the Philippians are thus
excellent. He was not the equal in gifts to Timothy,
but Paul used gladly the services of less gifted men.
Not all men can be leaders and pioneers. Moses had
Aaron, Luther had Melancthon (cf. Baskerville, *in
loco*).

But Paul had a specific reason [6] for sending Epaphroditus now. The simple truth was that Epaphroditus was intensely homesick. " He longed after you
all " [7] with yearning *pothos* and pathos. He " was

---

[1] ἀπόστολον. Here in the original and general sense of the
word, not one of the Twelve or like Paul (cf. 2 Cor. 8 : 23).

[2] λειτουργὸν.   [3] θυσίαν.

[4] λειτουργίας.

[5] On Paul's use of pagan terms see Ramsay, *Exp. Times*,
X, 1–5.

[6] ἐπειδή. Only in three other places in Paul's Epistles.
Cf. Robertson, " Grammar," p. 965.

[7] ἐπιποθῶν ἦν. Periphrastic imperfect adds to the notion of
continuance. Note ἐπι —— Cf. Phil. 1 : 8. It is a strong
word.

sore troubled"[1] in anguish of heart, either from dis-
gust at the situation or from a real case of homesick-
ness. At any rate he was sick at heart now "because
ye had heard that he was sick."[2] It is a common
feeling for the sick to conceal the serious nature of
the illness from their loved ones so as to avoid giving
pain. Perhaps the Philippians on hearing of the illness of Epaphroditus had written Paul a letter about
it. If so, Paul was now replying to that letter. As
it was, the heart of Epaphroditus was pierced to the
quick with anxiety. This touch of human sympathy
is life itself.

(*b*) *The Recent Peril of Epaphroditus* (verse 27).
Paul has put the thing too mildly, "for indeed"[3]
(really) "he was sick nigh unto death."[4] What this
sickness was we do not know. Epaphroditus may
have run great risk on his way to Rome. He may
have come in the hot season and have caught the
terrible Roman fever, a plague yet in spite of our
knowledge of the mosquito. Some have suggested
that Paul was more closely confined after the arrival

---

[1] ἀδημῶν. The etymology is wholly conjectural whether
from ἄδημος (away from home) or from ἀδήμων (distressed).

[2] διότι ἠκούσατε ὅτι ἠσθένησεν. Note διότι (causal) and
ὅτι (declarative) and the two aorists. He "fell sick" (ingressive aorist).

[3] καὶ γάρ. Ascensive force of καὶ. Cf. Robertson,
"Grammar," p. 1181.

[4] παραπλήσιον θανάτου. Most MSS. read θανάτῳ, but W
H follow B P here. Cf. Robertson, "Grammar," p. 646.
Cf. also p. 203 for change of ω and ου.

of Epaphroditus who had more exposure. But, whatever the cause, God took pity[1] on Epaphroditus and, Paul adds with delicacy of feeling, " on me also,"[2] and in particular, " that I might not have sorrow upon sorrow "[3] as if wave upon wave of woe would overwhelm Paul with a flood, Epaphroditus' death piled upon Paul's imprisonment. That would be more than Paul could stand. Isaiah spoke of " tribulation upon tribulation,"[4] the Psalms of Solomon of " sin upon sin,"[5] and Jesus of " stone upon stone."[6] We have a proverb about trouble: " It never rains, but it pours." But that is the philosophy of pessimism. The waves did stop rolling over Paul and Epaphroditus was spared.

(c) *Welcome for Epaphroditus* (verses 28 f.). The final recovery of Epaphroditus, added to the anxiety of the Philippians, led Paul to speed[7] in sending[8] him to the Philippians, to more[9] eagerness on Paul's part

[1] ἀλλὰ ὁ θεὸς ἠλέησεν.   [2] οὐκ αὐτὸν μόνον, ἀλλὰ καὶ ἐμέ.

[3] ἵνα μὴ λύπην ἐπὶ λύπην σχῶ.

[4] 28 : 10 θλίψιν ἐπὶ θλίψιν.

[5] 3 : 7 ἁμαρτία ἐπὶ ἁμαρτίαν.

[6] Matt. 24 : 2 λίθος ἐπὶ λίθον. The MSS. vary here in Phil. 2 : 27 between λύπη and λύπην with ἐπί. Either makes good sense. Cf. Robertson, " Grammar," pp. 602, 604. Note punctiliar idea in σχῶ, get.

[7] οὖν. Therefore, because of the circumstance.

[8] ἔπεμψα. Epistolary aorist.

[9] σπουδαιοτέρως. There is no reason for taking this comparative as a positive or even as a superlative. Cf. Robertson, " Grammar," pp. 664 f. The object of comparison is implied.

than he would have had. He has lost no time in
getting Epaphroditus off, " that, when ye see him
again, ye may rejoice." [1]   Paul is anxious for the
Philippians to recover their cheerfulness which had
been clouded by the sickness of Epaphroditus. Their
joy will react on Paul and make him happy. The
best way to be happy is to make others happy.
" And that I may be less sorrowful " [2] than I have
been. Paul states his own joy euphemistically. He
understands the yearning of Epaphroditus and the
anxiety of the Philippians. " Who is weak, and I
am not weak? Who is caused to stumble and I
burn not ? " (2 Cor. 11 : 29).

" Receive him therefore in the Lord with all joy." [3]
Give him a royal welcome. The command seems
superfluous, but none the less Paul makes it. He
only wishes he could have a share in it. We may
be sure that the Philippians did this thing and took
Epaphroditus to their hearts. He had come back
from the very grave and deserved a conqueror's
welcome. He had been a hero of faith. " Hold
such in honour." [4] This plea for the proper esteem
and treatment of soldiers of the cross is not without
point to-day. Certainly preachers get their share

---

[1] ἵνα ἰδόντες αὐτὸν πάλιν χαρῆτε.

[2] κἀγὼ ἀλυπότερος ὦ.

[3] προσδέχεσθε οὖν αὐτὸν μετὰ πάσης χαρᾶς. A continuous
welcome (present tense).

[4] τοὺς τοιούτους ἐντίμους ἔχετε. Keep on doing so (present tense).

of public esteem and criticism. They are outstanding targets and cannot escape a certain amount of
rough handling which is not wholly bad. As a rule
preachers get what love they deserve and often more.
It is well to insist that ministers deserve due appreciation because of the high and holy task committed
to them, particularly if they do their duty steadily
and faithfully. But, as a rule, preachers are paid a
pitiful salary and are expected to live on less than
most other people with economy and good appearances. There is something better than monuments
and that is right treatment while they live. In particular, one may note with pleasure the endowment
funds for aged ministers now under way in most
of the denominations. That is the least that can be
done and it ought to be done. Any decent nation
takes care of its old soldiers.

(d) *Risking All for the Work of Christ* (verse 30).
Epaphroditus deserves the welcome of a hero " because for the work of Christ he came nigh unto
death." [1] Already " the work " was getting a technical meaning like " the way," " the name." It signified " the cause " of Christ [2] and Paul used it
absolutely [3] in Acts 15 : 38 about John Mark who
" went not with them to the work." The courage

---

[1] ὅτι διὰ τὸ ἔργον Χριστοῦ μέχρι θανάτου ἤγγισεν. **Note**
causal conjunction ὅτι and preposition διά.

[2] Many MSS. have Κυρίου.

[3] As Ignatius does in Eph. 14, Rom. 3.

of Epaphroditus stands over against the timidity of
John Mark. Witness the heroes of faith in Revelation 12:11 who "loved not their life even unto
death." It is possible to be too careful of one's own
life at the cost of real usefulness. One does not wish
to be foolhardy, but soldiers dare danger as do doc-
tors and drummers and all sorts of men. So Epaphroditus really hazarded his life for the work of
Christ. Paul uses here a gambler's phrase. Epaphroditus gambled with his life in the risk that he ran
in coming to Rome, either from the Roman fever
or Nero's wrath or some unknown peril. The early
Christians called those who risked their lives for
Christ "Parabolani" or "the Riskers," the brotherhood of those who dared all for Christ as Aquila and
Priscilla risked their necks for Paul (Rom. 16:4).
Charles Kingsley pictures these "Riskers" for the
souls of men in Hypatia. Epaphroditus did this to
fill up[2] what was lacking[3] in the service[4] of the Philippians for Paul. They could not come themselves
in person and could only send their love by proxy.

[1] παραβολευσάμενος τῇ ψυχῇ. The verb παραβολεύομαι
is from the adjective παράβολος rash, reckless, gambling. Cf.
παραβαλέσθαι ταῖς ψυχαῖς in Diod. 3, 36, 4. In Roman
law the appellant deposited a stake (παράβολον) which he for-
feited if he lost his case. Deissmann ("Light from Ancient
East," p. 84) cites the verb from an inscription of II cent.
A. D. in sense of exposing oneself.

[2] ἀναπληρώσῃ. Cf. Col. 1:24. Fill up to the brim.

[3] ὑστέρημα. No reproach in this term.

[4] λειτουργίας. Sacrificial service.

But Epaphroditus dared all and did this sacrificial service which Paul would never forget. " For that which was lacking on your part they supplied " (1 Cor. 16: 17; cf. 2 Cor. 11 : 9). Paul's feeling towards the Corinthians is repeated in the case of the Philippians.

VIII

THE HOLY QUEST
(3:1-14)

THIS paragraph challenges comparison with the great one in 2:1-11 concerning the Person of Christ. Here the Passion of Paul for likeness to Christ is expressed with the utmost energy and yearning of his soul. Nowhere does his mysticism find a nobler statement. Paul is greatest when his intellect is set on fire with love for Christ. No Knight in search of the Holy Grail ever had such elevation of feeling as Paul here reveals. This is the true chivalry, the Passion for Christ.

1. Repetition of the Commonplace (verses 1-3).

It is possible that Paul at first meant to conclude his letter at this point, when he wrote " finally,[1] brethren," though that is by no means the necessary meaning of his language. The phrase literally means " what is left," " the rest " as in 1 Thessalonians 4:1 ; 2 Thessalonians 3:1. It may mean " henceforth "

[1] τὸ λοιπόν. The case is accusative of extent of time. Cf. Robertson, " Grammar," p. 470. For the use of λοιπόν like οὖν see p. 1146. For a similar use in Epictetus see *Class. Review*, III, p. 71.

as in Mark 14:41; 1 Corinthians 7:29; 2 Timothy
4:8. It may mean only " now " (*jam*) or " therefore " as in Matthew 26:45; Acts 27:20. The
meaning " finally " is also correct as in 2 Corinthians
13:11. On the whole I incline to the view that Paul
did not mean to close the Epistle, but simply turns
to the remaining topics before him with the repetition
of " rejoice." [1] Lightfoot translates by " farewell,"
a possible, though not probable rendering. Joy is the
dominant note in the Epistle so far and it rings on
to the end. But the refrain is joy " in the Lord " as
Paul so often says about all his experiences.

The next sentence puzzles the commentators no
little: " To write the same things to you,[2] to me indeed is not irksome, but for you it is safe." To what
does Paul refer? Is it the repetition of " rejoice " in
this same Epistle? To keep on writing this message
is not tedious[3] to me, " but for you it is safe."[4] It
makes you steadfast, or stable, able to stand. Does
Paul refer to a previous letter in which he gave warnings which he now repeats? That is possible, though
not certain.[5] Paul did write letters which we do not

[1] χαίρετε. Cf. 2:18; 4:4.
[2] τὰ αὐτὰ γράφειν ὑμῖν. Note linear action (present infinitive).
ὀκνηρόν. From ὀκνέω, to hesitate. Means sluggish,
slothful, " poky," tiresome. Does not make me tired. Cf.
Matt. 25:26; Rom. 12:11.
ἀσφαλές. Not to trip or to fall.
[5] Polycarp's use of ἐπιστολαί (*ad Phil.* iii.) does not prove
it as the plural was sometimes applied to single letters.

now possess (1 Cor. 5:9; 2 Cor. 10:10f.; 2 Thess. 2:15; 3:17). Whatever it is, Paul repeats it with a slight apology. Every speaker has a certain hesitancy in repeating things to the same audience, though it is more or less necessary if one is to be effective. Particularly do teachers find repetition necessary. Some people are almost immune to new ideas. They must be taught line upon line, precept upon precept. It is not pleasant to speak to people who do not care to hear. It is easier to write, but even so the edge of expectancy is dulled. But Paul is sustained by the great need of his warning on the part of the Philippians and goes right on.

It is quite possible that the tendency to dissension in the Philippians to which he has already several times alluded was complicated with the Judaizing heresy since Paul proceeds to warn his readers against the Judaizers in very pointed language. If so, it was eminently "safe" for the Philippians for Paul to repeat his warnings against these subtle and dangerous teachers. Three times with striking repetition "in the intense energy of his invective" (Kennedy) Paul makes his warning: "Beware, beware, beware."[1] It is more exactly "look out for,"[2] rather than "beware of," though that idea naturally follows.

[1] βλέπετε, βλέπετε, βλέπετε.
[2] With accusative τοὺς κύνας (as in 2 John 8) rather than with ἀπό (as in Mark 8:15). Cf. 2 Chron. 10:16 and Robertson, "Grammar," p. 471.

He is not describing three classes of opponents, but only one by the use of "the dogs, the evil workers, the concision." There can only be one group whom Paul would so picture and that is the Judaizers whom Paul had already termed "false apostles, deceitful workers, fashioning themselves into apostles of Christ" (2 Cor. 11 : 13). If one is shocked at Paul's use of the word dogs [1] for the Judaizers, he may be reminded that this was the common description of the Gentiles by the Jews. A Jew was forbidden to bring the price of a dog into the house of God to pay a vow (Deut. 23 : 18). Jesus Himself, though in a more or less playful vein, employed the word for "little dogs," [2] of the Gentiles in speaking to the Syro-Phœnician woman (Matt. 15 : 26) and she took no offence at it, but took it up as a pleasantry with the retort about "the little dogs" eating the crumbs under their masters' table (15 : 27). So then Paul is here but retorting to the Judaizers who are the real spiritual dogs while the Gentiles have understood the truth about Christ. Dogs were the common scavengers in the Oriental cities and were considered very unclean by Jews for obvious reasons. In Revelation 22 : 15 the term "dogs" is applied to those "whose impurity excludes them from the heavenly city" (Vincent). We need not split hairs over the precise point in the impurity that Paul means to bring out, whether shamelessness, insolence, cunning,

[1] τοὺς κύνας.   [2] τὰ κυνάρια.

greediness, roving tendencies and howling, snappish-ness. Certainly these Judaizing dogs had dogged Paul's steps all over the empire, snapping at his heels and barking after him at a distance. At any rate the moral impurity of the Judaizers is the subject of Paul's contempt. Look out for these dogs, for they will bite. *Cave canem.* That sign appears at the gate where dangerous dogs are to be found. These "dogs" are also "evil workers."[1] They are actively at work, but in the wrong direction. They are busy doing wrong, fine specimens of wasted energy. Paul calls them "hucksters"[2] in 2 Corinthians 2:17 with the implication of corruption and fraud so often true of those who put the best apples on the top of the barrel, the prettiest strawberries on the top of the basket. These Judaizers, like the Pharisees before them, com-passed sea and land to make one proselyte and made him twofold more a son of hell than they were (Matt. 23:15). Once more Paul speaks of the Judaizers as "the concision."[3] They had mutilated the ordinance of circumcision in making it essential

[1] τοὺς κακοὺς ἐργάτας. Cf. ἐργάται δόλιοι in 2 Cor. 11:13.   Crooked sticks at best.

[2] καπηλεύοντες.

[3] τὴν κατατομήν. The word in the LXX is used only of mu-tilations as in Lev. 21:5; 1 Kings 18:28. The *annominatio* here of κατατομή, περιτομή, is a common figure with Paul (cf. Rom. 12:3; 2 Thess. 3:11). Cf. Robertson, "Grammar," p. 1201. These plays on words are common. An ambassador to Spain said he was sent not to Spain, but to Pain. Coleridge called French philosophy "psilosophy."

to salvation. Christians are the true circumcision as Paul states elsewhere (Rom. 2: 25–29; Eph. 2: 11; Col. 2: 11), the circumcision of the heart which was symbolized by that of the flesh.

Paul gives three reasons for holding that Christians are the real circumcision. We "worship by the Spirit of God." This is the probable translation. The word[1] is the one used for ritual worship, but it means here the true worship of God who is spirit (John 4: 24) with our spirits by the help of the Spirit of God. Then again true Christians "glory in Christ Jesus."[2] This word glory or exult "expresses with great vividness the high level of Christian life" (Kennedy) and belongs to Paul's "triumphant mood." Once more, "we do not put our trust in the flesh."[3] By "flesh" here Paul means the unrenewed human nature, not in the state of grace, even if one is observing ritual ceremonies. It is a vivid picture of the mere ceremonialist who is unsaved. This use of "flesh" is common in Galatians and Romans (cf. Rom. 8: 4–8). In Galatians 5: 2–6 Paul places the mere ceremonialist outside of Christ.

2. **Religious Pride** (verses 4–6).

This pride of religion was at bottom the cause of the

---

[1] λατρεύοντες.

[2] καυχώμενοι ἐν χριστῳ Ἰησοῦ. Cf. Rom. 2: 17; 1 Cor. 1: 31; 2 Cor. 10: 17; Gal. 6: 14.

[3] καὶ οὐκ ἐν σαρκὶ πεποιθότες.

hatred of Paul by the Jews and the Judaizers. There
is much of it to-day, alas. John the Baptist smote
it hip and thigh when the proud Pharisees and Sadducees came to hear him down by the Jordan.
" Think not to say within yourselves, We have Abraham to our father" (Matt. 3 : 9). Instead of being
the spiritual children of Abraham by reason of
ecclesiastical privileges John called them a brood of
vipers as did Jesus later (Matt. 12 : 34) and also children of the devil (John 8 : 44). Paul understands
perfectly the standpoint of these Pharisaic disciples.
He had been there himself and once gloried in all
the things on which they now pride themselves. He
had once before made out an ironical bill of particulars
in ridicule of their carnal religious pride (2 Cor.
11 : 16–30), once when he played the fool for Christ's
sake, "that I also may glory a little." So now he
has as much right to boast of his Jewish prerogatives
as the Judaizers, " though I myself might have confidence even in the flesh." [1] Paul appreciates to the
full the dignity of being a Jew (Rom. 3 : 1 f.). He
places himself for the moment at the Jewish standpoint. " Seeing that many glory after the flesh, I
will glory also " (2 Cor. 11 : 18). He is here speaking " foolishly " and " not after the Lord." " If any
other man thinketh to have confidence in the flesh, I

---

[1] καίπερ ἐγὼ ἔχων πεποίθησιν καὶ ἐν σαρκί. Concessive
clause with καίπερ and the participle. Cf. Robertson,
" Grammar," p. 1129.

yet more." [1] " If they arrogate to themselves these
carnal privileges, I also arrogate them to myself"
(Lightfoot). I have as much right to do it as the
Judaizers.

Paul now proceeds to prove the point of his *argumentum ad hominem*. There is here the same depth
of feeling on Paul's part as in 2 Corinthians 11 : 21,
but less tumultuous eagerness and a more subdued
tone (Lightfoot). There is undoubtedly " a certain
natural pride in recounting his hereditary privileges "
(Kennedy), a pride exhibited even in the sadness of
heart with which they are recounted in Romans
9 : 3–5. " In circumcision eight days old." [2] This
was according to Jewish custom and Paul was thus
an orthodox Israelite (Gen. 17 :12; Lev. 12 : 3).
Circumcision was practiced in Egypt and the papyri
give instances of it. Ishmaelites postponed it till the
thirteenth year (Gen. 17 : 25). He was also " of the
stock of Israel." [3] He was not a proselyte (Vincent),
but belonged to the original stock of Jacob whose

---

[1] εἴ τις. δοκεῖ ἄλλος πεποιθέναι ἐν σαρκί, ἐγὼ μᾶλλον.
Condition of the first class, determined as fulfilled. Cf. Robertson, " Grammar," pp. 1007 ff. Cf. μὴ δόξητε in Matt.
3 : 9.

[2] περιτομῇ ὀκταήμερος. For the locative with adjectives
see Robertson, " Grammar," p. 523. For this use of the
temporal adjective like τεταρταῖος (John 11 : 39) see Robertson, " Grammar," p. 657.

[3] ἐκ γένους Ἰσραήλ. The use of ἐκ for class or country is
common (cf. John 3 : 1). Ἰσραήλ is appositive genitive. Cf.
Robertson, " Grammar," p. 498.

covenant name was Israel (Gen. 32 : 28). The Edom-
ites were descended from Isaac through Esau and
the Ishmaelites also from Abraham. Paul was a
genuine Israelite in the covenant of grace (Rom.
9 : 4; 2 Cor. 11 : 22). Once more Paul was " of the
tribe of Benjamin." [1]   Benjamin was the son of
Rachel, Jacob's beloved wife (Gen. 35 : 17 f.), and
alone of the sons of Jacob was born in Palestine.
The tribe of Benjamin gave the first king whose
name (Saul) Paul also bore (1 Sam. 9 : 1 f.). This
tribe also had the post of honour in battle. " After
thee Benjamin " (Judg. 5 : 14). Mordecai was a Ben-
jaminite. Benjamin alone remained faithful to Judah
when the kingdom was divided (1 Kings 12 : 21). After
the exile it was merged with Judah (Ezra 4 : 1). Paul
was evidently proud of his descent from this little tribe
(cf. Rom. 11 : 1 ; Acts 13 : 21). Paul was a true Ben-
jaminite as a persecutor before his conversion : " In
the morning he shall devour the prey and at night he
shall divide the spoil " (Gen. 49 : 27). Paul was also
" a Hebrew of the Hebrews." [2]   By this phrase Paul
means that he is a Hebrew sprung from Hebrews.
The word Hebrew originally meant " passed over "
in reference to Abram the Hebrew, as designated by
foreigners. It was first used then to distinguish
Abraham's descendants from other nations or
peoples. They themselves preferred the term Israel
or children of Israel. After the return from the ex-

[1] φυλῆς Βενιαμείν.   [2] Ἑβραῖος ἐξ Ἑβραίων.

ile " Jew " [1] came to be the common term in contrast
with Greek (cf. Rom. 1 : 16), " we being Jews by nature, and not sinners of the Gentiles " (Gal. 2 : 15).
Hebrew was now used chiefly for the language and
customs of the Jews rather than for the race. It
served to distinguish between two kinds of Jews.
Those that spoke only the Greek language and followed some of the Greek customs were termed
Hellenists,[2] while those who spoke Aramaic (Hebrew as in Acts 21 : 40; 22 : 2) were called Hebrews.
This distinction is drawn in Acts 6 : 1 between the
Hebrew and Hellenistic widows, both classes being
Jewish Christians. Paul lived in Tarsus, a great
Greek city of Cilicia, and spoke Greek, but he also
spoke Aramaic and was loyal to the Hebrew tra-
ditions of the fathers. He comes of the Aramæan
line, not the Hellenistic. He belonged to the purest
and most loyal type of Jews, the Hebrews. He was
both Hellenist and Hebrew.

But this is not all. In his own personal character-
istics the same fidelity is found, " as touching the
law, a Pharisee." [3] Besides the inherited privileges he
made his choice along the same line. He was in
truth the son of a Pharisee (Acts 23 : 6). But he was
a loyal and zealous Pharisee as opposed to the Sadducees. He was a diligent student of Pharisaism
(Gal. 1 : 14) at the feet of Gamaliel in Jerusalem

[1] $Ἰουδαῖος—Ἕλλην.$ [2] $Ἑλληνιστής.$
[3] $κατὰ νόμον Φαρισαῖος.$ Cf. Acts 22 : 3 ; 23 : 6 ; 26 : 5.

(Acts 22 : 3) and he lived a Pharisee "after the straitest sect of our religion" (Acts 26 : 5). Indeed, in some points Paul was always a Pharisee (Acts 23 : 6). They were not wrong in everything (cf. Matt. 23 : 3). Paul undoubtedly received a deep impress from the school of Hillel and he always revered the law of Moses as the law of God (Rom. 7 : 12, 14, etc.). The Pharisees in reality struck down the law of God by their tradition (Mark 15 : 2, 3, 6). "As touching zeal, persecuting the church."[1] Vincent takes this language as ironical. "I was so very zealous that I became a persecutor of the church." Certainly the early Christians knew full well how true it was. One of the outgrowths of Pharisaism was the Zealot party which brought on the war with Rome and the destruction of Jerusalem. Paul calls himself a Pharisaic zealot in Galatians 1 : 14. The story in Acts 8 : 1 ff. amply justifies Paul's ironical claim. Once Paul did exactly what the Judaizers are now doing to Paul. "As touching the righteousness which is in the law blameless."[2] He means ceremonially blameless, of course, for that was righteousness to the Pharisee. This doing of righteousness was denounced by Jesus in Matthew 6 : 1–18 as punctilious performance of outward rules "to be seen of men" (cf. also Matt. 23 : 5). This righteousness was tested by the stand-

---

[1] κατὰ ζῆλος διώκων τὴν ἐκκλησίαν. Note neuter form of ζῆλος here.

[2] κατὰ δικαιοσύνην τὴν ἐν νόμῳ γενόμενος ἄμεμπτος.

ard[1] of the law (cf. Ps. Sol. 9 : 9). Jewish thought
gave unusual prominence to righteousness.[2] In
Romans 7 Paul describes his own fruitless efforts to
satisfy his own conscience when once disturbed out
of its complacent attitude. The rich young ruler
(Mark 10 : 17–22) shows the self-satisfaction of the
average Jewish moralist whose religion consisted in
doing ritual and legal requirements. He felt himself
" blameless " though he loved self more than God.

Paul has made out such a good case for himself
that one may half-way believe that Paul regrets his
charge or at least thinks it useless. But he is simply
making good his claim of " I yet more " in verse 4.
He is trying to shame, if possible, those who, though
nominal Christians, still set up their own claims to
religious aristocracy. It is quite possible to-day for
Christians to have pride, forsooth, not in Christ, but
in themselves, in their social prestige, in the church to
which they belong, in their denomination, in the pastor, in the music, in the church architecture. Each
denomination may develop a special kind of pride
on a par with Paul's pride as a Pharisee. Certainly
each denomination has developed a special type of
piety and Christian life.

3. **Change of Values** (verses 7 f.).

This category of religious prerogatives which Paul

[1] κατὰ.
[2] Cf. Weber, " Lehren des Talmud," pp. 209 f.

has made in verses 5 and 6 once satisfied Paul's ideals. They were such things as "I used to count up with a miserly greed and reckon to my credit" (Lightfoot). Like a miser he took peculiar delight in the clink of each piece of gold. They were "gains,"[2] indeed, "profits" of race and religion and personal zeal, each item in the old credit side of the ledger once gave Paul peculiar zest as he counted them up to his own spiritual delectation. These items were, indeed, usually considered the greatest blessings of life. Sir W. Robertson Nicoll has discussed in *The British Weekly* (1913) the "Greatest Joys of Life" with his readers. They do not all agree, though most find joy in the spiritual values of life. It is a sum in profit and loss.

Now Paul has undergone an intellectual and spiritual revolution. "Howbeit,"[3] he says, in sharp contrast to the old standpoint, "what things were gains to me," "these have I counted loss for Christ."[4] His words are measured and deliberate. He has come to count and still counts (the present perfect tense, punctiliar-linear), but not as he used to count. Now he counts "for Christ's sake," the new factor in the situation, the new standard of values, the new reason

[1] ἅτινα almost = οἷα. Cf. Robertson, "Grammar," p. 727.
[2] κέρδη. The plural was usually used of money. Jebb, Soph. Antig., 1326.
[3] ἀλλά a real adversative here. Cf. Robertson, "Grammar," pp. 1186 f.
[4] ταῦτα ἥγημαι διὰ τὸν χριστὸν ζημίαν.

for life. Because of Christ, who has thus stepped in
between [1] Paul and his old ideals, Paul has reversed
his entire outlook on life. He has changed the head-
ing at the top of the ledger. He has erased " gains "
(credit) and written " loss " (debit). They are minus
in the sum of life and plus no more. This word loss
ends the sentence with a dull thud, but Paul is not
done with the subject.

He starts all over again with glowing eagerness
and passion, dropping the tone of irony above. He
piles up particles in the effort to express his vehement
emotion on the subject. The " yea, verily, and " very
imperfectly renders the Greek original [2] which is more
precisely, " But indeed therefore at least and." So
Paul repeats his verb in the present tense, " I do
count " [3] by the new standard of values, not merely
the religious prerogatives named above, but " all
things " [4] literally and emphatically as " loss " " for the
excellency of the knowledge of Christ Jesus my
Lord." [5] This is no momentary impulse, no spas-
modic rhapsody on Paul's part. Here he takes his
stand. This is his choice in life. Paul has weighed
the whole world (" all things ") beside Christ. He
has come to the same conclusion that Jesus an-

---

[1] διά.

[2] ἀλλὰ μὲν οὖν γε καὶ. Ellicott notes that ἀλλὰ contrasts,
μὲν confirms, οὖν epitomizes, γε intensifies, καὶ proceeds with
addition.   [3] ἡγοῦμαι.   [4] πάντα.

[5] διὰ τὸ ὑπερέχον τῆς γνώσεως Χριστοῦ Ἰησοῦ τοῦ Κυρίου
μου.

nounced as wisdom when He said : " For what shall
a man be profited if he shall gain[1] the whole world,
and forfeit[2] his life ? " (Matt. 16 : 26).   " For what
shall a man give in exchange[3] for his soul ? "   In
spiritual barter what is the price of a soul ?   Mr.
John D. Rockefeller is credited with wealth to the
amount of a billion dollars.   But what is that by the
side of his soul ?   The Czar of Russia was said to be
worth many billions of dollars with an incredible in-
come.   But what is that beside the worth of his
soul ?   And the Czar has had to abdicate his throne
before the wrath of his people.   The knowledge[4] of
Jesus, " the most excellent of the sciences," overtops[5]
all else, rising sheer above all else in life like the
highest mountain peak, dwarfing all other knowledge
and all of everything else on earth.   Christ is king
of the intellect as of the heart.   No other knowledge
is so exalting and so uplifting as that of Jesus the
Lord of life.   Christians ought to be the noblest of
men with such a commanding intellectual atmosphere
in Christ.   Theology is still the queen of the sciences
in subject and object of research.

Life is a mystery at best, full of change and sur-

---

[1] $\kappa\epsilon\rho\delta\dot{\eta}\sigma\eta$.   Cf. $\kappa\dot{\epsilon}\rho\delta\eta$.   [2] $\zeta\eta\mu\iota\omega\theta\tilde{\eta}$.   Cf. $\zeta\eta\mu\iota\alpha$.
[3] $\dot{\alpha}\nu\tau\dot{\alpha}\lambda\lambda\alpha\gamma\mu\alpha$.
[4] $\gamma\nu\tilde{\omega}\sigma\iota\varsigma$ experimental knowledge.
[5] $\tau\dot{\omicron}$ $\dot{\upsilon}\pi\epsilon\rho\dot{\epsilon}\chi\omicron\nu$.   The articular participle here, like the articular adjective, used as a substantive.   Cf. Robertson,
" Grammar," pp. 1108 f.   Cf. 1 Cor. 4 : 17 for $\tau\dot{\omicron}$ $\dot{\epsilon}\lambda\alpha\phi\rho\dot{\omicron}\nu$
$\tau\tilde{\eta}\varsigma$ $\theta\lambda\dot{\iota}\psi\epsilon\omega\varsigma$.

prises. Relative values in life change with the years. The child is happy with his Christmas toys. "When I was a child, I spake as a child, I felt as a child, I thought as a child; now that I am become a man, I have put away childish things" (1 Cor. 13:11). Paul is now a man in Christ Jesus who dominates the world of manhood for him, "Christ Jesus my Lord." For Christ's sake[1] Paul did suffer loss,[2] yea, the loss of "the all things,"[3] the sum-total of his old life's values. His own family probably regarded him as a disgrace to Judaism. His Pharisaic confrères considered him a deserter from the cause. The Jews in general treated him as a renegade and a turn-coat. He had paid the price for Christ's sake. But it is worth the price. He has no regrets. "I do count (the third use of this verb) but refuse"[4] beneath my feet, not as diadems for my head. These "pearls" Paul deliberately flings to the dogs, if not to the swine, as trash. It is sad to see the poor picking for treasures in the piles of refuse. Paul is not a madman in reckless disregard of all values. It is the greatest bargain of life. He does it "that I may gain Christ."[5] The new "gain" is Christ. He lost the Jewish world to gain Christ the Lord of all.

[1] δι' ὅν.
[2] ἐζημιώθην. Aorist ind. Definite period of his conversion.   [3] τὰ πάντα.
[4] σκύβαλα. Cf. Sirach 27 : 4. Either from εἰς κύνας βάλλω I fling to the dogs or from σκῶρ dung.
[5] ἵνα χριστὸν κερδήσω. Cf. κέρδη.

4. **Gaining Christ** (verses 9–11).

What is it to " gain Christ " ?   Paul gave up all to win more in Christ.   Lightfoot [1] properly notes that " the earnest reiteration of St. Paul's language here expresses the earnestness of his desire."   Paul knows the power of repetition on the mind.   It is a pity that verse 9 begins right in the middle of a subordinate clause, separating two verbs [2] (" gain," " be found ") used with the same final particle (" that " [3]). As a matter of fact the thought in verses 9–11 is simply the expansion of that in the last words of verse 8, " that I may gain Christ."   To be sure, Paul had gained Christ at once when he surrendered his Jewish prerogatives as sources of gain and pride.   But he had not exhausted the unsearchable riches in Christ (Eph. 3 : 8).   All the treasures of wisdom and knowledge are in Christ who is the mystery of God (Col. 2 : 2 f.).   There are riches untold still ahead of Paul which beckon him on.   These he can only enjoy when he has appropriated them and has made them his own.   These verses are so rich in ideas that they overlap and overflow.

" And be found in him." [4]   Dying is gaining [5] Christ, Paul has already told us (1 : 21), gaining Christ

---

[1] Thus κέρδη, κερδήσω—ἥγημαι, ἡγοῦμαι, ἡγοῦμαι—ζημίαν, ζημίαν, ἐζημιώθην—διά, διά, διά—πάντα, τὰ πάντα —γνώσεως, γνῶναι—Χριστὸν, Χριστοῦ, Χριστόν.

[2] κερδήσω, εὑρεθῶ.   [3] ἵνα.

[4] καὶ εὑρεθῶ ἐν αὐτῷ.   [5] κέρδος.

in full, though life is Christ to Paul. Paul is already
" in Christ " in the real mystic union. But Christ
had new riches for Paul each day. The word " be
found " has a semitechnical sense of " turn out
actually to be " (Kennedy) as in Galatians 2 : 17
(" we ourselves also were found sinners " [1]). This
complete identification of the believer with Christ is
" the central fact in Paul's religious life and thought "
(Kennedy). He probably here is thinking of the
consummation when we shall all stand before the
judgment seat of Christ (2 Cor. 5 : 10). Then in
reality Paul wishes it to be manifest to all that he is
in Christ. When death overtakes Paul he wishes to
be found by death in Christ. James Moffatt (*Expository Times*, October, 1912, p. 46) cites Epictetus [2]
as using " found " of death : " I want to be found in
right thoughts of God." It is a not uncommon
thought with people as to what they should like to
be doing when death finds them. Preachers are
sometimes stricken with death in the pulpit. Paul's
desire is that all shall know that then he is actually
in Christ. In particular he is clear that then he will
not have [3] a righteousness of his own,[4] that which is
of the law,[5] the sort that he once gloried in, the
Pharisaic righteousness of rules and ceremonial

[1] εὑρέθημεν καὶ αὐτοὶ ἁμαρτωλοί.
[2] εὑρεθῆναι. Cf. also Epictetus 4 : 10–12. Cf. Gen.
5 : 24 καὶ οὐχ ηὑρίσκετε διότι μετέθηκεν αὐτὸν ὁ θεός.
[3] μη ἔχων.
[4] ἐμὴν, δικαιοσύνην.   [5] τὴν ἐκ νόμου.

punctilios, "but that which is through faith in
Christ,"[1] in a word, "the righteousness which is from
God by faith,"[2] upon the basis[3] of faith and issuing
from[4] God, the God-kind of righteousness (Rom.
1 : 17), the only real righteousness in Gentile or
Jew (Rom. 1 : 18–3 : 20). Thus alone can one gain
a right relation (righteousness) with God. It is not
found outside of Christ. Only thus is God's standard met. This is God's gracious way of treating
those as righteous who have no righteousness of
their own. We may call it "forensic" if we wish,
but that description in no way nullifies the fact. It
is also ethical, for only thus is it possible for us to
become righteous ourselves. God's love and forgive-
ness start us on a new plane and guide us in the new
path. It is not a bald legal transaction, but "for-
giveness with the Forgiver in it" (Rainy, Exp. Bible
on Phil., p. 231). "The only way of entering on new
relations with God, or ourselves becoming new men,
is the way of faith" (Rainy, p. 233).

Paul repeats the passion of his soul, "that I may
know him,"[5] that I may come to know him by

---

[1] ἀλλὰ τὴν διὰ πίστεως Χριστοῦ.   Note the article here
which is almost demonstrative. Cf. Robertson, "Grammar," p. 780.   The genitive Χριστοῦ is objective. Cf. *ibid.*,
pp. 499 ff.

[2] τὴν ἐκ θεοῦ δικαιοσύνην ἐπὶ τῇ πίστει.

[3] ἐπὶ.   The medium is expressed by διά.

[4] ἐκ.

[5] τοῦ γνῶναι αὐτόν.   The infinitive of purpose (with τοῦ)
is common enough. Cf. Robertson, "Grammar," p. 1088.

richer experience.[1] He takes up the word "knowledge" from verse 8 and presses the idea home. Paul longs to "go in deeper" and to learn more of Christ by inner experience. He explains this knowledge as the natural result of winning Christ and being found in Him. "For with Paul this Christian Gnosis is the highest reach of Christian experience" (Kennedy). Paul takes up some of the items in the higher knowledge of Christ. "The power of his resurrection."[2] Paul is here thinking not of the historical fact of Christ's resurrection nor of his own resurrection after death. It is rather Paul's experimental knowledge of the power or force in Christ's resurrection in its influence on Paul's own inner life (Vincent). Cf. Romans 6: 4-11; Colossians 3: 1 ff. Lightfoot notes various aspects of this power as the assurance of immortality (Rom. 8: 11; 1 Cor. 15: 14 f.), as the triumph over sin and the pledge of justification (Rom. 4: 24 f.), as showing the dignity of the human body (1 Cor. 6: 13-15; Phil. 3: 21), as stimulating the whole moral and spiritual being (Rom. 6: 4; Gal. 2: 20; Col. 2: 12: Eph. 2: 5).[3] There is the dynamic of the Cross because of the Resurrection of Jesus. Paul felt the grip of this truth in its appeal to holy living. He adds "the

[1] γινώσκω is common in this sense. Cf. 1 Cor. 13: 12. Cf. Eph. 1: 17-20; John 17: 3.

[2] τὴν δύναμιν τῆς ἀναστάσεως αὐτοῦ. Cf. our dynamite.

[3] Cf. Westcott's "Gospel of the Resurrection," ii. § 31 f. Cf. Ellicott, in loco.

fellowship of his sufferings."[1]   It is " participation "
in the sufferings of Christ.   Certainly Paul is here
revealing " the deepest secrets " (Kennedy) of his own
Christian experience.   " Being in Christ involves
fellowship with Christ at all points—His obedient life,
His spirit, His sufferings, His death, and His glory "
(Vincent).   Paul is not thinking of martyrdom for
himself, but of the " spiritual process which is carried
on in the soul of him who is united to Christ "
(Kennedy).   As Paul understands the power of
Christ's death and resurrection, he is able to understand His sufferings and to enter into them with sympathy and spiritual blessing as we drink from the cup
that Christ drank (2 Cor. 4: 10; 1 Pet. 4: 13). The
climax is reached by Paul in the words " becoming
conformed unto his death."[2]   One thinks at once of
Romans 6: 3 " baptized into his death " and 5
" united with him in the likeness of his death " and
then also Galatians 2: 20: " I have been crucified
with Christ."   We are in Paul's Holy of Holies in his
relations with Christ.   He suffers when Christ suffers.
He dies when Christ dies.   He lives when Christ
lives.   The language is symbolic, to be sure, but
represents the deepest and highest things in life for
Paul.   This likeness to Christ is our destiny (Rom.
8: 29), but the process begins here.   If we are to

[1] κοινωνίαν παθημάτων αὐτοῦ.

[2] συμμοοφιζόμενος τῷ θανάτῳ αὐτοῦ. Cf. σύμμορφος in
Rom. 8: 29.

share in the glory of Jesus, we must also share in the
suffering (Rom. 8 : 17 f., 28 f.). So Paul rejoices to
fill up on his part the sufferings of Christ left over
for him (Col. 1 : 24). In dying on the Cross Christ
was regarded as sin (2 Cor. 5 : 21) and identified Himself with the sin of the world. So now we are
identified with Christ's sufferings and death.

Paul closes with the modest hope, not at all in
doubt, expressed in conditional form, " if by any
means I may attain unto the resurrection from the
dead." [1] Paul does not here deny the general resurrection of the dead which he teaches in 1 Corinthians
15 : 42. He is apparently here thinking only of the
glorious resurrection of the pious dead and expresses
the devout hope of sharing in that without throwing
doubt at all upon his confidence in the matter. At
any rate this passage makes it perfectly clear that
Paul had no positive conviction that Jesus would
come for him while alive before death. His language
in 1 Thessalonians 4 : 15 " we that are alive " does
not mean that. He simply groups himself with the

[1] εἴ πως καταντήσω εἰς τὴν ἐξανάστησιν τὴν ἐκ νεκρῶν.
The verb καταντήσω may be either future ind. or aorist subj.
The use of εἴπως expresses a half purpose also. The use of
ἐξανάστησιν rather than ἀνάστησιν has not been explained.
Lightfoot takes it to be because of ἐκ with νεκρῶν and to emphasize the resurrection of the righteous out from the dead.
Ellicott takes it to be the first resurrection as in Rev. 20 : 5,
and so interprets 1 Thess. 4 : 16 where, however, the contrast is between Christians living and dead. The point is not
made out (Vincent).

living for he is alive when he writes (cf. 1 Thess.
5 : 2; 2 Thess. 2 : 2). He hoped that Christ would
come soon, but he has nowhere said that He would
do so.

5. The Single Chase (verses 12–14).

Paul does not lose the sense of proportion in the
midst of his rhapsody. He is keenly conscious of a
possible misunderstanding of his language. He
seems to be thinking of " some at Philippi who were
claiming high sanctity and so affecting superior airs
towards their brethren " (Kennedy) with inevitable
irritations and jealousies. The reaction from Jewish
formalism easily went from liberty to license. It
was not a mere rhetorical question that Paul raised
when he said : " Shall we continue in sin that grace
may abound ? " (Rom. 6 : 1). The antinomian spirit
was a live thing then and now. One wing of the
Gnostics boldly argued that they were free from guilt
in sins of the body so long as the spirit communed
with the Lord. The so-called Christian Scientists
to-day deny the reality of and guilt for sin. Some
evolutionists treat sin not as a moral problem at all,
but simply as an animal inheritance, " nature red in
tooth and claw," not yet shaken off. Professional
perfectionists likewise to-day minimize their own
faults with all the skill of the Pharisees who " say
and do not " (Matt. 23 : 3). So Paul says pointedly :
" Not that I have already obtained, or am already

perfect." [1] Paul thus disclaims absolute perfection in unequivocal language. He gathers up in the verb "obtained"[2] or "attained" all his experiences and achievements thus far,[3] all that he has described in verses 8–11. He then explains more literally his figure by the simpler "or am already made perfect." The change of tense[4] is not accidental or a confusion of tenses. He means to express his present state of imperfection. Absolute perfection he expressly denies. By the present perfect tense he gathers up the whole past in its relation to the present. He has not yet reached the goal. He is here discussing moral and spiritual perfection in Christ. There is a relative perfection which was true of Paul and of all who grow in grace at all and are no longer babes in Christ (cf. 3 : 15). Paul is not speaking of that. This holy dissatisfaction with his spiritual attainments and eager longing for loftier heights in Christ we often see in Paul's writings (cf. Eph. 3 : 17–19; 4 : 13–16; Col. 1 : 28). Ignatius (Eph. iii) says: "I do not command you as though I were some-

---

[1] οὐχ ὅτι ἤδη ἔλαβον ἢ ἤδη τετελείωμαι. In New Testament οὐχ ὅτι is used to prevent misunderstanding, not as in classic Greek = not only, but. τελειόω is as common in Hebrews and means to bring to an end.

[2] ἔλαβον. Constative aorist. Cf. Robertson, "Grammar," pp. 831–834. Cf. John 17 : 4 ἐδόξασα.

[3] ἤδη.

[4] τετελείωμαι. Present perfect. This tense is kept distinct from the aorist in the New Testament. Cf. Robertson, "Grammar," pp. 898–902.

what, for even though I am in bonds for the Name's sake, I am not yet perfected in Christ."[1]

"But I press on."[2] The verb is used of the chase and of the race. Ellicott renders it: "But I am pressing onwards." The verb means literally "I pursue" or "I follow after" (A. V.). "The pursuit is no groping after something undefined, nor is it prosecuted with any feeling of doubt as to the attainment of its end" (Vincent). It is the eager pursuit of a definite goal.[3] Not every pursuit wins its object, but Paul is not doubtful about the outcome of this chase or race. "I press on," Paul says, "if so be that I may lay hold on that for which also I was laid hold on by Christ Jesus."[4] This is his definite object. This is his real goal. He points to his conversion as the event in his life which explains everything. That is the moving power in Paul's growth.

[1] οὐ διατάσσομαι ὑμῖν, ὡς ὤν τι εἰ γὰρ καὶ δέδεμαι ἐν τῷ ὀνόματι, οὔπω ἀπήρτισμαι ἐν Ἰησοῦ Χριστῷ.

[2] διώκω δέ. Paul is fond of διώκω (cf. Rom. 9:30 f.; 12:13; 14:19; 1 Cor. 14:1; 1 Thess. 5:15). A patricide fled into the desert and was pursued by a lion ἐδιῶκαιτο (ἐδιώκετο) ὑπὸ λέωντος. P. Grenf. II, 84? (cf. Moulton & Milligan, " Vocabulary," for other exx.).

[3] Lucian (Hermot., 77) has ὠκύτεροι παραπολὺ διώκοντες οὐ κατέλαβον. Cf. Ex. 15:9. In Rom. 9:30 both verbs occur together. Cf. 1 Cor. 9:24; Eccl. 11:10.

[4] εἰ καὶ καταλάβω, ἐφ᾽ ᾧ καὶ κατελήμφθην ὑπὸ Χριστοῦ Ἰησοῦ. Note the subjunctive here with εἰ (without ἄν), the deliberative subj., a sort of indirect question also, and a sort of correction to εἴ πως above (Kennedy). Cf. Robertson, "Grammar," pp. 934, 1017, 1044.

Christ changed him from persecutor to apostle. His
goal now is to fulfill the ideal that Christ had for him
in doing that (Vincent). " He desires to grasp that
for which he was grasped by Christ " (*ibid.*). He
has come far since that day on the Damascus road
when Jesus stopped his course and turned him right
about. The goal is still ahead, but Paul breathlessly
follows after. The word " grasp "[1] is a strong word
and is the one used of Christ's grasping Paul. He
means to seize and hold.[2] Christ holds Paul fast and
will not let him go. Hence Paul has confidence in
the success of his own pursuit of this goal. Christ
leads him on, ever beckoning as the fleeing goal moves
on ahead, but never so far ahead as to make Paul
lose heart and give up the chase. He is not chasing a
bag of gold at the end of a rainbow or a will-o'-the-
wisp in the bog. He is pressing on as Christ leads
him on and up towards full manhood in Christ Jesus.

Once more Paul pauses to explain that he has not
reached the top of this mountain. " Brethren, I
count not myself yet to have laid hold."[3] Success is

---

[1] καταλάβω. Milligan (" Greek Papyri," p. 5) quotes Ex.
Vol. Hercul. 176⁶ (iii. B. C.) καὶ ἐκεῖ κατειλήφαμεν in sense
of " finding " a friend.

[2] Note perfective use of κατα— The ἐφ' ᾧ either means
τοῦτο ἐφ' ᾧ that with a view to which or ἐπὶ τούτῳ ὅτι for
this reason that either makes good sense without much difference.

[3] ἀδελφοί, ἐγὼ ἐμαυτὸν οὕτω λογίζομαι κατειληφέναι. The
word λογίζομαι (common in Paul's Epistles) counts up calmly
the results of a process of reasoning. Cf. our " reckon."

certain, but still ahead of him. This is the third time
he uses this word "lay hold" and he employs it here
in the perfect tense. He disclaims the state of completion of his holy quest. The chase is not over.
He has no delusions about that. "I do not count
myself" at the end of the course. Later Paul did
feel that way (1 Tim. 4:7 f.) when he faces death.
Not yet has he grasped this flying goal. But does
he stop? Not he. Does he change his interest to
something else? Not Paul. "But one thing."[1]
There is power in concentration. The mark of an
educated man is just this power of concentration.
The one thing worth while for Paul is to win the
ideal set up for him by Christ, to grasp that goal.
He will not be diverted to anything else. He will
not be a quitter. He will not run off on side-issues
like a dog that jumps every trail and holds to none,
starting with a deer and ending the day barking at a
rat hole. He has no time for lesser interests. He
has "the expulsive power of a new affection" that
drives out all else. Paul vividly pictures his tension
in the chase, "forgetting the things which are behind."[2] He is not here thinking of his surrendered
Jewish prerogatives, but of that part of the Christian

---

[1] ἓν δέ. Ellipsis and a common one. Can supply ποιῶ or
any one of a number of verbs. Power in the ellipsis. Cf.
Robertson, "Grammar," p. 391.

[2] τὰ μὲν ὀπίσω ἐπιλανθανόμενος. Both gen. and acc. occur
with this verb. Cf. Robertson, "Grammar," p. 509. Acc.
very common in the κοινή.

course already run (Ellicott). The precise phrase is
used of the pre-Christian life as in Luke 9 : 62; John
6 : 66, but it does not follow that Paul so employs it
here. The point is not that Paul is ashamed of his
past career as a Christian, but simply that he does not
lull himself to ease and relaxation of effort because
of past achievements. These attainments are not to
serve as a spiritual soporific, but as a stimulus to
greater endeavour (cf. 1 Cor. 4 : 11–16; 9 : 19–27;
2 Cor. 11 : 23–12 : 6). Paul runs on " stretching forward to the things which are before." [1] He has no
time to look backward. The rather he reaches out
with a runner's eagerness, leaning forward to grasp
the goal with the forward pressing of his body. It is
the graphic word from the arena. The metaphor
applies naturally to the tension of the runner in the
foot race as he leans forward in his eagerness. " The
eye outstrips and draws onward the hand, and the
hand the foot" (Bengel). In sporting language he is
on " the home-stretch." Lightfoot notes that not
looking is fatal in the chariot race. Kennedy quotes
Jeremiah 7 : 24 of the stubborn disobedience of those
who " went backward and not forward." [2] Lucian [3]
describes " the good runner as only aiming at what
is before and concentrating his attention on the goal."

[1] τοῖς δὲ ἔμπροσθεν ἐπεκτεινόμενος. Note dative case.
Cf. Vulgate extendens meipsum.
[2] ἐγενήθησαν εἰς τὰ ὄπισθεν καὶ οὐκ εἰς τὰ ἔμπροσθεν.
[3] Calumn. 12 κἀκεῖ γὰρ ὁ μὲν ἀγαθὸς δρομεὺς—μόνον τοῦ
πρόσω ἐφιέμενος καὶ τὴν διάνοιαν ἀποτείνας πρὸς τὸ τέρμα.

Once more Paul gathers up his feelings on this great subject in a succinct repetition of the whole discussion: "I press on towards the goal unto the prize of the high calling of God in Christ Jesus." "I press on towards the goal," he says. I rush on bearing down upon the mark set before me, keeping my eye fixed on that and not turning aside to look at anything else. "He who pursues sees nothing but that towards which he is hastening, and passes by all things, the dearest and the most necessary" (Theophylact, *in loco*). He presses on "unto the prize of the high calling of God in Christ Jesus." The prize belongs to the calling. Paul uses the same word for prize[2] in 1 Corinthians 9:24, "know ye not that they that run in a race run all, but one obtaineth the prize? Even so run, that ye may attain." Paul is thinking of the crown of righteousness (2 Tim. 2:10 f.; 4:8), not the garland of leaves for the victor in the games. He calls this "the upward calling."[3] Paul speaks of "the hope

[1] κατὰ σκοπὸν διώκω. Cf. σκοποῦντες in Phil. 2:4 and ἀφορῶντες in Heb. 12:2. Σκοπός was used for the archer's mark (Job 16:13; Lam. 3:12). Cf. κατασκόπους for spies or scouts (Heb. 11:31) and κατασκοπῆσαι for spying out (Gal. 2:4).

[2] τὸ βραβεῖον. The technical word is ἆθλον, but βραβεύω is used of umpire in Col. 2:18; 3:15. But βραβεῖον in sense of " prize " occurs in Vettius Valens 174²¹, 288⁸ and in Priene Inscriptions 118⁸ (II B. C.). Cf. Moulton & Milligan, " Vocabulary."

[3] τῆς ἄνω κλήσεως. Cf. John 11:41; Heb. 12:15.

of the calling" (Eph. 1 : 18; 4 : 4) and in Hebrews
3 : 1 we have "the heavenly calling." It is still the
act [1] of calling. God is calling and beckoning us on
and up towards Himself (cf. Eph. 1 : 18). It is God's
calling in Christ Jesus (Heb. 12 : 1 f.). Chrysostom
(*in loco*) says the specially honoured among the athletes were not crowned "below in the stadium," [2]
" but the king calling them up crowns them there." [3]
That crown is laid up for all who run the race with
patience and love Christ's appearing (2 Tim. 4 : 8).
I have seen the English skylark leap up from the
meadow and have heard him sing his glorious way
upward out of sight into the empyrean.

[1] κλῆσις.   [2] ἐν τῷ σταδίῳ κάτω.
[3] ἀλλ' ἄνω καλέσας ὁ βασιλεὺς ἐκεῖ στεφανοῖ.

IX

FOLLOWING THE ROAD
(3: 15–21)

THE skylark comes down to earth again. Jesus brought Peter, James, and John down from the Mount of Transfiguration to the valley of sorrow and struggle where there was work to do. Even the aeroplane has to come back to earth to replenish its supplies. Paul does not work a figure to death. He still has in mind the question of Christian perfection which he discusses with less passion, but with equal force. His very calmness after the whirl of words adds vigour to the ending. The Holy Quest has its monotonous moments when one is tempted to give it up or is in danger of losing his way. Mysticism is in peril of becoming only a mist or fog.

1. **Getting the Right Point of View** (verse 15).

" Let us therefore, as many as are perfect, be thus minded." [1] This simple sentence fairly bristles with difficulties. It "shows the effect of the strong emotion which pervades the preceding passage" (Vincent). Paul had just categorically and repeatedly

---

[1] Ὅσοι οὖν τέλειοι, τοῦτο φρονῶμεν.

denied the attainment of "perfection" in his own case (verses 12 f.). And yet here he includes himself among the "perfect" in "let us be thus minded." Evidently it is not a matter of courtesy simply, but of sincerity. It does "seem strange" (Rainy, *in loco*). Besides, the very form of the expression "as many as are perfect" implies that some are perfect and some are not. But the explanation is not far to seek and one in harmony with Paul's disclaimer of absolute perfection above. The Greek word for "perfect" is here used in the sense of relative perfection, as is common in the New Testament, contrasting the mature Christians with the babes in Christ who lack the experience and development which others have obtained. By this word "grown men" in Christ are described as in 1 Corinthians 14 : 20 where "children" and "men" are contrasted[1] by the word "perfect" for "men." In Ephesians 4 : 13 we have the phrase "unto a full-grown man"[2] with the same word for "perfect." So in Hebrews 5 : 13 the writer contrasts "babes"[3] in Christ and "full-grown men"[4] who can stand strong meat. Once more in 1 Corinthians 13 : 10 f. Paul uses "the perfect" for absolute perfection and illustrates it by the other sense of relative perfection, the contrast between child and man. The case is made out therefore and the idiom is in accord with Paul's other descriptions of the

---

[1] παιδία—τέλετοι.
[2] εἰς ἄνδρα τέλετον.
[3] νήπιος.
[4] τελείων.

relatively advanced Christians, "the spiritual" (Gal.
6 : 1), "the strong" (Rom. 15 : 1). The absolute use
of perfect is further seen in Matthew 5 : 48; James
1 : 4; 3 : 2. It is the desire of Paul to present every
man "perfect in Christ" (Col. 1 : 28) at last. It is
here the ideal not yet realized in the full sense,
though there is a sense in which it is relatively true
of all those who have been initiated into the mystery
of Christ and have made progress in the knowledge of
Christ. It is not necessary to insist that Paul is
using the word "perfect" in the sense of the "mysteries" (cf. Kennedy, "St. Paul and the Mystery-
Religions"), though it is quite possible that his use
of the term is suggested by that common terminology.
There is at any rate a touch of irony in Paul's em-
ployment of "perfect" in the double sense (absolute
in verse 12, relative in verse 15). Those, like himself,
who claim relative perfection, he exhorts to think[1]
"this." What is "this" or "thus minded"? It is
what he has just been saying in the preceding verses,
viz.: that they have not yet attained to absolute perfection. The "full-grown men" in Christ are the
very ones who are tempted to think that they have
reached the goal of absolute perfection. There were
probably some of them in Philippi who needed this
delicate hint not to be satisfied with their present
attainments in grace and goodness, who need the
lesson of humility that Paul has enforced by the

[1] φρονῶμεν. Hortatory subjunctive. Linear action.

example of Christ and now by Paul's own attitude
of mind. Spiritual pride is very subtle and creeps
into the hearts of the most gifted saints if they are
not on the watch. Paul does not wish his readers to
think that they have already reached the goal because in one sense they belong to the ranks of the
mature. It is almost a pity that we have " perfect "
as the translation in verse 15. Cf. 1 Corinthians
14 : 20 where it is " men."

" And if in anything ye are otherwise minded," [1]
Paul goes on. He assumes that the Philippians will
agree with him in his general statement on the subject of Christian perfection. He adds, however, a
possible detail as exception. If you think otherwise
on any particular point that Paul has not mentioned
and so claim absolute perfection on that, then what ?
Well, then, " this also shall God reveal unto you." [2]
If they have followed Paul thus far, there is hope for
the rest of the way, even if it takes time. Paul trusts
God to " unveil " the particular problem, untie that
knot, unravel that mystery as He has done the rest.
Paul has patience with the merely inept and surely
we need it. Sanity on the subject of Christian perfection is sorely needed when we have one extreme
of antinomian license and the other of professional
perfectionism. A story is told by Spurgeon that one

[1] καὶ εἴ τι ἑτέρως φρονεῖτε.
[2] καὶ τοῦτο ὁ θεὸς ὑμῖν ἀποκαλύψει. It could be rendered
" even this."

Sunday morning a crank stepped into his study with
the remark that the Lord had revealed to him that
he was to preach for Spurgeon that morning.   Quick
as a flash Spurgeon replied that he had just received a
later revelation to show him the door, which he did.

The point of this often misunderstood verse is,
therefore, that we must get and keep the right standpoint.   We must read the sign-board aright and take
the right turn of the road.   We must not lose our
way in a bog of self-satisfaction and smug complacency or of cold indifference.   We must keep up the
struggle.   We may stick a peg here and there as we
go provided we do not stop with the peg.   We must
go on.   That is the main thing.

2.   Keeping On in the Path (verse 16).

Here we have an echo of " one thing I do " in
verse 14.   Paul is not impatient of minor differences
of opinion (verse 15) which are more or less inevitable
in men, provided the Philippians will stick to the main
road and go ahead.   " Only, whereunto we have attained let us keep on in the same path." [1]   The word
for " only " [2] is common in introducing a parenthesis
(Kennedy) or at the end of an argument to single out
the main point.[3]   " Just one thing more."   In opposing
the claim of absolute perfection Paul wishes no mis-

---

[1] πλὴν εἰς ὃ ἐφθάσαμεν, τῷ αὐτῷ στοιχεῖν.
[2] πλήν.   Probably from πλέον more.
[3] Cf. Robertson, " Grammar," p. 1187.

understanding. They must not give up the struggle in despair any more than they must stop because they think that they have already reached the end in view. Either were mockery. Weizsäcker hits it off correctly: "Only one thing. So far as we have come, keep the path." The translation "by the same rule" misses the point. We have come thus far on the way to the goal which is still ahead. What are we to do? There is but one thing to do, just go right on in the same path by which we have come thus far. The word for "walk"[2] means to "walk in file," to "keep the step." This is hard to do. It is climbing a sandy mountain often. We slip back almost as much as we go on and up. The notion of row[3] or alphabet appears in Galatians 4:3, 9. The tramp, tramp of the soldier is fine for a while, but in time one is weary and it is hard not to lag behind. One comes

---

[1] ἐφθάσαμεν is a dramatic aorist for present attainment. Cf. Robertson, "Grammar," pp. 841–843. This verb originally meant to arrive "before" some one else (as in 1 Thess. 4:15), but here it has lost all idea of anticipation and means simply "come" as in 2 Cor. 10:14. Cf. Robertson, "Grammar," p. 551.

[2] στοιχεῖν. For infinitive as imperative see Robertson, "Grammar," pp. 943 f. Cf. χαίρειν in James 1:1 and in the papyri. Kennedy notes that "to work" in English may be originally dative case, then exclamatory imperative, and then infinitive like the Greek absolute infinitive here.

[3] Cf. συνστοιχεῖ in Gal. 4:25. The verb στοιχεῖν occurs in Syll. 325[6] (ii. B. C.) in sense of walking in the steps of one's fathers (Moulton & Milligan, "Lexical Notes from the Papyri," *Expositor*, June, 1911).

to the jog-trot of the Christian life. The dull monotony of religious routine palls on one. But there
is but one thing to do and that is to keep on going[1]
in the same path.[2] This is the way the dog went to
Dover, leg over leg, step by step. " It's dogging as
does it." There is monotony in work, the tedium
of household cares, the grind of church services, the
petty details of pastoral life, the minutiæ of scholarship and all forms of Bible study, the treadmill of
spiritual exercises (prayer, reading the Scriptures,
singing, church attendance, work for Christ), the
humdrum of things like three meals a day and
going to bed every night—these things tend to pall
on the sensitive spirit. But we shall die if we do not
eat, sleep, walk, work, breathe. We shall die without the common details in the spiritual life. The
lesson for our time is precisely this, to keep at it. I
love to hear a boy whistle at his work or play. He
loves then to keep at it. Thus we can put new spirit
into the same old tasks, the same old church, the
same old preacher. Victory lies along the path by
which we have come. We must not merely "think"
right (verse 15). We must also keep up the practice
and keep on in the same path that leads to the goal.
Let us not forget that. Fidgetiness is not spiritual
activity. We are not to be restless spiritual " hobos,"
always on the jump and never getting on. It is the

[1] στοιχεῖν is linear action (pres. inf.).
[2] τῷ αὐτῷ locative case.

steady tread in the right path with the eye fixed on
Christ that tells the story of final achievement.

3. Keeping the Eye On the Guide (verse 17).

Paul had urged that they keep step [1] in the Christian walk.   He carries that idea further in his charge:
"Brethren, be ye imitators together of me." [2]   Lightfoot puts it better thus: " Vie with each other in im-
itating me."   In 1 Corinthians 11 : 1 Paul says: " Be
ye imitators of me, even as I also am of Christ."
That is precisely the point.   " Paul is compelled to
make his own example a norm of the new life "
(Kennedy).   Paul knows wherein he imitates Christ
who is the real standard of orthodoxy and ortho-
praxy (cf. 2 John 9).   But Jesus is no longer visible
in the flesh and people need an objective standard,
a secondary standard.   We copy the copy of the
original in most cases.   The preacher cannot escape
this side of his responsibility if he would.   He must
show the way by his walk as well as by his talk.
Paul made his own living in Thessalonica " to make
ourselves an ensample [3] unto you, that ye should imitate us " (2 Thess. 3 : 9).   He did it for that purpose.
Besides, says Paul, ye " yourselves know how ye
ought to imitate us " (2 Thess. 3 : 7).   Paul begs the
Corinthians to imitate him (1 Cor. 4 : 16).   The
pastor must lead and the people are to follow.   Paul

[1] στοιχεῖν.
[2] συνμιμηταί μου γίνεσθε, ἀδελφοί.   The word μιμητής is
our mimic.   [3] τύπον.

wishes not merely sporadic following, but "a whole company" of imitators (Ellicott).   There is no self-conceit in Paul's demand that they all follow him. It is like the Captain who says: "Follow me." Imitation plays a large part in all life.   Most that the child learns at home is unconscious imitation. The preacher is an object lesson to the church.   Like priest like people.   Children copy the preacher and the church members copy his shortcomings and often criticize his virtues.

"And mark them that so walk." [2]   Paul is not the only one who follows Christ.   There were many in Philippi who did so.   Keep your eye on those who keep to the same path by which you have come. The word here for "mark" [3] is sometimes used for watching and avoiding as in Romans 16: 17: "Mark them that are causing the divisions and occasions of stumbling, contrary to the doctrine which ye learned; and turn away from them."   But it may also be used for keeping the eye on good things as in 2 Corinthians 4: 18 where it is employed for the spiritual vision of the unseen as the guide of life.   It is dangerous to take the eye off of the guide in perilous mountain climbing or in tangled jungles.   Once lost, one is helpless.   Keep your eye on the goal if you can see

---

[1] συνμιμηταί.   *Co-imitores.*   Paul is fond of the preposition συν—in composition.   Cf. συνπολῖται in Eph. 2 : 19.   Plato (*Polit.*, p. 274D) has συμμιμεῖσθαι.

[2] καὶ σκοπεῖτε τοὺς οὕτως περιπατοῦντας.   Cf. σκοπός goal.   [3] σκοπεῖτε.   Cf. " Mark Twain."

it. If not, keep your eye on one who knows the way to the goal and who is going there. This is the only way to walk straight. Signs are useless if erased or doubtful. Many an accident is due to misreading of the signals by the engineer. It is still worse to follow false signs. Lights are used by wreckers to lure vessels on the breakers, false lights that point the way to death.

"Even as ye have us for an ensample."[1] Paul changes from "me" to "us" on purpose. Timothy and Epaphroditus were two certainly that we can name who besides Paul were ensamples to the Philippians. The word for "ensample"[2] was originally the impression left by a blow, the mark of the blow as in John 20 : 25 "the print of the nails." Then it was used of the thing that caused the mark as a type or mould or pattern (cf. our use of type in printing). Paul is fond of this word (cf. Rom. 5 : 14; 6 : 17; 1 Cor. 10 : 6, 11 ; 1 Thess. 1 : 7). There is the mould of doctrine (Rom. 6 : 17) and the mould of life as here. It is sad when a church is afraid to follow the preacher, still sadder when the church ought to refuse to follow his bad example, when he does not follow Christ. Blind guide he is then and those that follow him will fall with him into the pit.

4. **Missing the Path** (verses 18 f.).
"For many walk" evilly,[3] Paul means, though he

[1] καθὼς ἔχετε τύπον ἡμᾶς.   [2] τύπον.   From τύπτω strike.
[3] πολλοὶ γὰρ περιπατοῦσιν.   Vg. *ambulant.*

does not use the word. One is reminded of Psalm I. Perhaps Paul is even thinking of walking hypocritically, for he is hardly referring to the heathen. He either has in mind the Judaizers, the " dogs " of verse 2, or lackadaisical Christians, nominal church members, who bring reproach on Christ by their conduct, antinomian libertines, incipient Gnostics, immoral men with Epicurean philosophy. Something can be said for both of these views, though probably the latter suits the context more exactly. Action and reaction follow each other. The lax age of Charles the Second followed the age of the Puritans under Cromwell. Perhaps both extremes were represented in the church of Philippi. At any rate they had been warned by Paul of one of these classes, " of whom I told you often." [1] Paul had done his duty to them either when with them or in letters which we do not now possess (cf. 3 : 1). " And now tell you even weeping." [2] Once more Paul repeats his warning and it brings tears to his eyes to have to use such plain language about professed followers of Christ. Paul was a man of great heart and his emotional nature is often profoundly stirred. It was so once when he had to write with severity to the Corinthians (2 Cor. 2 : 4). He admonished the Ephesians with tears many times (Acts 20 : 31). It is a serious situation in Philippi and it stirs Paul's heart to the bottom. He is cut to the quick over the disgrace in

[1] οὓς πολλάκις ἔλεγον ὑμῖν.   [2] νῦν δὲ καὶ κλαίων λέγω.

this noble church to the name of Christ.   It is enough to break a preacher's heart to see so many Christians recreant and disloyal.   They are " the enemies of the cross of Christ." [1]   Both the Judaizers (Gal. 5 : 11 ; 6 : 12 f.) and the antinomian Gnostics (Col. 3 : 5 f. ; cf. 2 Cor. 1 : 5 f.) were hostile to the cross of Christ as were the Jews and Greeks generally (1 Cor. 1 : 17 f.).   But these persons took it as a personal affront and made themselves personal enemies of the cross of Christ which reflected on their lives of self-indulgence.   Polycarp (Phil. 7) speaks of " whoever does not confess the witness of the cross."   Rainy (Phil., p. 286) speaks of hangers-on who love " the suburban life of Zion," but who wish none of the limitations and responsibilities of the yoke of service.

But Paul is pitiless in his picture of these men " whose end is destruction." [2] End with them is both consummation and culmination.   It is more than mere termination (cf. Rom. 6 : 21 ; 2 Cor. 11 : 15).   The word for destruction does not necessarily mean annihilation.   It is rather a state of moral ruin.   It is used of the lost though physically alive (cf. Luke 19 : 10).   " Whose god is the belly," [3]

[1] τοὺς ἐχθροὺς τοῦ σταυροῦ τοῦ χριστοῦ.   The accusative here is in apposition to the relative οὕς (cf. 1 John 2 : 25) unless λέγω be taken as " call " (Kennedy) when it is predicate accus.   Cf. Robertson, " Grammar," pp. 416, 480.

[2] ὧν τὸ τέλος ἀπώλεια.   Paul gives σωτηρία as the end of the redeemed and ἀπώλεια of the lost (1 Cor. 1 : 18 ; 2 Cor. 2 : 15 f.).

[3] ὧν ὁ θεὸς ἡ κοιλία.   Vg. *quorum Deus Venter est.*

Paul adds.   In Romans 16 : 18 we have : " For they
that are such serve not our Lord Christ, but
their own belly." [1]   The comic poet Eupolis describes one as " a devotee of the belly," [2] who
makes a god of his belly.   The glutton or gour-
mand is on the road to this low estate.   Cicero tells
it on himself that once at a feast he took an emetic
that he might enjoy more of the dinner.   Perhaps
more people make a god of their stomachs than will
admit it.   We have a proverb to the effect that we
dig our graves with our teeth.   Paul says : " The
Kingdom of God is not eating and drinking " (Rom.
14 : 17), a truism about sticklers for certain kinds of
food, but equally true in this context.   The word for
belly is used for all sorts of sensual indulgence and
applies to drink and immorality also (wine and
women).   Once more Paul says, " whose glory is in
their shame." [3]   These moral perverts turn liberty
into license.   They throw moral pride to the winds
and became unmoral degenerates.   They revel in
the mire and mud like the hog, and rejoice in their
debasement.   The life of the underworld is a terrible
reality in all our large cities to-day, but Paul pictures
some persons in the church at Philippi as in the
grip of the same form of vice, which has mastered

[1] Seneca has : *Alius abdomini servit.*

[2] κοιλιοδαίμων.   In his Κόλακες Xenophon (Mem. 1 : 6,
8, etc.) has δουλεύειν γαστρί.   Cf. 2 Pet. 2 : 13.

[3] καὶ ἡ δόξα ἐν τῇ αἰσχύνῃ αὐτῶν.   Cf. Prov. 26 : 11 ;
Sirach 4 : 21.   It was apparently a current proverb.

them and bound them hand and foot, slaves of
sin. The last word that Paul has about these spiritual perverts is " who mind earthly things." [1] These
are just the opposite of Paul in his passion for the
upward calling (verse 14). They hear no call to fly
like the eagle in the cage, but, like Bunyan's man
with the muckrake, grovel in the dirt and glory in
the drivel and dust of earth. They have their minds
set on things of time and sense and on the lowest
plane of things here below. What do modern people care most about? Face the facts. Statistics
tell some things rightly. On any Sunday in our
modern cities the moving picture-shows will be
crowded when the churches are thinly attended. On
a pretty Sunday in the summer the baseball park
will be full. The horse races where still allowed have
no lack of crowds. People complain of hard times,
but have plenty of money for dress and for food and
for travel. The public talk is much more about these
things than about the Kingdom of God and righteousness upon earth. But there are " forward-looking
men," to use President Woodrow Wilson's striking
phrase, who do look up instead of down, onward instead of backward, inward instead of merely outward.

---

[1] οἱ τὰ ἐπίγεια φρονοῦντες. The use of the nominative
here after οὓς and ὧν is not unknown. In fact such an independent nominative in apposition is a rather common anaco-
luthon. Cf. οἱ κατέσθοντες in Mark 12 : 40. So also Mark
7 : 19; Acts 10 : 37; Rev. 1 : 5; 7 : 4; 20 : 2. Cf.
Robertson, " Grammar," pp. 414 f.

5. A Colony of Heaven (verse 20ᵃ).

" For our citizenship is in heaven." [1] This Paul
says in contrast with those who " mind earthly
things " (verse 19). The emphatic word is " our " in
opposition to the mundane and grovelling spirit of
the recreant Christians who make a god of the belly.
In 1 : 27 Paul had urged the duty of worthy conduct
as citizens. [2] The Vulgate here has *conversatio*
(A. V. conversation) which properly rendered one
aspect of the Greek word [3] as manner of life. Our
modern use of conversation for talk is simply one
phase (possibly the main one in some cases) of conduct. But it probably here means the commonwealth or state as in 2 Macc. 12 : 7 ; Philo, *de Jos.* ii.
p. 51 M and in the inscriptions. The Jews therefore
had adopted this word from the Greeks a good while
before Paul wrote (Kennedy). [4] Jesus told Pilate that
His kingdom was not of this world (John 18 : 36). The
heavenly Jerusalem (or that which is above) appears
in Galatians 4 : 26 and Mt. Zion is contrasted with
Mt. Sinai in Hebrews 12 : 20 ff. The New Jerusalem
is heaven in Revelation 21. The point with Paul
here is that we are now citizens of heaven even while

---

[1] ἡμῶν γὰρ τὸ πολίτευμα ἐν οὐρανοῖς ὑπάρχει. The Vulgate has *autem*, but *enim* is more exact for γὰρ.

[2] ἀξίως πολιτεύεσθε.

[3] πολίτευμα. Used practically in same sense as πολιτεία by
Aristotle. Cf. πολιτεία in Acts 22 : 28.

[4] Cf. Hicks, " Political Terms in the New Testament "
(*Classical Review*, i., 1, pp. 6–7).

living on earth. We are fellow-citizens[1] with the
saints and the household of God (Eph. 2 : 19). Our
life is hid with Christ in God (Col. 3 : 3). We like
the patriarchs look for a city which hath founda-
tions whose builder and maker is God (Heb. 11 : 10),
a better country, that is an heavenly (11 : 16), being
" strangers and pilgrims on the earth " (11 : 13). In
other words, our real citizenship is in the commonwealth of heaven, the Kingdom of God. We are a
colony of heaven here on earth (Moffatt), a pattern
of the heavenly for earthly citizens. Philippi was
itself a colony of Rome and would understand perfectly[2] this local touch in Paul's figure. Paul himself was proud of his Roman citizenship and had
found it an advantage in Philippi (Acts 16 : 37–39)
and in Jerusalem (Acts 21 and 22). Paul is not
speaking of an impossible Utopia or a vague ideal
like Plato's Republic or even as impractical a thing
as Augustine's City of God. Paul means that Christians must live now on earth as citizens of the
heavenly commonwealth, not merely that we shall be
heavenly citizens after death. The Christian commonwealth is a present reality in the world.[3] It
partly fulfills the prayer which Jesus taught the dis-

---

[1] συνπολῖται.

[2] They knew what the *jus Italicum* meant. Cf. Mar-
quardt, " Römische Staatsverwaltung," Bd. I, pp. 363 ff.

[3] In the Epistle to Diognetus we read of Christians this :
ἐπὶ γῆς διατρίβουσιν ἀλλ᾽ ἐν οὐρανῷ πολιτεύονται. Cf. Plato
" Republic," 592.

ciples to pray : " Thy Kingdom come. Thy will be
done, as in heaven, so on earth " (Matt. 6 : 10).   The
full consummation is to come at the end, but Christianity is the most powerful factor in the life that now
is.   We are in the world, but not of its spirit.   We
live under the principles, ideals, and laws of heaven.
We must apply them to the life in this world.   In a
word we are a patch of heaven on earth to help make
earth like heaven.   The roar of the guns in the
World's Great War only accentuates the words of
Paul.   We must drive war out of this world and
make men turn their swords into ploughshares.   The
war on war is long, but the Kingdom of God is
coming, always coming in power, and is here in the
hearts of those who feel themselves more citizens of
heaven than of earth.   The true patriotism is the
hunger for and loyalty to the real Fatherland, for
heaven is our home.

6.   Looking for the King (verse 20[b]).

Meanwhile we all know that earth is not yet
heaven.   There are colonies of heaven scattered here
and there over the world.   These are the joy and
hope of men.   The attitude of these colonies of
heaven is one of expectation.   At best earth still has
its sorrows.   Our eyes turn heavenward " whence
also we wait for a Saviour, the Lord Jesus Christ." [1]

---

[1] ἐξ οὗ καὶ σωτῆρα ἀπεκδεχόμεθα, Κύριον Ἰησοῦν Χριστόν.
Here ἐξ οὗ is probably adverbial and refers to οὐρανοῖς.

The Lord Jesus Christ (note all three words) is the King in the heavenly commonwealth or kingdom. He is coming back to complete His glorious work. Meanwhile we wait for Him " as Saviour." [1] He is needed as Saviour and He will come. He will complete the work of salvation and rescue men from sufferings and infirmities of the flesh (Rom. 8 : 19 ff.; 2 Cor. 5 : 4). The inscriptions often speak of the Roman Emperor as God and Saviour in fulsome flattery. But Paul's word " wait for " or " tarry for " [2] reveals the note of eager expectancy as if a wife steps out of the door in the evening and looks away down the lane for the husband who is late in coming. The King is coming. The tiptoe of anticipation is like that of the crowds at Delhi during the Durbar who waited for the appearance of their king from England. Christians have Christ's own promise that He will come back. As a colony of heaven they have a right to look for Him. This blessed hope exerted a powerful influence for holy living and Christian activity among the early Christians. Some of them misunderstood the promise as definitely made for their own time. The centuries have dimmed for many the brightness of this star of hope, but without

---

[1] Predicate accusative. Cf. Robertson, " Grammar," p. 480. The word σωτήρ is common in 2 Peter and the Pastoral Epistles for God.

[2] ἀπεκδεχόμεθα (common with Paul as in Gal. 5 : 5; 1 Thess. 1 : 10; Rom. 8 : 19, 23, 25. Cf. Heb. 9 : 28; 1 Pet. 3 : 20). Cf. ἀποκαραδοκία in Phil. 1 : 20.

reason, for a day with the Lord is as a thousand years and a thousand years as one day (2 Pet. 3 : 8). The promise of the first coming of the Messiah seemed long in realization, but Christ did come in the fullness of time. Christ's own word is that we be ready: "Watch" (Matt. 25 : 13). This is the attitude of which Paul speaks. We are still watching and waiting for the King.

7. The Body of Glory (verse 21).

The King will come and will finish His work. He "will fashion anew the body of our humiliation, that it may be conformed to the body of his glory."[1] Christ will "change the fashion" (cf. Rom. 12 : 2; 1 Cor. 4 : 6; 2 Cor. 11 : 13–15) of our body from corruption to incorruption (1 Cor. 15 : 44, 51). We shall be clothed upon (2 Cor. 5 : 4) with a spiritual body connected with this body which belongs to our state of humiliation (not "vile body") as seed-corn with harvest and yet not this same body of flesh and blood which cannot enter the Kingdom of God (1 Cor. 15 : 50). It is all a mystery, but modern science by no means discredits the kind of a resurrection of the body which Paul pictures here and in 1 Corinthians 15. Paul does not consider the body in which our spirit dwells as itself evil and only vile as the Gnostics held. On the contrary Paul urged

[1] ὃς μετασχηματίσει τὸ σῶμα τῆς ταπεινώσεως ἡμῶν σύμμορφον τῷ σώματι τῆς δόξης αὐτοῦ. Vg. has *corpus humilitatis.*

the dignity of the body as the abode of the redeemed
soul (1 Cor. 6: 12–20) and the temple of God (1 Cor.
3: 16).   Hence Paul urged that we must glorify God
in the body (1 Cor. 6: 20).   But though our bodies
are subject to infirmity, weakness, disease and death,
yet they have a glorious destiny as well as a high
honour now.   This body of our humiliation is to be
" conformed "[1] to the body of Christ's glory.   Our
renewed (refashioned) body will be like in essential
form that of Jesus.   We shall be made fit for the
family of God in heaven (cf. Rom. 8: 29 f.).   We
shall have on the wedding garment of glory.   We
shall have a spiritual body suitable for the new
environment in heaven.   Peter, James, and John saw
the glory of Jesus on the majestic mount of transfiguration.   The process of transformation of our
spirits has already begun here and we are transformed
from glory to glory (2 Cor. 3: 18).   This word
" glory " was used for the Shekinah.   Jesus is the
Glory (Jas. 2: 1) and we shall be like Him for we
shall see Him as He is (1 John 3: 2).   If one hesi-
tates at the stupendous claim that Paul makes
about the body he must recall the power at Christ's
disposal, " according to the working whereby he is
able even to subject all things into himself,"[2] accord-

---

[1] Predicate accusative.   Cf. Robertson, " Grammar," p.
480.   Cf. σύμμορφον here and μετασχηματίσει.

[2] κατὰ τὴν ἐνέργειαν τοῦ δύνασθαι αὐτὸν καὶ ὑποτάξαι αὐτῷ
τὰ πάντα.

ing to " the energy of his power." He not merely possesses inherent (latent) power, but He exercises this dynamic energy (Col. 1 : 29; 7 : 12; 2 Thess. 2 : 9) as Creator and Preserver of the Universe (Col. 1 : 16 f.). The glorious destiny of all things is to come fully under the sway of Christ's will. The Crowning Day is coming when God will sum up all things in Christ.

" The power or virtue which was in Christ when the woman touched the hem of his garment (Mark 5 : 30 ; Luke 8 : 46) was δύναμις. In the healing of the woman it became ἐνέργεια " (Vincent). In the New Testament ἐνέργεια is limited to superhuman activity (cf. Robinson, Eph., p. 242). Cf. περὶ τῆς ἐνεργείας θεοῦ Διός (OGIS 2624 iii. A. D.), Moulton & Milligan, " Lexical Notes from the Papyri," Expositor, March, 1909.

X

THE GARRISON OF PEACE
(4 : 1–9)

PEACE is one of the greatest of blessings. The peace that Christ gives is better than any "King's Peace" of the feudal times: "Peace I leave with you; my peace I give unto you: not as the world giveth, give I unto you" (John 14:27). This peace of Christ cannot be taken from us by our environment or by earthly circumstance. And yet peace in itself is not the first blessing. "But the wisdom that is from above is first pure, then peaceable" (Jas. 3:17). Righteousness, not peace, exalteth a nation. It is sometimes necessary to fight in order to have peace, a peace that rests on the triumph of right over wrong. The devil offered Jesus the copartnership of the world as a compromise on condition that Jesus recognize the devil's sovereignty and power. But Jesus chose war, eternal war, the path to the Cross. Thus He won the right and the power to bring peace to the sinner. Paul exhorted us all to live peaceably with all men, if possible, as far as it depends on us (Rom. 12:18). But we are not to be silent on great moral issues for the sake of a complacent peace with the powers of evil. Christ does not require us to

225

make peace at any price.   The rather He challenges
to victorious conquest of the forces of evil.   But we
are to fight even evil in the spirit of Christ and with
the weapons of righteousness and truth.   A dead
church can find no consolation in the peace of God.

1. Standing Fast (verse 1).

Paul applies his message about the heavenly citizenship (3:17–21) to the situation in Philippi.
" Wherefore,"[1] he pleads, because you are citizens of
heaven, have courage here on earth. " So stand fast
in the Lord."[2] " So " stand as becomes citizens of
heaven and as Paul has exhorted them.   Paul has
used the figures of running, of pursuing,[3] of walking,[4]
and now he adds that of standing.   It is often very
hard to stand still.   Attack is said to be much easier
than defense.   It is difficult to stand still and be shot
at.   In Ephesians 6 : 11, 13, 14 Paul repeats the command to "stand" as soldiers of Christ.   When others run away, it is hard to stand one's ground.   It is
not easy to stand against the flood-tide.   Paul makes
a tender plea for stability.   " My brethren beloved

---

[1] ὥστε. Common as inferential particle at beginning of
sentence with no effect on structure of the sentence. Cf.
Robertson, " Grammar," pp. 999 f.
[2] οὕτως στήκετε ἐν κυρίῳ. Paul uses ἐν κυρίῳ more than
forty times and it occurs nowhere else in the New Testament,
save in Rev. 14 : 13. The form στήκετε belongs to the col-
loquial κοινή, a present made on a perfect stem. Cf. Phil.
1 : 27.   [3] διώκω.   [4] στοιχέω.

and longed for." [1]   Here we see " a hint of the pain
caused by his separation from them" (Vincent).
" My joy and crown." [2]   They are now his joy and
they will be his crown of victory in the day of Christ,
showing that he did not labour in vain (Phil. 2 : 16).
The word here used for crown is that for the chaplet
of victory in the games, not the diadem[3] worn by
kings.   Paul spoke of the Thessalonians as his hope,
joy, crown (1 Thess. 2 : 19).   He repeats his affection-
ate appeal after the exhortation to steadfastness by
saying once more, " Beloved."   He is not ashamed
to show his love for the saints.   He is very much in
earnest that the Philippians shall be loyal to Christ in
this time of trial.   His words are enough to melt a
heart of stone and must have had a powerful effect on
the church.

2. Helping These Women (verses 2 f.).

" I exhort Euodia, and I exhort Syntyche, to be of
the same mind in the Lord."   Paul makes specific [4]
the general exhortation in 2 : 2.   Clearly these two
women were prominent in the church in Philippi and
may have been deaconesses like Phœbe of Cenchreæ

---

[1] ἀδελφοί μου ἀγαπητοὶ καὶ ἐπιπόθητοι.   Vulgate has
fratres mei carissimi, et desideratissimi.   The Latin super-
latives bring out the passion in the Greek adjectives.

[2] χαρὰ καὶ στέφανός μου.   Vg. has *gaudium meum et corona
mea.*

[3] διάδημα (Rev. 12 : 3).   The verb στεφανόω is used in
the κοινή for obtaining reward (Deissmann, " Bible Studies,"
p. 261).   [4] τὸ αὐτὸ φρονεῖν.

(Rom. 16 : 1).   They have beautiful names.   Euodia[1]
means " Prosperous Journey " (or " Sweet Fragrance "
if another text is followed) and Syntyche " Good
Luck."   He mentions the names with safety in public because he is in Rome and because the matter
was probably now a topic of public talk though not
advanced to open breach.   Klöpper thinks that sep-
arate factions of the church were meeting in the
homes of these two women as the church originally
met in the home of Lydia (Acts 16 : 40).   Women
were prominent in the foundation of the church in
Philippi (Acts 16 : 13 f.) and had special honour in this
Roman colony (cf. Lightfoot, *in loco*) as in Rome itself (Rom. 16).[2]   The activity of other Macedonian
women in Paul's work is seen in Acts 17 : 4, 12.
We do not know what the trouble was between these
women.   It may have been on the subject of perfection (cf. 3 : 13–16).   It may have been the very
question of woman's rights or it may have been a
matter of personal taste.   The cause may have been
trivial enough, for slight bickerings are easily magnified into great issues by the hypersensitive.   " It may
have been accidental friction between two energetic
Christian women " (Kennedy).   A slight breeze
would cause trouble in so noble a church.   I know

[1] Εὐοδία.   Some MSS. read Εὐωδίαν (cf. ὀσμὴν εὐωδίας in
4 : 18).   Both of these names occur in the inscriptions.
[2] Cf. Ferrero, " The Women of the Cæsars " and his " Char-
acters and Events of Roman History."

of a lovely woman who took umbrage because a dear friend refused to speak on meeting her in the street. But the guilty woman was near-sighted and did not see her friend! Paul is perfectly impartial in his exhortation and repeats the verb[1] with each name. Perhaps each was to blame in part. They can come together in the Lord at any rate. They expect to be one in Christ in heaven. They had best be so here and now.

But these good women need help and Paul intercedes with some one to do this delicate piece of work. The work of peacemaker has a high reward (Matt. 5 : 9) and is like the work of God in Christ (Eph. 2 : 14). "Yea, I beseech thee also, true yoke-fellow."[2] Paul introduces "a third party" (Vincent). Who is this third party? The suggestions are numerous. Epaphroditus, the bearer of the letter, is considered most probable by Lightfoot. Ellicott thinks it is the chief bishop of Philippi. Clement of Alexandria thinks it is Paul's own wife[3] who is addressed as "true yoke-fellow." Others have guessed Luke, Silas, Timothy, and even Christ. It is most likely that

[1] παρακαλῶ. It means to call to one's side. The Vulgate has *Evodiam rogo, et Syntychen deprecor*, a needless distinction in the verbs.

[2] ναὶ ἐρωτῶ καὶ σέ, γνήσιε σύνζυγε. For ναὶ see Matt. 15 : 27; Rom. 3 : 29. Ἐρωτῶ like *rogo* is used of equals and αἰτῶ like *peto* towards a superior. The Vulgate has *germane compar*.

[3] But γνήσιε is masculine.

Syzygus is a proper name and that " true " is a reference to the meaning of " yoke-fellow." Live up to
your name, a joiner together. The name does not
occur in known inscriptions, but Zygos is found as a
Jewish name. At any rate " help these women."[2]
" Take hold together with them." The implication
clearly is that Euodia and Syntyche wanted to lay
aside their differences, but found it somewhat embarrassing to make a start. Take hold of the problem
and help them to solve it. Speak the first word
towards peace. Be a peacemaker, not a peace-
breaker. Much of the best work that we do is in
helping others to agree. It is always a noble thing
to help the women, " for they laboured with me in
the gospel."[3] These women were spiritual athletes,[4]
better than the Amazons of story, along with Paul.
The ministry of women is a prominent feature of early
Christian work as is plain in the Gospels, Acts, and
Epistles. It is not made clear precisely what these
women did, but their activity is unquestionable. Indeed, to-day too many men are willing for the women
to do it all. They say " Ladies first " at the wrong

[1] γνήσιε genuine, true to the name σύνζυγε. For a similar
play on the name see Philemon 11 and 12 ('Ονήσιμον,
εὔχρηστον, ἄχρηστον). See P. Epph. 63 B. C. 311–310 for
γυναῖκα γνησίαν for " legal wife," " genuine wife."

[2] συνλαμβάνου αὐταῖς. Literally, " help them." Note
middle voice.

[3] αἵτινες ἐν τῷ εὐαγγελίῳ συνήθλησάν μοι. Causal use of
αἵτινες. Cf. Robertson, " Grammar," p. 960. Cf. Phil.
3 : 7.   [4] συνήθλησαν. Cf. 1 : 27.

time.   Here Clement and "the rest of my fellow-
workers"[1] come after the women.   We do not know
who these fellow-workers were, "whose names are in
the book of life."[2]   Possibly these workers are dead
when Paul writes.   Paul is always grateful for his
co-labourers.

3.   Gladness (verse 4).

Here we have again the key-note of the Epistle.
Over and over Paul strikes this note of joy.   Recently
I read an article on " The Joyous Life " in a physical
culture magazine.   The writer was pleading for a more
outspoken manifestation of good-will and hilarity, a
rather coarse and boisterous view of happiness.   Paul
knew the joyous life, the mood of cheerfulness, the
serenity and calmness of spirit possible only to the
soul stayed on God.   So he strikes this refrain :
" Rejoice in the Lord always."[3]   There is no other
ground of perpetual optimism that is not blind indifference.   Only " in the Lord " is it possible to get
a view of life as a whole that will stand the shock of
sorrow and sin.   Paul knows that he has said " always " and that this word covers the darker side of
human life.   So he says it over again, after pausing
in contemplation of sorrow, "Again I will say,
Rejoice."[4]   This philosophy of life is no ephemeral
emotion, but a settled principle, a deeper feeling that

---

[1] τῶν λοιπῶν συνεργῶν μου.   Cf. 2 : 25.

[2] ὧν τὰ ὀνόματα ἐν βίβλῳ ζωῆς.   This is an Old Testament
figure.   Cf. Ex. 32 : 32 ; Isa. 4 : 3 ; Ezek. 13 : 9.

[3] χαίρετε, ἐν κυρίῳ πάντοτε.   [4] πάλιν ερῶ, χαίρετε.

underlies all the storm-tossed waves on the surface.
Paul's joy is not grounded in earthly conditions, but
in Christ.   No one can rob Paul of Christ or of his
joy in Christ.   Christ satisfies Paul's soul.   Christ is
his all and in all.   He needs naught else to make his
soul sing aloud for sheer joy, to sing aloud and to
sing long.   Men differ in their opinion as to the
sweetest song-bird.   Some say the nightingale, some
the mocking-bird, some the English skylark, some
the Kentucky cardinal, some the wood-robin.   Each
bird has his individual note, but each has the note
of joy.   Christians have not risen to their privileges
in the matter of conquering joy.   It is resistless as a
witness for Christ and as an antidote for grief.

4. Gentleness (verse 5).

Joy and graciousness go together. " Let your forbearance (gentleness, margin of R. V.) be known unto
all men." [1]   The word for forbearance and gentleness
is translated in various ways as moderation (A. V.) [2]

---

[1] τὸ ἐπιεικὲς ὑμῶν γνωσθήτω πᾶσιν ἀνθρώποις. The neuter
adjective with article τὸ ἐπιεικὲς is used as abstract quality like
ἐπιείκεια. Cf. τὸ χρηστὸν (Rom. 2 : 4) and τὸ μωρὸν (1 Cor.
1 : 25).   See Robertson, " Grammar," p. 654.

[2] Cf. Modestia of the Vulgate.   Aristotle (Nich. Eth. V.
10) contrasts the word with ἀκριβοδίκαιος judging severely.
In 1 Pet. 2 : 18 and Jas. 3 : 17 it is connected with ἀγαθός
and εὐπειθής, in 1 Tim. 3 : 3 and Tit. 3 : 2 with ἄμαχος,
in 2 Cor. 10 : 1 with πραΰτης. The word is from εἰκός reasonable, fitting, likely, equitable, fair, mild, gentle.   The
stem of ἔοικα is εἴκω the same as εἴκω to yield, concede,
though they are not associated by the lexicons.   The fundamental ideas are similar.

reasonabieness (Kennedy), " sweet reasonableness "
(Matthew Arnold, " Literature and Dogma," pp.
66, 138).   Courtesy is not far from the true idea.   It
is graciousness with strength and poise of character.
It is the opposite of obstinacy.   The word is not
negative restraint simply, but positive giving up to
the reasonable desires of others.   It is the mildness
of disposition that leads one to be fair and to go beyond the letter of the law.   The best type of the
ancients prided themselves on this trait of moderation.   Christianity carried it much further and gave
a touch that was not there before, the grace of giving
up to the weaker.   Kennedy pertinently quotes from
Pater's " Marius the Epicurean," (ii., p. 120): " As
if by way of a due recognition of some immeasurable
Divine condescension manifest in a certain historic
fact, its influence was felt more especially at those
points which demanded some sacrifice of one's self,
for the weak, for the aged, for little children, and
even for the dead. And then, for its constant
outward token, its significant manner or index, it
issued in a certain debonair grace, and a certain
mystic attractiveness or courtesy, which made Marius
doubt whether that famed Greek blitheness or gaiety
or grace in the handling of life had been, after all, an
unrivalled success."   In a word, what Paul here urges
is the grace of giving up, not because one has to
surrender to superior force, but because of the nobler

[1] Like ἀνοχή (from ἀνέχω, hold back).

impulses of generosity and gentleness.   Ignatius [1] has
it when he pleads : " Let us be found their brothers
by our forbearance."   It includes the chivalry of the
true man towards a woman, his own sister or mother
or wife, or any one's sister or mother or wife.   A
gentleman is a gentle man.   " Thy gentleness hath
made me great " (2 Sam. 22 : 36), said David of God's
dealings with him.   The great illustration is the example of Jesus.   " Now I Paul myself entreat you by
the meekness and gentleness [2] of Christ, I who in
your presence am lowly among you, but being absent
am of good courage towards you " (2 Cor. 10 : 1).
The gentleness of Jesus appeals to us to be gentle
also, not only to Christians, but to all so far as we can.

   " The Lord is at hand," [3] Paul adds.   The phrase
can mean that " The Lord is near " in space as in
Psalm 145 : 18.   " The Lord is nigh unto all that
call upon him." [4]   But it is more likely that (cf. Rom.
13 : 12 ; Jas. 5 : 8) Paul here means Christ by Lord as
he usually does and is referring to the expected
return of the Lord Jesus.   Indeed, this expression
was a sort of watchword with Paul (Lightfoot), a
password for the elect.   Cf. the Aramaic " Marana
tha " [5] or " O Lord, come " (1 Cor. 16 : 22).   The

---

[1] *Eph.* X ἀδελφοὶ αὐτῶν εὑρεθῶμεν τῇ ἐπιεικείᾳ.

[2] διὰ τῆς πραύτητος καὶ ἐπιεικείας τοῦ Χριστοῦ.

[3] ὁ Κύριος ἐγγύς.

[4] ἐγγὺς Κύριος πᾶσι τοῖς ἐπικαλουμένοις αὐτόν.

[5] Μαρανὰ θά or Μαρὰν ἀθά " The Lord will come " or
" The Lord is here."

manner of Christ is a reason for repose of spirit (see next verses) and for gentleness towards others. The clause here is taken by some with verse 5, by some with verse 6, by some with both. It is true of the continued presence of Jesus with us by the Holy Spirit (Matt. 28 : 20) as well as of the blessed hope of His second coming. " Lo, I am with you all the days, even unto the consummation of the age." Jesus is coming again, but Jesus is also here and near us all the varied days. of our checkered human life, here to cheer us and to beckon. us on to follow in His steps.

5. **The Heart at Rest** (verses 6 f.).

Paul has risen to the pure empyrean of spiritual repose above carking cares. He soars like the eagle above the storms below. " In nothing be anxious."[1] It is a common word in the Gospels for harassing care that Paul here uses (cf. Matt. 6 : 25). It suggests brooding and pondering into which our human nature so easily falls (1 Pet. 5 : 7). It is the anxious solicitude[2] that one finds hard to avoid in time of real trouble as well as " the little foxes that eat away the vine." Christ is the only cure for anxiety of heart. He can calm the fluttering heart that palpitates with worry and dread (cf. John 14: 1, " Let not your heart be troubled "). Christ's panacea for heart

[1] μηδὲν μεριμνᾶτε. Cf. Homeric μερμηρίζειν to debate anxiously.

[2] Vulgate has *nihil solliciti sitis*.

trouble is trust in Him as in God. Paul suggests prayer to God. At bottom the solution is the same. " Let your requests be made known unto God." [1] Come into the presence of God and open your heart to Him just as if God did not know all about it. The mother loves to have the sobbing child tell all the trouble to her. She understands and the child is sure of sympathy and help. The difficulties will be smoothed out in mother's arms. God loves to hear the tale of our woes " by prayer and supplication." [3] It should be in the spirit of gratitude. " Thanksgiving is the background, the predominant tone of the Christian life " (Kennedy). We are to pray " with thanksgiving." [4] This is an essential element, for dissatisfaction with God will " clip the wings of prayer " (Kennedy). " Remembrance and supplication are the two necessary elements of every Christian prayer " (Rilliet). " Thankfulness for past blessings is a necessary condition of acceptance in preferring new petitions " (Lightfoot). We are to make known our requests to God " in everything." [5] We are not to pick our ground too sharply, but to have wholehearted abandonment to the will of God in every

---

[1] τὰ αἰτήματα ὑμῶν γνωριζέσθω πρὸς τὸν θεόν. Vulgate has *petitiones*.

[2] πρὸς face to face with.

[3] τῇ προσευχῇ καὶ τῇ δεήσει. The general term for prayer and the particular word for petition.

[4] μετ᾽ εὐχαριστίας. Cf. our word Eucharist.

[5] ἐν παντί.

situation. We are to know that all things work together for our good (Rom. 8 : 28), whether we can perceive it in this particular instance or not.

"And the peace of God, which passeth all understanding, shall guard your hearts and your thoughts in Christ Jesus." The blessing here offered is the result[1] of the attitude of prayer in verse 6. God is the God of peace (Phil. 4 : 9) and His peace [2] is the inward peace of the soul that is grounded in God's presence and promise (Vincent). Paul here assumes that we have made our peace with God in Christ and now we are enjoying our peace with God (Rom. 5 : 1). This *pax Dei* is the tranquillity possible only to the soul that has found rest in the bosom of Christ. "Come unto me, all ye that labour and are heavy laden, and I will give you rest" (Matt. 11 : 28). "This peace is like some magic mirror, by the dimness growing on which we may discern the breath of an unclean spirit that would work us ill" (Rendel Harris, "Memoranda Sacra," p. 130). This inward peace fills the heart "with all joy and peace in believing" (Rom. 15 : 13); "for the Kingdom of God is not eating and drinking, but righteousness and peace and joy in the Holy Spirit" (Rom. 14 : 17). This peace of God "passes all understanding.'[3] Like a

[1] καὶ is here consecutive = "and so" or inferential = "then." Cf. Robertson, "Grammar," p. 1183.

[2] ἡ εἰρήνη τοῦ θεοῦ.

[3] ἡ ὑπερέχουσα πάντα νοῦν. Intellectual grasp (νοῦς). ὑπερέχω is to overtop, to surpass. Cf. 2 : 3; 3 : 8.

granite peak it rises sheer above the mists and clouds
of human speculation. Intellectual apprehension fails
to grasp the height of it. The intellect is a noble
gift and is to be honoured and used, but it is not in-
fallible and at best is a feeble instrument of knowledge. The emotions and the will are more fundamental and more reliable. I stand by the rights of
the intellect in criticism and in life. We are bound
to do so or to abdicate the throne of reason. But,
after all is said and done, the intellect is like a bird
with a broken wing. Faith can fly farther and faster
and more surely. We must learn to trust the primal
instincts as well as the reason. The peace of God
rises above the sphere of intellect (*sensum*, Vulgate). This peace of God shall act as a garrison[1]
to the soul. This is a promise, not a prayer (Vincent). It is a military term. Hicks (" Classical Review," i., pp. 7 f., suggests the garrisoning of the
towns by the Roman soldiers as a familiar sight.
The successors of Alexander the Great made a feature of such garrisons in the towns of Asia Minor.
Philippi was a Roman colony and a military outpost.

> "Love is and was my King and Lord,
>   And will be, though as yet I keep
>   Within his court on earth, and sleep
> Encompassed by his faithful guard,

---

[1] φρουρήσει. Vg. *custodiat.* Cf. 1 Pet. 1 : 5 τοὺς ἐν
δυνάμει θεοῦ φρουρουμένους.

> And hear at times a sentinel
> Who moves about from place to place,
> And whispers to the worlds of space,
> In the deep night that all is well."
>   —*Tennyson.*

So the sentinel of God's peace mounts guard over our hearts and thoughts. One recalls the comfort of the voice of the sentinel who walks the bridge of the ship at night in time of storm and calls out that all is well.   The little child is sometimes unable to sleep without the pressure of mother's hand and the soothing melody of mother's voice.   This peace of God quiets both our hearts and our thoughts. When insomnia comes, the mind is abnormally active and the brain whirls round and round.   When fear grips the heart, rest is gone.   Both heart and thoughts are soothed to calm and rest as Jesus stilled the sea of Galilee in spite of wind and storm.   Beautiful tranquillity comes to him whose soul rests in Christ Jesus for the peace of God keeps watch over his life.

6.   High Thinking (verse 8).

Paul is now thinking of the close of the Epistle. " Finally, brethren," [1] he says, but with no reference to 3:1 where he used similar language.   It is not a second finally in the strict sense, though Lightfoot says that once more the Apostle attempts to conclude. Paul thus introduces a noble exhortation to the high-

---

[1] τὸ λοιπόν, ἀδελφοί.

est ideals of thought and endeavour. It is a final
recapitulation of themes for meditation and practice
(Ellicott). The Stoics had their four cardinal virtues
(prudence, temperance, justice, fortitude). We are
not to think that Paul is here giving a list of Christian virtues on a par with these. In truth, he attempts no inclusive list of spiritual ideals, but gives
in rapid fashion two groups, one introduced by
" whatsoever," [1] the other by " if." [2] Lightfoot sees
a descending scale in the words. Perhaps so, and
the two " if " clauses may be an afterthought. The
list is rather too beautiful for one to enjoy minute
dissection. We may pause a moment on each of the
words. " True " [3] is to be taken in the widest sense,
far more than simply veracious. " God is the norm
of truth " (Vincent) and Jesus is the truth (John
14: 6). The moral ideal of Christianity rests on reality and aims at reality as it answers to the nature
of God. Truth is the very core of Christ's teaching.
It is no mere value judgment. " Honourable " [4] is
more exactly venerable or reverend or " nobly serious " (Matthew Arnold [5]) as opposed to that flippancy
that lacks " intellectual seriousness." Reverence is a
sadly needed virtue in many quarters to-day. " Just " [6]

[1] ὅσα. Quæcunque.
[2] εἴ τις. Si qua.
[3] ἀληθῆ. Vera.
[4] σεμνά. From σέβομαι to worship. Vg. pudica. Opposed to κοῦφος lightness.
[5] " God and the Bible," Preface XXII.
[6] δίκαια. From δίκη. Vg. justa.

or righteous is applied to both God and man. It is the right way of looking at things, right *per se* (cf. Rom. 2 : 13), according to God's standard. These three qualities are fundamental in Christian ideals, the deep down things that go to the roots of right living. " Pure "[1] is stainless, chaste, unsullied as a pure virgin. " Lovely "[2] is whatever calls forth love, attracts to itself, the graciousness that wins and charms. Cf. the Beauty of Holiness in the Psalms and the Beautiful and the Good of the Greeks. " Of good report "[3] is " fair-sounding " (Vincent), almost our " high-toned "[4] (Kennedy). Whatever rings true to the previous notes is not out of tune with the Christian standard of morality. There are ever new and changing questions that have to be tested by the Christian's spiritual tuning-fork. The piano must be kept in tune. So must our sensitive spiritual nature be kept clean and sweet. " Virtue "[5] is moral excellence, a common heathen term that Paul seems generally to avoid (Lightfoot). The word originally meant only courage or manly skill or excellence with no moral quality. It gradually came to be used in a variety of ways.[6] Peter uses it of

[1] ἁγνά. Vg. *sancta*. ἅγιος is holy, consecrated, but ἁγνός is pure, untouched of evil, undefiled.

[2] προσφιλῆ. Vg. *amabilia*. Alone here in the New Testament. Cf. Sir. 4 : 7 ; 20 : 13.

[3] εὔφημα. Vg. *bonæ famæ*.

[4] " Was einen guten Klang hat " (Lipsius).

[5] ἀρετή. *Virtus* (Vg.).

[6] Cf. Deissmann, " Bible Studies," pp. 90 ff.

God (1 Pet. 2:9; 2 Pet. 1:3) and treats it as a
Christian grace (2 Pet. 1:4). Paul says: " Quit you
like men,[1] be strong" (1 Cor. 16:13). Christianity
does appeal to the elemental virtues in young manhood (cf. 1 John 2:13 f.), the sense of the heroic, the
nobility of service for others. It has taken over this
heathen virtue and applied it to a higher cause.
" Praise "[2] is the moral approbation from the practice
of virtue (cf. 1 Cor. 13). Put your mind[3] on these
things just mentioned. It is not the mere flash of
thought like the flitting of a sparrow, but deliberate
and prolonged contemplation as if one is weighing a
mathematical problem. Reckon up the *pros* and
cons of the moral values in life. Too many fail just
here. They do not give Christ worthy consideration.
Make your mind move in the realm of elevated
thoughts. High thinking is essential to holy living.
We must let Christ control our thoughts, " casting
down imaginations and every high thing that is exalted against the knowledge of God, and bringing
every thought into captivity to the obedience of
Christ " (2 Cor. 10:5).

7. **High Endeavour** (verse 9).
" These do."[4] These practice as a habit. These
put into practice and keep on doing them. Noble

---

[1] ἀνδρίζεσθε.   [2] ἔπαινος. Vg. *laus disciplinæ*.
[3] λογίζεσθε. Vg. *cogitate*. Present (linear action) tense.
[4] ταῦτα πράσσετε. Linear present. Sometimes distin-
guished from ποιεῖν to accomplish. Vg. *haec agite*.

ideals will come to naught unless translated into
deeds.   Performance surpasses mere preaching.   The
physician must practice his theories and heal himself.
So Paul turns from generalities to particulars.[1]   Paul
has given above proper subjects for meditation.   He
now presents a proper line of action (Lightfoot).   It
is now a scheme of duties (Vincent), not a list of
mottoes.   It is not necessary to say with Ellicott
that Paul has precisely the same ideas in mind in
verse 9 as in verse 8, but certainly the general outline is the same.   Paul urges that the Philippians
transmute aspiration into actuality, profession into
performance.   He even claims that he has given them
a suitable example for their imitation.   The expo-
nents of so-called " New Thought" at least have
grasped the truth of the relation between thought and
life.   Paul was a practical idealist, a pragmatist in the
best sense of that term.   He gave them proper pre-
cepts similar to the list in verse 8 : " The things
which ye both learned and received."[2]   They had
taken their lesson well from Paul as the transmitter.
Paul had also given them the concrete expression of
abstract truth : " and heard and saw in me."[3]   They
knew his life among them which was an open book
to them.   This is the Bible that the world eagerly

---

[1] " Facit transitionem a generalibus ad Paulina " (Bengel).

[2] ἃ καὶ ἐμάθετε καὶ παρελάβετε.   Vg. *quæ et didicistis, et accepistis.*

[3] καὶ ἠκούσατε καὶ εἴδετε ἐν ἐμοί.   Vg. *et audistis, et vi- distis in me.*

reads, the epistle that is known and read of all men, the life of Christ in God's people. There is no escape from it. Paul humbly points to his life in Christ as an aid to the Philippians in following after the great ideals set before them, " And the God of peace shall be with you."[1] This is proper preparedness to make peace with God by surrender to His will and then to find peace and power in God through Christ.

---

[1] καὶ ὁ θεὸς τῆς εἰρήνης ἔσται μεθ᾿ ὑμῶν. Vg. *Deus pacis erit vobiscum.* For this phrase (God of peace) see also Rom. 15 : 33 ; 16 : 20 ; 1 Thess. 5 : 23 ; Heb. 13 : 20.

XI

THE SECRET OF HAPPINESS
(4 : 10–23)

THIS Epistle is not long, but it is very rich in thought and fertile in suggestion. There seems little order save the introduction, the body of the Epistle, and the close, but Paul has an orderly method in his own mind in spite of the apparently easy and incidental way in which he goes on his way.

1. Delicate Appreciation (verse 10).

"But I rejoice in the Lord greatly,"[1] Paul adds with no apology for his repeated expression of joy in the Lord, great[2] joy this time, "that now at length ye have revived your thought for me."[3] Paul had indeed alluded to the generosity of the Philippians in the gift which Epaphroditus had brought (1 : 5, 7 ; 2 : 30), but he had not formally thanked them for their kindness. He seemed about to forget it in his

---

[1] ἐχάρην δὲ ἐν κυρίῳ μεγάλως. The epistolary aorist (Robertson, "Grammar," p. 845). "The δὲ arrests a subject which is in danger of escaping" (Lightfoot).

[2] Polycarp ad Phil. i. has συνεχάρην ὑμῖν μεγάλως ἐν Κυρίῳ ἡμῶν Ἰησοῦ Χριστοῦ.

[3] ὅτι ἤδη ποτὲ ἀνεθάλετε τὸ ὑπὲρ ἐμοῦ φρονεῖν.

eager discussion of other things and so he checked himself before it was too late. They had sent the gift in the Lord and he had received it in the Lord and he now is grateful in the Lord. Kennedy thinks that Paul here discusses his attitude towards the gift of the Philippians because of the base slanders about him elsewhere. The " cloak of covetousness " was a phrase flung at him in Thessalonica that stuck and hurt this proud and sensitive man (1 Thess. 2 : 5). It is an old canard that preachers preach for money. If so, very few ever get the object of their ambition. Paul defended his right to full pay for his preaching (1 Cor. 9 : 3–18; Gal. 6 : 6), but because of the foolish misrepresentations of his work in Corinth he made the gospel message there without charge. Some even criticized him for this refusal to receive pay, but Paul continued to preach the Gospel for naught in Corinth to cut off occasion from those who desire occasion (2 Cor. 11 : 8–12). He even " robbed other churches " to do this thing. But even so he did not escape, for he was accused of using Titus to raise a fund for himself under pretense of getting money for the poor saints in Jerusalem (2 Cor. 12 : 16–18). It is a humiliating experience for a preacher to have to make public appeal for his own support. Paul refused to stoop to that level and worked with his own hands (1 Thess. 2 : 9; Acts 20 : 33 f.) in order to be independent of those who were so ready to impute wrong motives to him. He rejoiced in the church at Phi-

lippi because they trusted him and understood him.
They gladly and frequently made contributions for
the support of his work elsewhere. For some time
the Philippians had not remembered Paul in this
way. He had been a prisoner in Cæsarea for over
two years. Then came the voyage and shipwreck
and the imprisonment in Rome. A considerable interval had elapsed since the last time (cf. 2 Cor. 11 : 9)
before Epaphroditus came. It has seemed long
("now at length") to Paul as he looked back over it
all. The coming of Epaphroditus seemed like a
genuine revival of interest on the part of the Philippians. It was like old times to hear from them again
in this way. " Ye let your thought of me sprout up [1]
now once again" like a plant in spring (the miracle
of spring!). Their thought of Paul had blossomed
again like the first crocuses of spring. Like a bunch
of roses their gift spoke volumes. It was sweet to
Paul to be remembered again by his old friends in
his hour of trial. People sometimes take the pastor
too much as a matter of course. It did my soul
good one day to hear a deacon say of his pastor :
" He is worth his weight in gold." I told the pastor
what the deacon had said and it cheered him greatly.

But Paul's delicate nature shrinks from the implication that they had really forgotten him. "Wherein
ye did indeed take thought, but ye lacked oppor-

---

[1] ἀνεθάλετε. Rare second aorist form and probably transitive as in Ezek. 17 : 24. Ingressive aorist.

tunity." [1] Paul's sensitive concern makes him with-
draw the implied rebuke for their apparent neglect.
They may not have known always where he was or
they may have had no messenger till Epaphroditus
came. The word for " lacked opportunity " could
mean " lacked means." Expression of thanks is
often embarrassing, but Paul keeps his poise and
misses the pitfalls.

2. **Manly Independence** (verses 11ᵃ, 17ᵃ).

Paul is not free from fear about being misunderstood on the subject of money. It is in truth a
thorny problem. He has set straight his appreciation of the continued interest and love of the
Philippians. But he shrinks again from the fear
that they will think that he is hinting for future
favours. " Not that I speak in respect of want." [2]
He repeats the same *caveat* in verse 17ᵃ : " Not that
I seek for the gift." [3] Paul does not wish his joy
at this fresh proof of their love to be understood
as mere satisfaction at relief from want or begging
for a repetition of like generosity. He is not sug-

[1] ἐφ᾽ ᾧ καὶ ἐφρονεῖτε, ἠκαιρεῖσθε δέ. The imperfects picture the state of mind of the Philippians. Liddell and Scott
give only one instance (Diod. Siculus) of ἀκαιρέω. Moulton
& Milligan's " Vocabulary " gives no instance in the papyri
and inscriptions, but does give ἀκαίρως and ἀκαιρία. Εὐ-
καιρέω in sense of favourable opportunity occurs in the papyri.

[2] Οὐχ ὅτι καθ᾽ ὑστέρησιν λέγω. Cf. 3 : 12 for similar use
of οὐχ ὅτι to guard against misapprehension. The Vg. has
non quasi propter penuriam dico.

[3] Οὐχ ὅτι ἐπιζητῶ τὸ δόμα. Note the force of ἐπί.

gesting that they do it again. Many another
preacher has had similar emotions as he expresses
appreciation of the kindnesses received at the hands
of friends. Paul is sensitive on the point of his
financial independence. He vindicated his right to
adequate remuneration for his work in Corinth, as we
have seen (1 Cor. 9 : 6–20), but all the same he would
not allow them to pay him because of their suspicion
and perversion of his conduct. So he toiled on at
his trade of tent-making and supported himself in the
main, though he did accept the gifts from the Philippians. Many of the pioneer American preachers
were confronted with precisely this situation. In
order to preach at all they had to support themselves. Usually the pioneer preacher had a farm.
Sometimes he was a merchant, a lawyer, or a physician. All honour to the courageous men who met
abnormal conditions and knew how to preach Christ
in spite of ignorance and prejudice. We are not yet
past this mistreatment of preachers who are paid in
most cases a pitiful salary and are not allowed to
splice it out by secular business. If preachers do not
live well on a pittance, they are considered poor
business men. If they do make some money, they
are charged with being fond of filthy lucre, as, alas,
is sometimes true. But the modern minister must
keep out of debt, pay his bills promptly, make a good
appearance and so dress well, entertain largely, edu-
cate his children, lead his church in beneficence, and

save some money for old age when no church wants his services. It is a vicious circle and leads too often to debt and loss of financial standing and almost of self-respect. The whole business cheapens the preacher. Paul felt it all keenly. It rankled in his breast. He would be manly and self-reliant. He would be independent and stand on his own feet. It is openly charged to-day against the ministry that they are often afraid to speak out against crying evils (like the liquor business, the divorce evil, the wrongs done to labouring men), because the preacher's salary is largely paid by men guilty of some of these social sins. It is probably sometimes true, but the great mass of modern preachers are loyal to their ideals and risk all for their message. Pay the preacher a decent salary.

3. Learning the Secret (verses 11ᵇ, 12).

The ministry has its limitations. They are the limits of efficiency and service also. It is no life of self-indulgent affluence. Many things must be given up. Happy is the man who learns this lesson soon. Paul had learned the joy of doing without. " For I have learned, in whatsoever state I am, therein to be content." [1] Paul had to learn it for himself[2] as we all do. He still knows[3] his lesson.

[1] ἐγὼ γὰρ ἔμαθον ἐν οἷς εἰμὶ αὐτάρκης εἶναι.

[2] Note emphasis of ἐγὼ γάρ.

[3] ἔμαθον is aorist indicative, but a timeless aorist. It is the constative aorist and sums up all the life of Paul as one experience. Cf. Robertson, " Grammar," pp. 831–834.

" The tuition has extended over his whole experience up to the present" (Vincent). It is now his blessed possession and helps to explain his sense of manly independence. One can be too complacent for any use and lack ambition. One can be content only when he has reached the goal of his desires. Happy is the man who keeps the golden mean, who is not slothful, who is not resentful. There is a holy discontent. The Stoics made a good deal out of the virtue of self-sufficiency or independence of external circumstances[1] They held that a man should be sufficient in and unto himself in all things. When asked who was the wealthiest, Socrates said: " He who is content with least, for self-sufficiency is nature's wealth" (Stob. *Flor.* v. 43). Plato (*Tim.* 33 D) held that a being who was self-sufficient was far superior to one that lacked anything.[2] But, though Paul uses the Stoic word, he has more than the Stoic idea. He expressly disclaims this mere self-sufficiency : " Not that we are sufficient of ourselves, to account anything as from ourselves ; but our sufficiency is from God " (2 Cor. 3:5). " And

[1] This is the true meaning of αὐτάρκης (αὐτός and ἀρκέω). So Marcus Aurelius i. 16 τὸ αὔταρκες ἐν παντί. Seneca to Gallio *De Vita Beata* 6 Beatus est præsentibus, quæliacunque sunt, contentus.

[2] Cf. also *Repub.* 369 B. The papyri naturally give no examples of this philosophic use of αὐτάρκης. Sharp quotes Epictetus (" Epictetus and the New Testament," p. 124) : " Rejoice in what you have and be content (ἀγάπα) with those things for which it is the season."

God is able to make all grace abound unto you; that ye, having always all sufficiency in everything, may abound unto every good work " (2 Cor. 9 : 8). Paul's sufficiency is in Christ (Phil. 4 : 13) who makes a new self out of the old. Christ in Paul is the secret. It is godliness with contentment that is great gain (1 Tim. 6 : 6) over Stoicism and the so-called Christian Science of to-day which ignores and denies the facts of life. Paul is fully aware of the state in which he is, but he has learned how to rise above circumstance and environment and to be superior to these external matters. It is easy enough to be content somewhere else and in a different set of circumstances. But, caught in the net of evil chance, what is one to do, driven on by the *Sturm und Drang* of things? The problem with us all is precisely how to find content in the midst of things that ought to be changed. We should change what ought to be changed and can be changed for the better. What cannot be cured has to be endured. Do it with a smiling face. This is the lesson learned by Paul. This is the secret of a happy life. Kennedy quotes Boswell's " Johnson " (Globe ed., p. 351): " Dr. Johnson talked with approbation of one who had attained to the state of the philosophical wise man, that is, to have no want of anything. ' Then, sir,' said I, ' the savage is a wise man.' ' Sir,' said he, ' I do not mean simply being without,—but not having a want.' "

" I know how to be abased, and I know also how

to abound." [1]   Some people can stand adversity who
are ruined by prosperity.   Poverty imposes a certain
restraint that is swept away by the flood-tide of
riches.   Some are happy with plenty and grow bitter in spirit when want knocks at the door.   Some
wealthy men give most of their money away in order
to save their sons from the peril of money.   The
discipline of life is worth more than ease to make a
man that is worth while.   " Give me neither poverty
nor riches."   Yes, but life does not flow in such a
placid stream as that.   Drouth follows flood.   The
Nile runs low (Diod. i. 36) and the water has to be
conserved by irrigation now as of old.   One must
learn how to endure either famine or plenty, the lean
years and the fat.   The pendulum swings back and
forth.   Poise of character must keep us steady when
either extreme comes.   " Or did I commit a sin in
abasing myself that ye might be exalted?" Paul
asks the Corinthians with keen irony (2 Cor. 11 : 7).[2]

" In everything and in all things have I learned the
secret." [3]   Paul uses the particular and the general
in an effort to cover completely the whole of life's
varied experiences.   " In every way have we made

[1] οἶδα καὶ ταπεινοῦσθαι, οἶδα καὶ περισσεύειν.   " The one
καὶ must be correlative to the other " (Kennedy).   Cf. Robertson, " Grammar," pp. 1180 f.

[2] Here ὑφοῦν is the antithesis of ταπεινοῦν as is usual, but in
Phil. 4 : 12 it is περισσεύειν.

[3] ἐν παντὶ καὶ ἐν πᾶσιν μεμύημαι.   In Allem und Jedem.
Vg. wrongly translates ubique et in omnibus institutus sum.

this manifest unto you in all things " (2 Cor. 11 : 6).
The word for learning the secret [1] here means " I
have been initiated " or " I possess the secret." It
was used of initiation into the Eleusinian mysteries.[2]
Our very word mystery [3] is this Greek word. The
Mithraists also used it for their secret rites. Paul
takes the word and employs it of the mystic initiation into the life in Christ which makes him superior
to all the accidents that come and go. " The
secret of the Lord is with them that fear him " (Ps.
25 : 14). The wisdom of Solomon (8 : 4) speaks of
our being initiated into the knowledge of God.[4] Ignatius [5] speaks of those who are " co-mystics with
Paul the sanctified." The initiate kept his secret.
Paul gloried in the mystery of God (Christ) in whom
all the treasures of knowledge are hidden (Col. 2 : 2 f. ;
cf. also 1 : 26 f.). The baptized Christian came to be
called the initiated one. Paul had his initiation into
the mystery of happiness in the ups and downs of
his life for Christ in the Roman world. " Both to be
filled and to be hungry," [6] says Paul, both to have
plenty like a horse with plenty of fodder or grass
and to be hungry with no grass at all. " Both to

---

[1] μεμύημαι from μυέω to close or shut (cf. *mutus,* mute) is
the present perfect passive.
[2] Cf. Herod. ii. 51 ; Plato, *Gorg.* 497 C. ; Aristoph. *Plut.*
846 ; Plut. *Mor.* p. 795 E.   [3] μυστήριον.
[4] μύστις γάρ ἐστιν τῆς τοῦ θεοῦ ἐπιστήμης.
[5] *Eph.* XII. Παύλου συμμύσται τοῦ ἡγιασμένου.
[6] καὶ χορτάζεσθαι καὶ πεινᾶν.

abound and to be in want,"[1] he concludes, both to
overflow like a river and be dry like a desert. Alas,
how familiar the second word is to many preachers
who know what it is to be behind in one's accounts
with nothing in the bank to draw on. To be in want
and have no way to supply the necessary demands
of life is a tragedy. One can see the pretty things in
the stores and pass them by, the new books in the
shops and let them go. But it is hard to see one's
own family suffer for food and raiment and fuel.
Paul had learned how to do without many things,
not even to want them, and yet to be happy. He
had all in Christ and abounded.

4. Paul's Dynamo (verse 13).

In dodging this and that misapprehension Paul
has avowed his independence of material comforts.
It is not a new attitude for Paul: He has long come
to feel that the unseen, not the seen, is the proper
goal of endeavour (2 Cor. 4 : 17 f.). " I can do all
things in him that strengtheneth me."[2] Paul feels
able not only to do what he had said in verse 12, but
also to meet all demands of a similar nature. It is
sublime egotism surely. But is that all ? Is it true ?
" I have strength for all things,"[3] he means. This

---

[1] καὶ περισσεύειν καὶ ὑστερεῖσθαι.

[2] πάντα ἰσχύω ἐν τῷ ἐνδυναμοῦντί με. Vg. has *Omnia possum
in eo, qui me confortat.*

[3] Cf. Jas. 5 : 16. πολὺ ἰσχύει. Cf. also Gal. 5 : 6. The
accusative is due to the verb and is not adverbial. Δύναμις
is manifested in ἰσχύς.

strength resides in Christ who furnishes the power
for the exercise of this spiritual prowess. Christ
" empowers "② Paul, surcharges him with energy.
Christ is Paul's dynamo potential and actual. Christ
" infuses strength " (Vincent) into Paul and hence he
has it in all abundance. Paul uses this great word
elsewhere also of Christ's relation to him. " I thank
him that enabled [3] me, Christ Jesus our Lord "
(1 Tim. 1 : 12). " But the Lord stood by me, and
strengthened me " [4] (2 Tim. 4 : 17). Paul has spiritual power for life because Christ is his life. " Be
strong in the Lord " [5] (Eph. 6 : 10). This power is
accessible to all who will yield themselves to Christ,
who unreservedly place themselves at the service of
Jesus, who make the full surrender to God. So then
it is not an idle boast that Paul is making. It is no
boast at all. He does not mean that he always has
his way. Far from it. He has learned to do without
his way and to find his joy in God's way so that no
one can rob him of this joy in Christ. Men can kill
him, but they cannot deprive him of the love and the
power of Christ in his life (Rom. 8 : 35–39). Paul
leads the victorious life because he lets Christ reign
and rule in his heart. The power of Christ in Paul
is not for the gratification of Paul's whims, but for

[1] ἐν here is more than the so-called instrumental use.

[2] ἐνδυναμόω is a rare word. It occurs in Judg. 6 : 34
(Codex A) πνεῦμα θεοῦ ἐνεδυνάμωσεν τὸν Γεδεών.

[3] τῷ ἐνδυναμώσαντί με.

[4] ἐνεδυνάμωσέν με.   [5] ἐνδυναμοῦσθε ἐν κυρίῳ.

the carrying out of Christ's will. In a real sense
therefore the Christian is a reproduction of Christ.
A small dynamo can retain its energy if continually
replenished. Christians themselves are spiritual
dynamos, but they must be in constant touch with
the source of life and energy. Ignatius [1] said : " I
undergo all things, since he himself strengthens me
who is perfect man." The constant inflow of power
from Christ allows Paul to be a continuous supply of
energy for others.

5. Courteous Thanks (verses 14–18).

Once more Paul catches himself before he creates
the impression that he does not really care for the
gift of the Philippians. He is independent and self-
reliant and able to meet every emergency by the
grace and power of Jesus Christ. But this does not
mean that he does not suffer privation and affliction.
It is not " thankless thanks " as Holsten argues.
" Howbeit ye did well that ye had fellowship with
my affliction." [2] The gift was not superfluous for
Paul was still a prisoner and in affliction. He as-

---

[1] *Smyrn.* IV.   πάντα ὑπομένω, αὐτοῦ με ἐνδυναμοῦντος τοῦ
τελείου ἀνθρώπου.

[2] πλὴν καλῶς ἐποιήσατε συνκοινωνήσαντές μου τῇ θλίψει.
On πλὴν see I : 18 ; 3 : 16. For this idiomatic use of καλῶς
and the participle see Acts 10 : 33 ; 2 Pet. 1 : 19 ; 3 John 6.
For εὖ see Acts 15 : 29. It is the supplementary participle.
Robertson, " Grammar," p. 1121. Hort. on 1 Pet. 2 : 12
says that καλός " denotes that kind of goodness which is at
once seen to be good."

serted his independence as the rule of his whole life in Christ, not as a reflection on the generosity of the Philippians. So Paul's appreciation is hearty and sincere and not ironical. The Philippians had made common cause[1] with Paul in his long imprisonment and this fact Paul would never forget. They "went shares" with Paul (Lightfoot on Gal. 6 : 6). Vincent quotes Ben Johnson's use of " communicate " in the old sense of "share," " thousands that communicate our loss."

Paul gives the Philippians their crown of glory as the first of the apostolic churches to rise to the full height of complete coöperation in the missionary enterprise. The church at Jerusalem had a powerful Pharisaic element in it, the Judaizers (" they that were of the circumcision "), who arraigned Peter for preaching to and associating with Cornelius (Acts 11 : 1–18) and who challenged the missionary propaganda of Paul and Barnabas among the Gentiles (Acts 15 : 1–35). In Antioch itself Barnabas and Saul won sympathy, but no financial support (Acts 13 and 14), a great advance on Jerusalem. But it was the Philippians who first made contributions to the support of Paul in his great work. " And ye yourselves also know, ye Philippians."[2]   Ye men of

---

[1] συνκοινωνήσαντες. Paul makes abundant use of compounds with σύν like the κοινή generally, in spite of its rarity as a preposition.   Cf. Robertson, " Grammar," pp. 626 ff.

[2] οἴδατε δὲ καὶ ὑμεῖς, Φιλιππήσιοι.   Cf. 1 Thess. 2 : 1.

Philippi know this as well as I, Paul explains. It
was no secret. " In the beginning of the gospel,
when I departed from Macedonia, no church had
fellowship with me in the matter of giving and receiving but ye only."[1] Paul is not apologizing for a
disappointment in the later cessation of their gifts,
but enlarging the scope of his appreciation. The
rather he praises them in that they had opened an
account with Paul, a credit and debit page, " in the
matter of giving and receiving." This is a common
expression for pecuniary transactions (Sir. 41 : 19;
42 : 7; Epictetus ii. : 9; Hermas *Mand.* v. 2). The
" beginning of the gospel " refers evidently to the
early stage of the work in Macedonia about ten
years before this letter, not the origin of the gospel
work in Palestine. We know precisely then that the
Philippians helped Paul while he was in Corinth (cf.
2 Cor. 11 : 8 f.). But he here shows that even while
in Macedonia the church at Philippi had helped Paul.
" For even in Thessalonica ye sent once and again
unto my need."[2] Paul had left Timothy in Philippi
when he and Silas left (Acts 16 : 40; 17 : 4), but he
was in Beroea with Silas when Paul went on to

[1] ὅτι ἐν ἀρχῇ τοῦ εὐαγγελίου, ὅτε ἐξῆλθον ἀπὸ Μακεδονίας,
οὐδεμία μοι ἐκκλησία ἐκοινώνησεν εἰς λόγον δόσεως καὶ
λήμψεως εἰ μὴ ὑμεῖς μόνοι. The papyri give λόγος in sense
of " account " as εἰς λόγον ἱματισμοῦ on account of clothing.
P. Oxy. 275²¹ A. D. 66.
[2] ὅτι καὶ ἐν Θεσσαλονίκη καὶ ἅπαξ καὶ δὶς εἰς τὴν χρείαν
μου ἐπέμψατε. Cf. 1 Thess. 2 : 18 for ἅπαξ καὶ δίς.

Athens (Acts 17 : 14 f.). Probably Timothy had brought gifts, but even in Thessalonica they had sent contributions more than once. They kept it up after Paul went to Corinth as we have seen (2 Cor. 11 : 8 f.), though Thessalonica and Berœa may now have joined with Philippi in the gifts to Paul since Paul speaks of " other churches " (2 Cor. 11 : 8). Timothy and Silas may have brought gifts from all these churches when they came to Corinth (cf. Acts 18 : 5). " Not only on my departure, but even before I departed you were mindful of my necessities " (Vincent).

" Not that I seek for the gift." " Again the Apostle's nervous anxiety to clear himself interposes " (Lightfoot). He is not hinting for more gifts. They must excuse him for saying that again (4 : 11). " But I seek for the fruit that increaseth to your account."[1] It is not the gift so much as the giving that has brought joy to Paul's heart (Kennedy). A raven could bring a gift as to Elijah. But the real " interest "[2] on their investment is the spiritual fruit that comes to them. This is the real credit side of the ledger. " It is more blessed to give than to receive " as Jesus said (Acts 20 : 35). The way to lay up treasure in heaven is to give it away while on

---

[1] ἀλλὰ ἐπιζητῶ τὸν καρπὸν τὸν πλεονάζοντα εἰς λόγον ὑμῶν. Cf. 2 Cor. 9 : 6.

[2] Chrysostom explains all these terms here by the money-market. He says : ὁ καρπὸς ἐκείνοις τίκτεται.

earth. " Ye have your fruit unto sanctification, and the end eternal life " (Rom. 6 : 22). It is literally true that we only save what we give. It is also true that without giving we cannot grow in grace as we ought. If the Gospel could be preached to the world free of all cost, it would be a misfortune to the churches for they would be denied this spiritual growth that comes from hearty giving to the Lord's cause.

" But I have all things, and abound."[1] " I have the receipt in full." Deissmann [2] finds " countless in-stances" of the verb in the ostraca and papyri in the sense of receipt in full. Paul can give them this re-ceipt in full for their gifts. He overflows with their love. He has more than he could desire. " Who is rich ? He that is contented with his lot " (C. Taylor, " Sayings of Jewish Fathers," p. 64). " I am filled, having received from Epaphroditus the things from you."[3] Paul can stand no more for the present, so bountifully have the Philippians supplied his needs. In giving to Paul they have given unto God, " an odour of a sweet smell, a sacrifice acceptable, well-pleasing unto God."[4] Their gift is like the fragrance

---

[1] ἀπέχω δὲ πάντα καὶ περισσεύω.

[2] " Light from the Ancient East," p. 110. Like ἀπέχων παρὰ σοῦ τέλες(ος) ἐπιξένου (ostracon), ἀπέχω παρ' ὑμῶν τὸν φόρον (Fayûm Pap. A. D. 57). Cf. Matt. 6 : 2. It is the aoristic present. Cf. Robertson, " Grammar," pp. 864–870.

[3] πεπλήρωμαι δεξάμενος παρὰ Ἐπαφροδίτου τὰ παρ' ὑμῶν. Note tense of πεπλήρωμαι (state of completion), full satisfac-tion.

[4] ὀσμὴν εὐωδίας, θυσίαν δεκτήν, εὐαρεστὸν τῷ θεῷ.

of sweet incense (cf. Eph. 5 : 2). The figure is very
common of the sacrifices in the Old Testament (Gen.
8 : 21 ; Ex. 29 : 18). The gift is a spiritual sacrifice.
They were not actually buying grace, but they
pleased God with this proof of their love and loyalty
(cf. Rom. 12 : 1 f. ; Heb. 13 : 16 ; 1 Pet. 2 : 5). Surely
Paul has given golden words for the loving tokens
from the Philippians.

6. Riches in Glory (verses 19 f.).

Paul adds God's blessing with all his heart and
with full confidence. " God's treatment of them cor-
responds to their treatment of Paul " (Kennedy).
" And my God shall supply every need of yours." [1]
You have filled my cup to overflowing [2] (verse 18).
God shall fill [3] yours to the brim and over. Paul
says " my God " because he had tested and tried
God as his own Protector and Father. He has not
forgotten me, and He will not forget you. There is
implied also God's " practical approval " (Vincent)
of the conduct of the Philippians towards Paul. But,
just as Paul had received his highest blessing in his
independence of his environment, so the Philippians
will receive blessings from God " according to his
riches in glory in Christ Jesus." [4]   God has unlimited
resources and unbounded love. The measure [5] of His
beneficence is " the riches in glory in Christ Jesus,"

[1] ὁ δὲ θεός μου πληρώσει πᾶσαν χρείαν ὑμῶν.

[2] πεπλήρωμαι.   [3] πληρώσει.

[4] κατὰ τὸ πλοῦτος αὐτοῦ ἐν δόξῃ ἐν Χριστῷ Ἰησοῦ.   [5] κατά.

" the unsearchable riches of Christ " [1] (Eph. 3 : 8),
the " unspeakable gift " [2] (2 Cor. 9 : 15).   God's blessing will be both temporal and spiritual, but the weight
of glory of the spiritual far surpasses the light affliction of the present (2 Cor. 4 : 17).   The Philippians
had not done what they did as a matter of spiritual
barter with God.   Paul does not take it so.   The dignity and delicacy of his words here are above all praise.
He expresses his own independence without harshness
while he exhibits the utmost courtesy and gratitude
towards his benefactors for this fresh expression of their
love.   Blessings on those who have done so many
kindnesses to ministers of Christ.   They gave the cup
of cold water in the name of a disciple and it did not
escape the eye of Christ.   The preacher has to learn
to fix his eye upon the spiritual values in life as his
chief reward (2 Cor. 4 : 18).   The riches in glory in
Christ are the real wealth of the world after all and
this treasure is offered to all disciples of Jesus who do
the work of Christ in the spirit of Christ.   " Now unto
our God and Father be the glory for ever and ever.
Amen."   This is a suitable doxology.   " The glory " [3]
belongs to God as our Father.   Let us freely give it
to Him.   The word is used in the Septuagint for the
glory of the Shekinah or Presence of God.   Peter,
James, and John saw Jesus bathed in this glory on
the mount of transfiguration.   Our glory in the end

---

[1] τὸ ἀνεξιχνίαστον πλοῦτος τοῦ χριστοῦ.

[2] τῇ ἀνεκδιηγήτῳ αὐτοῦ δωρεᾷ.   [3] ἡ δόξα.

of the day will be to see Jesus crowned King of kings
and Lord of lords.   That will be glory for us.

7. Paul's Farewell (verses 21–23).

The time has come for Paul to say good-bye to the
Philippians.   The Epistle is after all very brief, but
rich in thought.   He may have written these last
words with his own hand (cf. Gal. 6:11; 2 Thess.
3:17).   The Epistle was probably read to the
whole church.   " Salute every saint in Christ." [1]
The humblest man or woman who loves Christ has
a claim on Paul's love.   By " saint," as we have
already seen, Paul does not mean the " professional "
saint who prates of his piety which nobody else can
recognize, nor does he mean the best of the Christians in Philippi.   He includes all true disciples of
Christ.   Saint is the inclusive name for followers
of Jesus with the obligation to holiness involved in
the name.   " The brethren that are with me salute
you." [2]   Those Roman Christians who helped Paul
in his work [3] are here described as well as his personal companions and fellow-travellers.   " All the
saints salute you." [4]   Here the whole Roman brotherhood is included.   " Especially they that are of Cæsar's
household." [5]   Cæsar's personal family is not meant,

[1] ἀσπάσασθε πάντα ἅγιον ἐν Χριστῷ Ἰησοῦ.
[2] ἀσπάζονται ὑμᾶς οἱ σὺν ἐμοί ἀδελφοί.
[3] McGiffert, " Apostolic Age," p. 397.
[4] ἀσπάζονται ὑμᾶς πάντες οἱ ἅγιοι.
[5] μάλιστα δὲ οἱ ἐκ τῆς Καίσαρος οἰκίας.   Vg. maxime
autem, qui de Cæsaris domo sunt.

but the great imperial establishment which was very
extensive, including slaves, freedmen, household servants, dependents, and retainers of various kinds.[1]
Some of the prætorian guard may have been included (Phil. 1 : 13). Many of the emperor's servants came from the east and some of these could very
well be Christians (cf. Rom. 16) even before Paul came
to Rome and all the more so now. Sanday and
Headlam on Romans show that many of the names
in Romans 16 occur in the *Corpus* of Latin Inscriptions as members of the imperial household. Evidently Christ has come near to Cæsar in Rome.
Christ is challenging Cæsar in his own home. These
Christian slaves can do something to leaven the lump
even there. We do not know why Paul puts in
" especially." Some of this number may have come
originally from Philippi or may have been known to
some of the Philippians. " The grace of the Lord
Jesus Christ be with your spirit."[2] This is Paul's
last word and one of his favourite benedictions (cf.
Phile. 25 ; Gal. 6 : 18). Paul's emphasis is on grace,
grace from the Lord Jesus Christ, Son of God and
Son of man, grace that ennobles and enriches the
human spirit as the abode of God's Spirit.

[1] Cf. Lanciani, " Ancient Rome in the Light of Recent Ex-
cavations," pp. 128 ff. See also Lightfoot's Comm. on Philippians.

[2] ἡ Χάρις τοῦ Κυρίου Ἰησοῦ Χριστοῦ μετὰ τοῦ πνεύματος
ὑμῶν.

196 Those who think infant "immortal sin" &. Adam via
genetics etc so masters of being a moral choice, a guess
inwittingly instit' evolutional who die now is an anan's
inheritance

146 & " God must be supreme to be God at all
us   man .. .. free   . . .. man .. ..

144 " Energy is the scientific name for God:

150 " Theirs not to make reply
" " " reason why
Their but to do & die"

151 one need to experiencel w/ evil in order to appreciate
good.

261 STEW

58 on Galatians
93 114 on (Zam to lewis is X st; ours sense)

95 a good funeral quote

Thesis on Paul : X's deity p 49-50 &

Maybe write Carl Trapp points out how

224 ενεργια
energy